Involuntary Unemployment

Involuntary Unemployment

Macroeconomics from a Keynesian Perspective

J. A. Trevithick
Fellow of King's College, Cambridge

HARVESTER
WHEATSHEAF

New York   London   Toronto   Sydney   Tokyo   Singapore

First published 1992 by
Harvester Wheatsheaf
Campus 400, Maylands Avenue,
Hemel Hempstead
Hertfordshire HP2 7EZ
A division of
Simon & Schuster International Group

Typeset in 10/12pt Times by
Keyset Composition, Colchester, Essex

Printed and bound in Great Britain by
BPCC Wheatons Ltd, Exeter

British Library Cataloguing in Publication Data

Trevithick, J. A.
  Involuntary unemployment: Macroeconomics from a
  Keynesian perspective.
  I. Title
  339.5

  ISBN 0-7450-0055-X
  ISBN 0-7450-0056-8 pbk

4 5 96 95 94 93

Contents

Preface   vii

1   Introduction   1

2   Old classical macroeconomics: Say's Law   5

3   Old classical macroeconomics: the quantity theory of money
    and its descendants   22

4   The Keynesian revolution   48

5   Keynes and the labour market   92

6   Inflation and the labour market   118

7   Rational expectations and the new classical
    macroeconomics   146

8   Recent developments in Keynesian macroeconomics   180

9   Concluding observations   217

References   236

Index   241

Preface

This book has evolved from a set of sixteen lectures which I have delivered for the Economics Faculty in Cambridge over the last few years. The audience I had in mind when writing this book was similar to my Cambridge audience: a combination of first-year undergraduates specializing in economics and second-year undergraduates in their first term. Although there are many excellent texts currently available to intermediate students, I have found it difficult to recommend a single book which adequately approaches modern macroeconomics from the point of view of the evolution of the history of ideas. The approach I have adopted in this book is certainly unorthodox, but I hope it does not strike the reader as quirky or idiosyncratic.

I have received support from so many friends, colleagues and students that it would be invidious to single out individuals for special thanks. However I must break this self-denying ordinance in respect of Geoff Harcourt and Luigi Pasinetti who were unstinting in their advice and help, particularly as the book neared its final stages. As usual the constructive criticism of undergraduates has been a constant source of new ideas and, equally important, new slants on old ideas. In particular, I should like to acknowledge the help and advice of Matthew Dyson and Stuart Whipp of King's College.

But above all I should like to express my appreciation for the constant inspiration of the late R. F. Kahn a close friend as well as one of the founders of the modern discipline of macroeconomics.

James Trevithick
King's College,
Cambridge
July 1991

vii

1

Introduction

The turmoil and confusion which has surrounded debates in macroeconomics over the last two decades has been unprecedented in the history of economics. Supporters of rival theories proffer widely differing diagnoses of the origins of the problems which confront the market economies of the Western world. Not surprisingly, in the light of these differing diagnoses, the cures for, for example, inflation and unemployment, diverge from each other in many vital respects. The controversy which followed the publication of Keynes's *General Theory* in 1936 would be reckoned to be merely minor turbulence by the standards of the early 1990s.

So what sense is the student of economics to make of the seemingly irreconcilable positions espoused by rival schools of thought? How will the student be able to form a balanced judgment of the relative merits and demerits of, for example, the Keynesian and the monetarist approaches to macroeconomics? More fundamentally, what *is* a Keynesian and how does a Keynesian differ from a monetarist or a new classical macroeconomist?

It will be the principal objective of this book to show how answers to these and similar questions cannot be given in an historical vacuum. Different theories of macroeconomics arose out of a dissatisfaction with the shortcomings, real or imputed, of the dominant paradigm of the time. Keynes's dissatisfaction with old classical theory gave rise to the Keynesian income–expenditure model; dissatisfaction with the income–expenditure model's supposed neglect of inflation gave rise to monetarism; and the suspicion that monetarism remained tainted with many Keynesian features gave rise to the new classical macroeconomics which sought to return to 'purer', i.e. pre-Keynesian, methods of analysis. The wheel has turned full circle.

So history, or at least the history of economic thought, might not be bunk after all. But where, our student may be asking, should we start our inquiry? Since this book aims to show how classical modes of thought continually break through in macroeconomic debate, we shall make our starting-point the mid-eighteenth century and the writings of David Hume. In Chapters 2 and 3 we shall see how a reasonably accurate and coherent picture of the structure of the old classical macroeconomic model can be pieced together. Three essential propositions lie at the heart of old classical macroeconomics: (a) that alterations in the relation between the desire to save and the desire to invest do not produce alterations in the overall levels of output and employment, as they do in the Keynesian system, but result solely in variations in the rate of interest; (b) that, for arbitrarily given initial levels of output and employment, variations in the real wage rate in a competitive economy will ensure that there will exist a strong tendency towards a state of overall full employment; (c) that the absolute price level is determined by the nominal quantity of money.

We shall see in Chapter 4 how Keynes sought to undermine propositions (a) and (c). He proposed: (a′) that the rate of interest was a 'monetary' and not a 'real' phenomenon, this observation giving rise to the distinct possibility that alterations in the relation between the desire to save and the desire to invest would result in alterations in the general levels of output and employment; and (c′) that the basic prediction of the quantity theory of money that an $x\%$ increase in the money supply would lead to an $x\%$ increase in absolute prices only held true in the special case where the economy was already in a state of full employment. Keynes's criticisms of proposition (b) of classical theory, in which variations in the real wage rate are assigned a role of paramount importance in ensuring that 'lapses' from full employment remain only 'lapses', is examined in Chapter 5. Much of the recent disenchantment with Keynesian economics arises from what is perceived to be rather casual treatment of the labour market in the *General Theory*. In fact Keynes's treatment is far from casual, though it must be admitted that the *General Theory* model is far from pellucid. Much of Keynes's labour market analysis is difficult to comprehend, and is occasionally confused, but it does make sense, particularly when it is borne in mind that Keynes was referring to the workings of a money using economy in which money is definitely not a 'veil'. In this chapter a full appreciation of the 'involuntariness', to use an ugly word, of Keynesian unemployment becomes apparent for the first time.

Up to this point we shall have had little to say about inflation. The failure to articulate an adequate theory of prices comparable with the quantity theory of money in classical economics has often been regarded as the

Achilles' heel of Keynesian economics. This problem appeared to have been overcome by the discovery in 1958 of the Phillips curve which related to the rate of change of money wages to the pressure of demand in the economy, the latter being proxied by the unemployment rate. But this discovery, which is the subject matter of Chapter 6, was to bring in its wake more problems than it solved. By the time it came under attack by Friedman, the Phillips curve had come to be regarded as an indispensable item in the tool-kit of Keynesian economics. A great deal of effort was invested in demolishing both the theoretical and the empirical credentials of the Phillips curve by a group of economists who were generally described as monetarists. The assault on the Phillips curve was part of a broader attack on the foundations of Keynesian economics even though the Keynesian system had thrived for many years without it. The monetarist concept of the natural unemployment rate came into vogue in a wide variety of circles in the late 1960s. It seemed at the time to sound the death knell for Keynesian demand management to alleviate unemployment or to curb inflation.

In the mid-1970s a more virulent strain of monetarism was beginning to surface in the form of the new classical macroeconomics which is discussed in Chapter 7. New classical macroeconomists simply *assume*, without demonstration or proof, that competitive markets clear. Their conviction in the power of markets to eliminate excess supply or excess demand at the microeconomic level is carried over on to the macroeconomic level: the forces of competition in the aggregate labour market ensure that deviations from a state of overall full employment will only be very temporary. We are not told *why* this should be the case: it just is. Moreover the new classical writers appear to be blissfully innocent of Keynes's rebuttal of exactly this proposition in his critique of the old classical theory of aggregate labour market adjustment.

In Chapter 8 we shall examine two important recent developments in macroeconomics. The first concerns the distinction between classical and Keynesian unemployment. It is no longer taken for granted, as it had been in the earlier heyday of Keynesian economics, that any abnormally high level of unemployment must be due to a deficiency of aggregate demand. It is now recognized that a new category of general unemployment – *classical* unemployment resulting from excessively high real wages – should also be taken into account. The second recent development is the notion of hysteresis. Most mainstream theories of inflation had laid the blame for the high rates of inflation from the 1960s onwards at the door of excess demand; the monetarist school is the most vocal branch of this demand–pull approach to inflation. However the mainstream theories found it increasingly difficult to explain how the remarkable rise in unemployment during the 1970s and 1980s had resulted in such modest reductions in the rate of inflation. Is the equilibrium level of unemployment itself rising and, if so, why? The concept of hysteresis attempts to provide answers to these and other questions.

2

Old classical macroeconomics: Say's Law

One of the most resilient ideas in the history of economic thought is the proposition that, if left to its own devices, a freely functioning competitive economy will automatically produce a state of full employment. It was a fundamental tenet of what Keynes rather cavalierly and inaccurately dubbed 'classical economics' that divergences from the normal condition of full employment were the result of, or referred to as, 'temporary derangements of markets' (J. S. Mill, 1862, p. 97). Temporary derangements apart, the classical writers denied the possibility of overproduction or underproduction: the output of commodities and the overall demand for commodities would always move in step with each other.

The essence of J. S. Mill's position is succinctly captured in the following passage:

> Could we but suddenly double the productive powers of the country, we should double the supply of commodities in every market; but we should, by the same stroke, double the purchasing power. Everybody would bring a double demand as well as supply: everybody would be able to buy twice as much, because everyone would have twice as much to offer in exchange. (J. S. Mill, 1862, p. 93)

In other words, an increase in output generates an equal increase in incomes; and the whole of the increase in incomes is spent on the increase in output.

The classical vision found expression in the famous dictum known as Say's Law, after J.-B. Say (1767–1832): supply creates its own demand. As with many cryptic adages, this principle has produced its fair share of confusion. On the one hand it is taken to imply that each act of production necessarily involves the creation of an equivalent demand for output as a whole. We shall refer to this as the *weak* version of Say's Law. On the other hand there is the *strong* version of Say's Law which states that, in an economy where the forces of competition are allowed to operate unimpeded, there will be an automatic tendency for all resources, including the resources of the available labour force, to be fully employed.

The basic hypothesis embodied in the weak version of Say's Law – that each increment in production necessarily creates an equal increment in the demand for commodities – can be grasped quite easily with the aid of the familiar 45° line analysis of elementary macroeconomic theory.[1] The overall demand for commodities, E, is measured on the vertical axis and the output of commodities, Y, is measured on the horizontal axis. Output and demand are equal to each other at all points along the 45° line. A spontaneous rise in the output of commodities, say from Y_1 to Y_2, will generate an equal increase in aggregate demand: expenditure on commodities will rise from E_1 to E_2. The economy can never be in danger of 'slipping off' the 45° line. It moves from point A to point B but never to a point such as point C since such a move would imply that some of the extra output would remain as unsold stocks of finished goods in the hands of producers. In Keynesian parlance this version of Say's Law postulates that the aggregate expenditure function is *identical* to the 45° line. The marginal propensity to spend out of income is exactly equal to one.

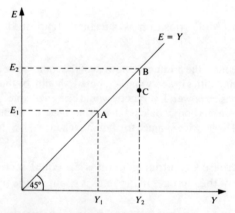

Figure 2.1   Weak version of Say's Law

[1] Those readers who are unfamiliar with this apparatus should consult any elementary text on macroeconomics, e.g. Trevithick, 1983, Chapter 3.

What was the analytical basis for the classical assertion that each successive act of production would generate *exactly* equal increases in demand? What justified the view that there could never be any injections into or leakages from the circular flow of income? Since the publication of the *General Theory* economists have become accustomed to the idea that certain exogenous shocks, such as sudden changes in the propensity to save or in the desire to invest, could produce temporary divergences between aggregate output and aggregate demand. What forces hermetically seal the classical system in such a way as to make it impervious to those shocks which, in the Keynesian system, lead to changes in aggregate demand and hence to changes in output and employment? In the author's view the answer lies mainly in the classical theory of interest.

Saving, investment and the rate of interest

One of the main points of contention between Keynes and his classical predecessors concerned the theory of saving and investment and, in particular, the forces that brought these two flows into equilibrium. For Keynes, saving and investment were brought into equality with each other through variations in the level of income. More generally, imbalances between injections and leakages were, in the first instance, rectified by quantity, not price, responses. By way of contrast the classical writers saw the rate of interest as playing this critical role of equilibrating saving and investment. A stylized account of the classical theory of interest is illustrated in Figure 2.2. The rate of interest, r, is measured on

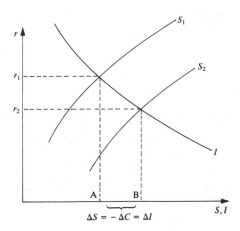

Figure 2.2　Classical theory of interest

the vertical axis and the flows of saving, S, and investment, I, are measured on the horizontal axis.[2] The positive slope of the saving schedule shows how the willingness of savers to make resources available to investors rises as the rate of interest rises. The saving schedule represents graphically the extent to which savers are willing to forgo present consumption at different rates of interest. The higher the rate of interest, the more willing will savers be to substitute present consumption in favour of enhanced future consumption. The rate of interest was hence regarded as the reward for abstaining from present consumption: it was variously described as the 'reward for abstinence', 'the reward for thrift' or 'the reward for waiting'. We shall very loosely[3] refer to the flow of saving as the supply of investible funds.

The demand for investible funds, represented in Figure 2.2 by the investment schedule, is also quite straightforward. The downward slope of the investment schedule indicates how the demand of entrepreneurs for the investible funds made available by savers rises as the rate of interest falls. As the rate of interest falls, more investment projects, which previously had been unprofitable, now become profitable. Entrepreneurs, spurred on by the prospect of profit, will therefore demand a higher flow of investible funds from savers as the rate of interest falls.

We have now postulated two sorts of relation, one a demand-side relation (the investment schedule), and the other as supply-side relation (the saving schedule). For the classical economist the most obvious way to examine how these twin blades of the Marshallian supply–demand scissors are brought together is to look at the behaviour of the price upon which both depend. In the light of Figure 2.2 it should come as no surprise to discover that the price which was accorded pride of place in bringing the desire to save into harmony with the desire to invest was the rate of interest. If the relevant saving and investment schedules are S_1 and I respectively, the equilibrium rate of interest (usually referred to as the

---

[2]For the moment we are drawing no distinction between the real rate of interest and the nominal (or money) rate of interest: that is, we are assuming for simplicity that the rate of inflation is zero.

[3]Some may regard this usage as inexcusably loose since we are entering into very perilous definitional territory. The most obvious alternative phrase would be the 'supply of loanable funds'. However those economists most associated with the loanable funds theory of interest – most notable among whom was Sir Dennis Robertson – would insist that the supply of loanable funds should include other elements in addition to private saving. For example, newly created bank credit is normally regarded as a net addition to the supply of loanable funds. Net dishoarding of inactive balances is another source of loanable funds. Nevertheless the 'loanable funds versus liquidity preference' controversy over the determination of the rate of interest, fascinating though it is to the historian of monetary economics, is too complex to be done full justice here.

natural interest rate) is r_1. At any rate of interest other than r_1 there will exist either an excess supply of or an excess demand for investible funds. The forces of competition, working through variations in the rate of interest, ensure that states of excess supply or demand in the market for investible funds will not persist for long. The natural rate of interest is at once a measure of the productivity of investment and the reward for thrift.

Much of the debate which followed the publication of the *General Theory* was concerned with evaluating the role played by these twin forces of productivity (the demand for investible funds) and thrift (the supply of investible funds) in determining the rate of interest. Keynes repeatedly denied that they played any direct role. (His obstinate reluctance to recognize any direct influence of saving and investment on the rate of interest was to be radically tempered in the debate which followed the publication of the *General Theory*. In the author's view, Sir Dennis Robertson was to emerge the victor in this confused and confusing interchange.) Others, most notably the economists of the Stockholm School and, of course, Robertson, doggedly insisted that changes in the desire to save or to invest would have direct, first-round repercussions on the rate of interest, not solely the second-round effects via the level of income which Keynes had emphasized. But more of this in Chapter 4 when we examine the Keynesian theory of interest in greater detail.

The full power of the classical theory of interest emerges very clearly when the effects of an increased propensity to save are scrutinized. In Figure 2.2, a shift in the saving schedule from S_1 to S_2 indicates that, at all rates of interest, savers are now willing to place a larger proportion of their incomes at the disposal of investors. In Keynesian theory such a parametric change will lead to a fall in expenditure and income and to a rise in unemployment. Not so in classical theory. Initially there will be an excess supply of investible funds but this will very quickly serve to depress the rate of interest until a new natural rate, r_2, is established. In the new equilibrium, the flow of investment will have risen by an amount exactly equal to the rise in the flow of saving. In the absence of rigidities and stickiness in adjustment, divergences between saving and investment, though conceptually possible since saving is no longer *identified* with investment, as it had been in the works of many early classical writers, will not occur: the rate of interest will serve continually to reconcile the desire to save with the desire to invest even if one or both of the functions are shifting erratically. Keynes's preoccupation with the fickleness of the investment decision, and with its susceptibility to sudden bouts of optimism and pessimism, would have been regarded as groundless within this framework.[4] In contrast to the predictions of the Keynesian model, a shift in either the saving or the investment schedule will not alter the overall magnitude of final output, though obviously these shifts will alter the division of that output between the production of capital goods and the production of consumption goods. That is, the components of Y may alter (in our example consumption falls and investment rises) but Y itself does not change.

In order to see how this result is arrived at, let us examine Figure 2.2 once again. Consumption expenditure (C) is defined as that part of income which is not saved. That is, $C = Y - S$. In the new equilibrium at a natural interest rate r_2, saving has risen by an amount AB and this is exactly mirrored in an equal fall in consumption. For Keynes this fall in consumption would have been regarded as prejudicial to general economic welfare: national income would fall and unemployment would rise. The classical writers saw things differently: the rise in the propensity to save and the fall in the propensity to consume could not be considered in isolation from their direct effects on the desire to invest. To be more specific, corresponding to the decline in consumption expenditure there will be an equal rise in investment expenditure. The horizontal distance AB not only measures the decline in consumption; it also measures the rise in investment. In symbols, since $Y = C + I$, $\Delta Y = \Delta C + \Delta I$, where ΔY, ΔC and ΔI are the changes in income, consumption and investment respectively. (The Δ operator will be used to denote a small change in a variable.) But since $\Delta I = \Delta C$, $\Delta Y = 0$. The rise in the propensity to save therefore produces a switch in the structure of final demand away from consumer goods towards investment goods.

Since a change in the propensity to consume or in the desire to invest cannot affect the level of national income, no practical implications followed from the Keynesian distinction between an injection into the circular flow of income and a leakage from it. Divergences between injections and leakages could only be temporary and would provoke a price response not, as in Keynesian theory, a quantity response. To use a hydraulic metaphor, variations in the rate of interest serve both to 'plug

---

[4]On the other hand Marshall's theory of the trade cycle attributed the origins of fluctuations in economic activity to these waves of optimism and pessimism. Apart from the assumption of frictions in adjustment, it is unclear to this author how Marshall reconciled his short-run theory of the cycle with the underlying long-run saving/investment/interest rate nexus. Perhaps the answer lies in Marshall's (and Wicksell's) famous distinction between the market and natural rates of interest: bouts of excessive optimism or pessimism could produce a divergence between the two rates which, in turn, could generate upturns or downturns in economic activity. See Chapter 3 for a fuller discussion of the Wicksell–Marshall monetary transmission mechanism.

up' potential leakages and to 'siphon off' potential injections. The rate of interest behaves in such a way as to convert an act of abstinence from expenditure – saving – into an act of expenditure – investment. In this way the classical economists were able to dispose of 'oversaving' or 'under-consumption' theories of crisis in capitalist economies which had been widely current in the nineteenth century, particularly among radical writers.

The classical theory of interest in action: the Treasury view

The experience of persistent mass unemployment in Britain in the period between the two world wars led to repeated demands from many quarters for the implementation of a programme of public works to create new jobs for the unemployed. Keynes (1929), in his famous pamphlet (written with Hubert Henderson) *Can Lloyd George Do It?*, argued forcefully for increased expenditure on public works. Such schemes were dismissed as futile by the British Treasury at the time. Although undoubtedly sympathetic to the plight of the unemployed, the Treasury resisted pressure for fiscal intervention to relieve unemployment. The Treasury view held that, while increased government expenditure would certainly create jobs in some sectors of the economy, such expenditure would just as certainly destroy jobs in other sectors of the economy since it would deprive private investors of adequate access to the limited supply of investible funds.

In popular discussion of macroeconomic policy nowadays, calls for an enhanced programme of public investment (as public works were often referred to) are usually associated with the ideas of Keynes and his followers. For the interwar period this was far from being the case since these calls did not emanate exclusively, or even principally, from the more eccentric reaches of the economics profession. For example, Professor A. C. Pigou, usually regarded as the doyen of classical economics at the time, added the weight of his influential opinion to the call for public works to relieve unemployment. As Blaug (1962, Chapter 15) has pointed out '[Sir Ralph] Hawtrey alone of all British economists of the 1920s opposed the case for public works on theoretical grounds.' (Lionel Robbins and many of his colleagues at the London School of Economics were also vigorous opponents of public works). Despite this intellectual isolation, however, Hawtrey's hostility to public works was to dominate thinking in the British Treasury in the years following the First World War. For Hawtrey the problem of general unemployment was, to borrow a phrase made famous in a different context, a 'monetary phenomenon'. As such it could only be cured by monetary means.

Expansionary fiscal policies would be powerless in relieving the acknowledged evil of mass unemployment.[5]

The analytical basis for the Treasury view was never set out in any detail,
but it appears to have rested upon an application of the classical theory of
interest. Government spending, G, was seen to constitute a source of
demand for investible funds in addition to private investment. Hence in
Figure 2.3 a rise in government expenditure from G_1 to G_2 shifts the
demand schedule for investible funds from $(I + G_1)$ to $(I + G_2)$. Private
investors must now compete for the savings of the private sector with a
government embarked on expansionary fiscal policies. As a result the
rate of interest is pushed up from r_1 to r_2. This has two effects: (a) it raises
the supply of investible funds, that is, saving rises; (b) it reduces the
private sector demand for investible funds, that is, investment falls.
However the rise in saving (effect (a)) is, once again, exactly mirrored by
an equal fall in consumption ($\Delta S = -\Delta C$). This fall in consumption,
when added to the fall in investment, leaves the overall level of
expenditure unchanged. Symbolically, since $Y = C + I + G$, and since
$\Delta G = -(\Delta C + \Delta I)$, then $\Delta Y = 0$. In modern terminology, increased
government spending is said to *crowd out* private spending. The division
of the fall in private spending between consumption expenditure and
investment expenditure will depend upon firstly the interest elasticity of
the saving schedule and secondly upon the interest elasticity of the
investment schedule.

A particular version of the Treasury view – a version which has enjoyed
a revival of professional currency in recent years – asserts that increased
government spending will be matched, dollar for dollar, by reduced
private investment. Implicitly this version is assuming that the saving
schedule is vertical, that is, that the decision of households over how to
allocate their current income between saving and consumption is
invariant with respect to the interest rate. This special case is depicted in
Figure 2.4.[6] It is important to distinguish this version of the crowding out
hypothesis from the better-known modern version popularized by

---

[5]The mainstream economists of the interwar period were, almost without exception,
united in recognizing general unemployment as a problem which purely microeconomic
measures – for example schemes to improve the mobility of labour between occupations or
regions – would be incapable of alleviating. In this respect their approach differs radically
from that of their new classical successors. For an excellent account of the historical
background of the public works debate see Peter Clarke (1988).

[6]Although Marshall was a leading proponent of the view that the rate of interest was the
reward for abstaining from present consumption, he nevertheless did not regard saving
behaviour as being particularly sensitive to variations in the rate of interest. For Marshall
the desire to save was more the outcome of habit and of 'family affection'.

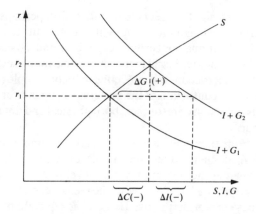

Figure 2.3 The effects of an increase in government expenditure in classical theory

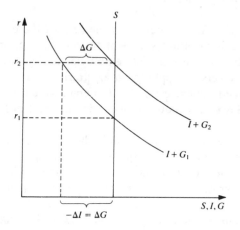

Figure 2.4 Special case: vertical saving schedule

present-day monetarists (see Chapter 4). In the Treasury view it is the *direct* pressure which extra government spending exerts upon the rate of interest which displaces private spending. The Treasury view has nothing whatsoever to do with money, though it does generate a prediction which is very congenial to monetarists, namely that fiscal policy is ineffective in altering the level of national income.

So a theory which, at first sight, appears to be rather dry, perhaps only of interest to historians of economic thought, turns out to carry wide-ranging policy implications concerning the scope and efficacy of state intervention in the economy. Fiscal activism is worse than useless: it fails to achieve its stated macroeconomic objective of higher employment but it results in the artificial contortion of the patterns of expenditure and production through its diversion of resources, both physical and financial, from the private sector.

It should be clear from the above exposition that the simple dictum 'supply creates its own demand' does not enable us to infer that the economy will settle down at the full employment level of output, which we shall denote by the symbol Y^*. Nothing in the weak version of Say's Law can justify Keynes's claim that 'Say's Law . . . is equivalent to the proposition that there is no obstacle to full employment.' Only the strong version of the Law can bear the weight of this inference.

Say's Law and the labour market

The weak version of Say's Law is a necessary element of the classical system but, taken by itself, it is not sufficient to imply an automatic tendency towards a state of rest at full employment. The central propositions of the weak version apply to an arbitrarily given level of income, a level which need not correspond to full employment income. The strong version of Say's Law requires an explicit account of labour market adjustment.

Unfortunately, as Keynes found to his dismay, there was virtually no systematic treatment of labour market adjustment in the works of the classical writers. The major exception was contained in the works of A. C. Pigou. Although he wrote extensively on the subject of unemployment, we shall confine our attention principally to two books: *Unemployment* (1913) and *The Theory of Unemployment* (1933). The classical theory of employment critically turns on the interaction between two functional relationships: a real supply curve of labour, linking the number of men offering themselves for employment to the real wage rate; and a real demand curve for labour linking the number of men that employers would ideally like to hire to the real wage rate.

The usual assumption behind the labour supply curve was that it would have a positive slope, reflecting the hypothesis that the higher the real wage rate the more willing workers would be to accept jobs or to work longer hours. The curve could in principle be vertical, in which case the negative income effect of a wage change exactly cancels out the positive substitution effect.[7] It could even be backward bending if the income effect were strongly negative – though it should not be *too* backward bending if the danger of instability was to be averted. Nevertheless, since it makes very little difference in what follows, we shall retain the usual assumption of a positively sloped labour supply curve.

Assuming perfect competition, the real demand curve for labour can be shown to coincide with the curve relating the marginal physical product of labour to the employment of labour. This proposition lies at the heart of the classical theory of employment and was one of the small number of classical postulates which Keynes retained in the *General Theory*. The economy possesses a unique short-run production function showing the maximum output which can be produced by varying the input of labour. All other factors of production, and most particularly the capital stock, are taken to be constant in the short run and the state of technological knowledge is also assumed to be given. The short-run production function is represented diagrammatically in Figure 2.5(a) in which Y is the real value of national income and L is the level of employment. The shape of the short-run production function (concave to the horizontal axis) reflects a hypothesis which had been an integral part of classical thought since the time of Ricardo: as the level of employment increases, each additional worker employed will add less to the total level of output than did his predecessor. In other words the ratio $\Delta Y/\Delta L$ will decline as the level of employment rises. The ratio $\Delta Y/\Delta L$ is known as the marginal physical product of labour. The inverse relationship between the marginal physical product of labour and the level of employment is illustrated in Figure 2.5(b).

It should be noted that both the short-run production function and the marginal product of labour curve are purely technological relationships. Economic considerations enter as soon as we pose the following question: for an arbitrarily given real wage rate – for example w_1 in Figure 2.5(b) – how many man would profit-maximizing employers wish to employ? Since the marginal product of labour and the real wage rate are both measured in terms of output, the real wage rate may also be measured along the vertical axis of Figure 2.5(b). It can be easily shown that a necessary condition for profit maximization is that the level of employment should be such that the marginal product of labour be equal to the real wage rate. In perfect competition a real wage rate w_1 will entail a demand for labour L_1. If, for whatever reason, the real wage rate were to

---

[7] Readers who are unfamiliar with the concepts of the income effect and the substitution effect should consult Samuelson and Nordhaus (1985), Chapters 19 and 28.

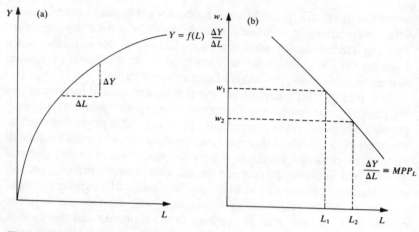

Figure 2.5 (a) Short-run production function; (b) relationship between marginal physical product of labour and employment

fall to w_2, the demand for labour would rise to L_2. Repeating the same experiment for an infinite set of values for the real wage rate yields a demand for labour curve which exactly coincides with the marginal physical product of labour curve. The hypothesis of diminishing marginal productivity[8] endows the demand curve for labour with the reassuringly negative slope of orthodox price theory.

The stage is now set for the construction of a diagram around which the whole of the classical theory of employment revolves. The real wage rate is measured on the vertical axis and the demand for and supply of labour, L^d and L^s respectively, are measured on the horizontal axis. In addition to the classical theory of interest which forms the basis for the weak version of Say's Law, the strong version of that Law requires that whenever there is an imbalance between the supply of, and the demand for, labour, the real wage rate will react in such a way as to eliminate this imbalance. For example in Figure 2.6 the general unemployment[9] associated with a real wage rate w_1 will be removed as a result of the operation of competitive forces which serve to depress the real wage rate downwards until it reaches w^*. Inspection of the diagram reveals that, at

---

[8]This hypothesis is often unhappily referred to as 'the law of diminishing returns'. This usage is avoided in this book since it can easily lead to confusion with the completely separate concepts of the diminishing/constant/increasing returns to scale.

[9]One can measure the extent of the excess supply in the labour market in two ways. It is either the horizontal distance ($L^s - L^d$) or the horizontal distance ($L^* - L^d$). For present purposes it matters little which measure is chosen.

a real wage rate w^*, there will no longer be any discrepancy between the overall demand for and the overall supply of labour: w^* is the market clearing real wage rate. Such measured unemployment as exists at this real wage rate is purely microeconomic in origin. We would nowadays call such unemployment 'frictional and structural'.

The really pivotal assumption in the above account – the assumption to which Keynes was to take grave exception – was that the real wage rate is a variable capable of direct adjustment by the process of bargaining between employers and workers. At first sight this assumption seems almost self-evidently plausible. Indeed it appears to be so painfully obvious to many modern monetarists that it requires little or no further amplification (see, for example, Friedman, 1968). The classical economists analyzed the functioning of the labour market as they would that of any other market. The labour market has a demand side, dominated largely by considerations of technology, and a supply side, dominated by the preferences of workers between work and leisure. The price which brings demand and supply into equality is the own relative price relevant to the labour market, the real wage rate. Applying the principles of partial equilibrium analysis to the economy as a whole, they inferred that competitive forces, if left free to operate without interference or friction, will automatically depress the real wage rate in the presence of general unemployment. What applied on a microeconomic plane in respect of individual labour markets was supposed to carry over to a macroeconomic plane in respect of the overall labour market. Keynes objected strongly to what he perceived to be a fallacy of composition.

In a competitive barter economy the real wage rate will clearly perform the role ascribed to it by the classical writers. If workers genuinely desire to work, that is if they are 'off' their supply curve at a point such as point A in Figure 2.6, they can always offer their labour services at a lower real wage so as to arrive back 'on' their supply curve at point D. Being paid in kind, there is no barrier to workers effecting a reduction in their rate of remuneration. They will voluntarily accept fewer loaves of bread or sacks of widgets in exchange for their labour. Moreover the distinction between the money wage and the real wage, so vital in the analysis of a money using economy, is meaningless: money, regarded as an intermediate vehicle of exchange, does not exist by definition.[10]

---

[10] Another way of viewing barter is as an economic system in which *all* goods are money in the sense that any one good may be exchanged for any other good without first being exchanged for another means of exchange. There is simply no need for such a unique medium of exchange in barter. This is how Clower (1967) perceives exchange relations in pure barter.

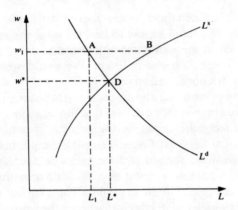

Figure 2.6   Classical theory of labour market adjustment

One of the cardinal elements of Keynes's *General Theory* was the repudiation of any such equilibrating role for the real wage rate in the context of a money using economy. Central to his critique of the classical theory of labour market adjustment was the proposition that, in a money using economy, workers and employers bargain over the level of money wages; and that a revision of the money wage bargain would have no direct effect on the level of real wages, though there might be indirect effects arising from the repercussions that a revision of the money wage contract might have on the level of aggregate demand. In other words, excess supply in the labour market might indeed put downward pressure on money wages, but without a collateral theory of the determinants of the price level no valid inference concerning the behaviour of the real wage rate could be made. Keynes was firmly of the view, for reasons which will become clear in Chapter 5, that the first-round effects of money wage cuts would be to leave the real wage rate largely unaltered.

Keynes's observation that workers and employers negotiate together to determine the level of money wages would not, in itself, have ruffled many classical feathers. Thank you, Mr Keynes, but do not waste our time by stating the obvious. Where Keynes parted company with, for example, Pigou was in his denial of any effect of money wage reductions on the real wage rate. (Note that for Keynes, as for Pigou, a reduction in the real wage rate was a necessary condition for a sustained rise in the level of employment.) But why did Pigou take it for granted that a fall in money wages would lead to a fall in real wages? This can only be a matter of conjecture but, in the author's view, three possible explanations present themselves. The first is that the classical writers tended to focus attention on the problems of an open economy in which the exchange rate was fixed with the rest of the world through an array of parities with gold. In such an economy, a reduction in the level of money wages (assuming unchanged levels of money wages in the rest of the world) will lead to a fall in the real wage rate. In the *General Theory*, however, Keynes was analyzing the effects of money wage reductions in a closed economy.

A second possible explanation has already been mentioned, namely that the classical writers were guilty of a fallacy of composition: what holds true for individual industries, regions or occupations does not hold true at the aggregate level. There is some evidence that the classical writers glided rather carelessly between micro and macro analysis. (Much the same can be said of their successors, the adherents of the new classical macroeconomics: see Chapter 7.)

A third explanation is the all important part that the quantity theory of money (see Chapter 3 below) played in the macroeconomic analysis of nearly all mainstream economists before Keynes. It is hard to over-estimate the pervasive sway that the quantity theory had held for at least two centuries. We see its influence very clearly today in the writings of the monetarists and the new classical macroeconomists. Its influence was no less powerful in the early decades of this century. Consider the example that Pigou (1913, p. 80) gives of a hypothetical economy which, starting from an initial state of full employment, suddenly experiences an outflow of gold. (The open economy analysis once again.) If money wages fail to decline *pro tanto*, the real wage will rise and, according to the marginal productivity theory of the demand for labour, employment will fall. If only money wages were perfectly 'plastic' (Pigou's usage), no general unemployment would ever occur. (The same argument applies on a microeconomic level: if wages between occupations, regions and industries, etc., were perfectly plastic, frictional and structural unemployment would remain at very low levels.) General unemployment is therefore caused by a misalignment between the general level of money wages and the quantity of money, the latter variable governing the absolute price level. Unemployment can be reduced either as a result of a reduction in money wages or an increase in the quantity of money in circulation.[11]

All in all the classical treatment of labour market adjustment at a macroeconomic level is something of a hotchpotch. It starts to make sense when the proposition that the absolute price level is determined by

---

[11]A similar conclusion, reached through a very different chain of reasoning, was to find expression in the consensus of opinion among economists which gradually evolved after the publication of the *General Theory*. Thus Modigliani (1944) wrote: 'The low level of investment and employment are both the effect of the same cause, namely a basic maladjustment between the quantity of money and the wage rate.' This is an early example of an approach which came to be known as the neoclassical synthesis.

factors other than the general level of money wages is accepted. For the majority of the classical writers this was accomplished by invoking the quantity theory of money. Once it is accepted that the quantity of money determines the absolute price level, and that the bargaining process determines the general level of money wages, then the door is open for a theory that attributes excessively high levels of unemployment to excessively high money wages. In such a theory a fall in money wages necessarily translates itself into a fall in real wages which, in turn, will induce employers to take on more labour. On the other hand if the absolute price level is determined, not by the quantity of money in circulation, but by the general level of money wages, then money wage cuts will not lead to the required reduction in the real wage, the demand for labour will not be stimulated, and the general level of employment will remain unchanged. But more of this in Chapter 5.

Conclusion

We saw in the first part of this chapter how the simple adage that 'supply creates its own demand', which we have called the weak version of Say's Law, does not carry the implication which Keynes imputed to it, namely an inherent tendency for a competitive economy to converge to a position of full employment. The weak version of Say's Law is grounded on a particular theory of the relationship of saving and investment to the rate of interest and to each other: the rate of interest moves in such a way as to ensure continual equality between saving and investment at arbitrarily given levels of income and employment. Stated slightly differently, the rate of interest adjusts in such a way as to prevent changes in the desire to save or invest from having any effect on the overall level of economic activity. In consequence the marginal propensity to spend is unity.

The strong version of Say's Law only makes sense once the weak version is supplemented by the classical theory of labour market adjustment. However, even if one accepts the functional relationships underlying this theory (in particular the marginal productivity theory of the demand for labour), the classical model of the functioning of the labour market in a closed economy is valid in only two specific circumstances. The first is where the economy under scrutiny is a competitive barter economy where the wage rate is, by definition, negotiated in real terms. The second is the case of a money using economy in which money wages and prices are determined independently of each other, money wages being determined in the bargaining process and the price level being determined by the quantity of money in circulation. It is small wonder that Keynes was at such loss to find a clear, unambiguous statement of the determinants of the real wage rate in the works of the classical economists. He surmised that the reason for this could have been that they were held captive 'partly by the settled conviction that labour is in a position to determine its own real wage and partly, perhaps, by preoccupation with the idea that prices depend on the quantity of money' (*General Theory*, p. 12).

Say's Law has left a trail of confusion in macroeconomics, so much so that W. J. Baumol (1977) has been able to track down at least eight distinct versions or interpretations of it.[12] According to the great historian of economic thought, Joseph Schumpeter (1954), J.-B. Say 'hardly understood his discovery himself and not only expressed it faultily but also misused it.'

---

[12]Thomas Sowell's entry in the *New Palgrave Dictionary of Economics* under the heading 'Say's Law' graphically illustrates the scope for confusion to which 'even intelligent thinkers of honesty and good will' are subject.

3

Old classical macroeconomics: the quantity theory of money and its descendants

In Chapter 2 we focused attention on what might be called the real sector of the classical system in that we were concerned with the determinants of certain real magnitudes – real income (Y), the general level of employment (L), the real wage rate (w), the flows of saving (S) and investment (I), and the real rate of interest (r). The factors determining certain important nominal or monetary magnitudes such as the level of money wages (W), the absolute price level (P), and the money rate of interest (i) were mentioned only in passing. The characteristics of the monetary sector of the classical system remain to be explored.

The classical dichotomy and the quantity theory of money

The fact that the real sector of the classical system can be analyzed with only the scantest reference to the monetary sector is the result of the celebrated classical dichotomy. Economics was conceived of as existing in two separate compartments each of which was hermetically sealed from the other. On the one hand there was the theory of value to which the powerful tools of marginal analysis were applied with increasing success.[1]

---

[1]Marginal analysis is the distinctive contribution of the *neo*classical school of economics. Keynes's practice of bundling all mainstream economists who preceded him into the catch-all category of 'classical economists' is highly misleading and has attracted a great deal of warranted criticism. The analytical methods of, for example, Jevons, Marshall, Fisher and Walras, and the types of problem to which they applied these methods, were light years removed from those of Adam Smith and David Ricardo. Nevertheless for the sake of exposition we shall reluctantly retain the epithet 'classical' when what we often mean is 'neoclassical'.

On the other hand there was the theory of money which concerned itself with problems such as the trade cycle and the determination of the price level. Microeconomics and macroeconomics, to use a modern distinction, comprised two entirely distinct spheres of intellectual inquiry. Few attempts were made to forge links between the two compartments. East is East and West is West, and ne'er the twain managed to meet.

The classical system can be solved sequentially, taking the real sector first and proceeding to the monetary sector. Once the magnitudes of certain real variables are known – in particular once we have ascertained the magnitudes of Y, w, ($= W/P$) and r – we are in a position to examine the contents of the monetary sector so as to be able to isolate the factors which determine the corresponding monetary magnitudes, namely, W, P, PY and i.

A necessary implication of the separation of the theory of value from the theory of money led the classical writers to claim that money is *neutral*: the magnitudes of real variables are independent of the size of the money stock. Changes in the money supply can have no lasting[2] effect on real variables. Real factors determine real variables and monetary factors determine nominal variables. At least in the longer run monetary factors have no effect whatsoever in determining the values of real variables.

The centre point of classical monetary theory was the quantity of theory of money. This was a theory of such venerable antiquity and impeccable pedigree that it came to occupy almost an axiomatic status. Expounded by such intellectual giants as David Hume,[3] David Ricardo and, in certain passages, even by Karl Marx, the simple proposition that the general price level is determined by the quantity of money in circulation, and that changes in the quantity of money lead to (more or less) equiproportionate changes in the price level, was regarded as the essential starting-point for any more detailed inquiry into monetary matters. Scholars could (and did) refine and investigate further the practical and theoretical details of monetary economics,[4] but the essential truth of the quantity theory was held to be beyond dispute.

---

[2]This is an important caveat. Most of the classical writers recognized that money may not be neutral in the short run. See the sections on Hume's *Essays* (1741–2) and on the Marshallian–Wicksellian transmission mechanism below. Once again the reasonableness of the old classical position is in marked contrast to the extreme views expressed by some members of the new classical school who regard money as neutral even in the short run.

[3]In view of the way in which Adam Smith has been appropriated as one of their own by monetarists and libertarians in recent years, it is interesting to note how strongly Smith disagreed with Hume on the need to control the growth of bank credit as a means of containing upward pressure on the price level. Smith appeared to regard an elastic supply of bank credit as a supportive concomitant to the smooth expansion of trade.

[4]Keynes's *A Tract on Monetary Reform* (1923) and *Treatise on Money* (1930) are often regarded as exemplars of this line of research.

There are two distinct formal statements of the quantity theory to be found in the literature on monetary economics. The first is the transactions approach contained in Irving Fisher's famous equation of exchange, $MV' = P'T$; the second is the Cambridge cash-balances approach summarized in the relation $M = kPY$.

Fisher's equation of exchange

The characteristic feature of Fisher's version of the quantity theory of money was his concentration on all of the monetary transactions which take place in an economy over some prespecified period of time. Let the total number of transactions be T and let P' be the average price of each transaction; $P'T$ will then be the total money value of all transactions which take place during some prespecified period of time, say a year.

In a money using economy most transactions are effected through a medium of exchange, that is, money. It is not a necessary feature of a money using economy that *all* transactions require the intermediation of money to become effective. Some transactions may be in kind. For example an individual may repair his neighbour's garden fence in exchange for some of the fruit and vegetables grown in it. No money will change hands. Nevertheless in a money using economy such transactions will be quantitatively insignificant, the great majority of transactions requiring a medium of exchange – money – to become effective.

Money is a stock which turns over a certain number of times over a period (we shall assume that the period in question is one year). Let M be the stock of money and V' be the rate at which one unit of money turns over in one year in effecting all transactions. Then obviously

$$MV' = P'T \tag{3.1}$$

However, until we start placing restrictions on this relation, it remains a pure tautology, an arithmetic necessity. An important step in transforming identity (3.1) into a theory of the price level involves placing restrictions on T and V' and in making an assumption regarding the determination of M.

The first restriction has already been encountered in a slightly different guise. The total volume of transactions, T, is determined in the real sector of the classical system. Although T and Y are far from being identical magnitudes (see the income version of the Fisher equation below), the reasons why T was regarded as invariant with respect to changes in the quantity of money were exactly the same as those that pertained to the level of real income. We saw in Chapter 2 that the real factors which determined Y were, *inter alia*, the size of the capital stock and the labour force; the state of technological knowledge; preferences between work and leisure, etc. Monetary considerations did not figure at all. Just as, in a competitive economy, Y was supposed to gravitate towards Y^*, so T will gravitate towards T^*, the number of transactions required to keep the labour force and the capital stock fully employed.

The second restriction is that V' is an institutionally determined datum in the short to medium run.[5] In the transactions approach to the quantity theory the obvious focus of attention for the determination of V' was the degree of synchronization of payments and receipts. For example, if workers are paid on a weekly basis we should expect V' to be higher than if they were paid on a monthly basis. But since there is little reason to believe that the time profile of income and expenditure in the various sectors of the economy is in any way affected by the size of the money stock, it was taken to be a plausible first approximation to assume that V' was given.[6]

Finally, the assumption concerning the behaviour of the supply of money is that M is determined independently of $P'T$. The money stock is an exogenous variable which does not respond to variations in $P'T$, as many Keynesians were to argue later. The direction of causation runs from M to $P'T$ and not vice versa. This is obviously true for a closed economy in which the sole medium of exchange is some sort of commodity money such as gold and in which the supply of commodity money cannot be augmented in any way (the gold mines have been exhausted). In this case the sheer physical impracticability of increasing the supply of the medium of exchange rules out any question of M being determined endogenously by $P'T$. But the idea that the money supply is an exogenous variable is less obviously true for an economy with a central bank – it is hard to think of many economies which are *without* a central bank – whose actions may be geared to using monetary policy to pursue intermediate objectives such as interest rate or exchange rate stability.[7]

---

[5]Note that many pre-Keynesian quantity theorists did not accept this restriction. They saw the *volatility* of V' as being a major source of monetary dislocation.

[6]Caveat: in times of substantial inflation the assumption of a constant V' was regarded as no longer tenable even as a first approximation. The enormous rise in V' during the German hyperinflation had made a great impression on professional opinion.

[7]We are wading into murky waters here. Under a regime of fixed exchange rates many monetarists – adherents to the 'monetary approach to the balance of payments' – believe that the supply of money is demand determined. That is, M^s is determined by M^d and M^d is determined by a string of variables, prominent among which will be $P'T$. With freely floating exchange rates, on the other hand, they believe that the money supply can be made to behave as a truly exogenous variable, provided that the central bank does not embark on futile attempts at controlling interest rates and concentrates on monetary aggregates alone. But even in this case the *real* money supply, i.e. the nominal money supply deflated by the absolute price level, will be demand determined.

What may hold true for an economy whose sole means of exchange is commodity money does not necessarily hold true for an economy where most transactions require the intermediation of banks and similar institutions. Nevertheless, since they were writing at a time when most advanced economies were on the gold standard, the classical writers tended to treat all money as if it were commodity money: after all, until the early years of this century,[8] bank notes, etc., could be exchanged for gold on demand at the central bank and the supply of 'other monies' was regulated in relation to the stock of gold.

It follows that, if M, V' and T are all predetermined variables, the only variable left to be determined is P'. The central proposition of the quantity theory of money follows by simple arithmetic: variations in M will produce equiproportionate variations in P' so that, in an economy with a zero rate of economic growth, the rate of inflation (dP/P) will be determined by the rate of monetary expansion (dM/M). This proposition also forms the basic tenet of modern monetarism, namely, that an inflationary process is set in motion by the actions of the central bank which, for a variety of reasons, pursues a monetary policy which results in an 'excessive' rate of growth of the money supply.

Moreover, if we accept that the real rate of interest is also invariant with respect to changes in the money stock, as it must be if money is neutral, the money rate of interest, i, will be equal to the sum of the natural (real) interest rate and the rate of inflation. That is

$$i = r_n + (dP/P) = r_n + (dM/M) \tag{3.2}$$

It must be continually borne in mind that the classical writers did not regard equation (3.2) as necessarily holding good in the short run: it was a medium- to long-run relationship.

The income version of Fisher's equation

The magnitude $P'T$ measures the money value of *all* transactions taking place in the economy over a particular period of time. For example, $P'T$ includes all intermediate transactions such as the payment of workers' wages as well as the expenditure of those wages on the final output of the economy. Many of the classical economists felt ill at ease with this rather cumbersome variable, preferring instead to emphasize only final money

---

[8]The United States and Britain came off the internal gold standard in 1914 and, after experimenting with a modified version of it after the Great War, abandoned it in the early 1930s.

income transactions, PY, where P is now a price index different from P': it is the price level of final output, what we would nowadays call the GDP deflator. They recast Fisher's equation in a form which highlighted a particular subset of all transactions, namely those transactions which involved expenditure on, and the sale of, the final output of the economy. All intermediate transactions were thereby excluded. The income version of Fisher's equation thus became

$$MV = PY \qquad (3.3)$$

where V is the income velocity of circulation of money, distinct from V', the transactions velocity of circulation in (3.1). Once again the same restrictions applied to (3.3) as applied to (3.1): Y is at its full employment value Y^*; V is fixed by the institutional arrangements of the economy; and M is, as before, the exogenously determined money stock.

The Cambridge cash-balance version of the quantity theory of money

The development of Fisher's version of the quantity theory was paralleled in Britain by the formulation of an alternative version by Alfred Marshall and his followers in Cambridge, most notable among whom was A. C. Pigou. The Cambridge writers regarded money not only as a means of exchange (the function stressed in the Fisherian approach); they regarded money as also performing the function of 'a temporary abode of purchasing power'. Money possessed qualities which were unique to itself. In particular money, unlike other stores of value, was highly liquid. It could be immediately used to effect transactions on an extensive range of goods, services and assets for which no other store of value would normally be acceptable. The convenience imparted by the quality of liquidity made money desirable as an asset to hold in its own right. The holding of money balances was regarded as an alternative to the holding of other, less liquid stores of value such as non-monetary financial assets or physical capital. The individual would weigh up the pros and cons of holding more or less money in relation to other stores of value.

In other words the Cambridge writers concentrated on the factors which would determine the *demand* for money. Given their emphasis on the 'temporary abode of purchasing power' function of money, the Cambridge School attached particular importance to individuals' expenditure flows that had to be 'serviced' by the money stock. At an aggregate level this was tantamount to singling out the money value of aggregate expenditure as the primary determinant of the demand for money. Since, in a closed economy, money expenditure equals money national income, this is equivalent to postulating that PY, the nominal value of national income, was the most important argument to be included in a demand for money function. Other factors were occasionally recognized as influencing the demand for money – most obviously the rate of interest – but pride of place was accorded to money national income. In symbols

$$M^d = kPY \tag{3.4}$$

where M^d is the demand for nominal money balances and k, often referred to as the Marshallian or Cambridge k, is interpreted as the desired ratio of the stock of money to the flow of money income.

A comparison of the Cambridge equation with the income variant of Fisher's equation might, at first blush, appear to suggest that they are equivalent since k appears to be simply the reciprocal of the income velocity of circulation of money, i.e. $k = 1/V$. On a purely formal level equations (3.3) and (3.4) are indeed identical if one ignores the 'd' superscript in (3.4). However, this apparent formal equivalence is misleading since the Cambridge equation is, as it stands, simply a theory of the demand for money: one cannot ignore the 'd' superscript. The magnitude of M^d cannot be directly observed.[9] On the other hand in equation (3.3), M is the actual, measured stock of money in circulation. Only in a state of full monetary equilibrium will M be equal to M^d. Indeed one of the reasons why subsequent monetary theorists have preferred the Cambridge version of the quantity theory over the Fisherian version is that it makes an explicit separation of the factors which determine the demand for money from the factors which determine the supply of money. Fisher's approach, with its emphasis on the institutional determinants of V and hence of k, was regarded as rather mechanical and hydraulic: something might happen to M on the left-hand side of equation (3.3) which would, if only as a result of the combination of a few restrictive assumptions with basic arithmetic, have repercussions on the right-hand side. In the Cambridge version a clear distinction is drawn between the demand for money and the supply of money. The great advantage of the Cambridge version over its Fisherian alternative is that it enabled the Cambridge School to provide a clearer account of the process by which a change in supply of money will alter the level of income. The path was clear for Marshallian supply–demand analysis: by what mechanism is M^d brought into equilibrium with M^s?

---

[9]More precisely, the demand for money can only be observed if certain assumptions concerning the determination of the supply of money and the mechanisms by which the supply of and demand for money are brought into equilibrium with each other are explicitly introduced into a fuller model.

The cash-balance transmission mechanism

Restrictions similar to those which were imposed on the income version of Fisher's equation of exchange, equation (3.3), must also be imposed, in a slightly different guise, on the Cambridge equation. Once again Y will tend towards its full employment value Y^*; the Marshallian k is, as a first approximation, assumed to be given. But there is one difference: M^d is not necessarily equal to M^s. Equation (3.4) is only one of the blades of the Marshallian scissors. The other blade, the examination of the factors determining the supply of money, was furnished by the usual summary practice of the quantity theorists: take it as a datum.

The problem which the Cambridge writers then proceeded to tackle was this: if, for whatever reason, the supply of money is not equal to the demand for money, by what mechanism will monetary equilibrium be established? In order to appreciate the process by which monetary equilibrium is attained, let us consider a specific example. Assume that the economy is initially in a state of monetary equilibrium, i.e. $M^d = M^s$. Let there be a sudden step increase in the supply of money. Since in the first instance the factors affecting the demand for money have not changed, the increase in the supply of money will produce a state of monetary disequilibrium such that $M^s > kPY^*$: there is now an excess supply of money. However this state of monetary disequilibrium will not persist because the community as a whole, holding a greater volume of nominal balances than it collectively wishes to hold, will attempt to rid itself of these excessive money balances in the only way which is available to it, namely by its increasing expenditure on a wide variety of assets and commodities. But the increase in the level of desired expenditure will hit up against supply-side barriers in the form of a fixed level of output and fixed stocks of financial and physical assets. The excess supply of money will be mirrored in   general excess demand for goods and assets which cannot, from the neutrality assumption of classical theory, be met from increased supplies of goods and assets. Prices start to rise in consequence and continue to rise for as long as there is an excess supply of money. That the inflationary process is only temporary is due to the fact that the rise in the price level itself tends to bridge the gap between the supply of and demand for money: rising prices raise the nominal demand for money and, provided that the money supply increases no further, M^d will rise until it eventually reaches the new, higher value for M^s. Once monetary equilibrium has been restored, the excess demand for goods and assets will vanish and prices will cease to rise.

Output responses in the short and long run: Hume's analysis

In his *Essays Moral, Political and Literary*, first published in 1741 and 1742, David Hume gave us what, for the time, was the clearest statement of the fundamental tenets of the quantity theory of money. His starting-point was the affirmation of his belief in the neutrality of money:

> It is indeed evident, that money is nothing but the representation of labour and commodities, and serves only as a method of rating or estimating them. Where coin is in greater plenty; as a greater quantity of it is required to represent the same quantity of goods; it can have no effect, either good or bad, taking the nation within itself . . .

However, despite his acceptance of the proposition that money is neutral[10] in the long run, Hume noted certain short-run phenomena associated with changes in the quantity of money which, at first sight, were 'not easily to be accounted for'. He observed that, in countries which had run a trading surplus with the rest of the world and which consequently had been net importers of gold, industry and agriculture were stimulated alike and output and employment rose.

But surely this observation constitutes a *prima facie* contradiction of the hypothesis that money is neutral: output and employment should remain unaffected by increases in the stock of gold. Not at all, responded Hume: the positive association between changes in the money supply and changes in output were purely transitory.

The essence of Hume's short-run/long-run distinction may be grasped quite easily from his own example. Let us assume that there is a sudden increase in exports over imports so that the economy becomes a net importer of gold. The export sector is the first to benefit from this favourable shift in the balance of trade. Exporters' incomes rise and they take steps to raise their output; they employ more labour and bid up money wages in the export sector so as to attract workers from other sectors of the economy. This rise in money wages also constitutes a rise in real wages in the export sector since the general price level has not yet risen. The increase in real wages in the export sector soon raises the demand for domestically produced commodities and their prices start to rise. There is thus a ripple effect, originating in the export sector and extending to the farthest corner of the economy. When the outermost ring of the ripple has adjusted to the increase in nominal demand, all money wages and prices are proportionately higher but the overall level

---

[10]Of course Hume would not have used this word. Similarly the phrase 'the quantity theory of money' would have been unknown to him.

and structure of real wages revert to their initial values. Similarly output and employment return to their initial levels and the balance of trade surplus vanishes as a result of the change in the terms of trade occasioned by the increase in domestic prices. Clearly Hume saw no logical contradiction in recognizing output and employment responses to a monetary disturbance in the short run and in accepting the medium- to long-run neutrality of money.

The Marshallian–Wicksellian monetary transmission mechanism

The cash-balance mechanism is a direct mechanism linking changes in the quantity of money to changes in the price level. Under the gold standard, where changes in the quantity of money come about mainly as a result of the net import or export of gold, this mechanism, coupled with the normal classical assumption of full employment, is quite helpful, as we have just seen in Hume's example. An increase in the rate of inflow of money which results from a rise in the trade surplus corresponds to a higher income flow directly accruing to the export sector.[11] The important point to note about the Hume example is that the increases in the money supply take the form of increases in income. The question which has bedevilled monetary economics for the last fifty years – through what channels does a change in the supply of money affect expenditure and nominal income? – is irrelevant in this context since a change in the money supply is simply the financial counterpart of the change in nominal income itself. Both changes are merely different ways of expressing the outcome of the same process. The increase in nominal income will lead to increased demands for goods and assets which cannot be satisfied on account of zero supply elasticities in the medium run. And this is precisely the mechanism which the cash-balance approach is so useful in eluci-dating.

Whatever the merits of the cash-balance mechanism in tracing the process of adjustment to monetary disequilibrium brought about by trade imbalances under the gold standard, it gradually came to be realized that this mechanism failed to encompass many of the indirect influences that changes in the money supply, originating from other sources, might exert. For example, it is difficult to see how the cash-balance mechanism provides an adequate account of the effects of open market operations.

---

[11]We are assuming that the improvement in the trade balance is the result of a rise in exports, not of a fall in imports.

Consider the case of an open market purchase by the central bank. When it engages in an open market purchase the bank is buying part of the holding of illiquid assets (bonds for short) in the hands of the private sector in exchange for money. The consolidated portfolio of the private sector now contains more money and fewer bonds than previously. In contrast to Hume's example in which the increase in the supply of money accrues to exporters in the form of higher income, the increase in the supply of money brought about by an open market purchase has no direct effect on the incomes of any section of society: in the first instance it leads simply to a rearrangement of private sector portfolios.

However, as Marshall and Wicksell were quick to point out, matters do not stop there since, in order to buy bonds, the central bank will normally be obliged to make it worthwhile for the private sector to surrender part of its holding of bonds in exchange for money. In general, therefore, the central bank will bid up the price of bonds as a result of its once and for all open market purchase. The yield on bonds consequently falls, as do the yields on other financial assets. In other words an open market purchase will tend to depress the general level of interest rates throughout the economy.

But surely the observation that variations in the supply of money can affect the rate of interest violates one of the basic tenets of classical economics, namely that the rate of interest is a real phenomenon, determined by the twin forces of productivity and thrift. Does it not call into question the neutrality of money? Neither Marshall nor Wicksell saw any contradiction here. The recognition that monetary factors could dominate real factors in determining the interest rate rested once again on the distinction between the short run and the medium to long run. Consider the two parts of Figure 3.1. The first part, Figure 3.1(a), has been encountered already in Chapter 2. It shows the dependence of the rate of interest on the forces of productivity and thrift. The second part, Figure 3.1(b), is less familiar and employs a concept which neither Marshall nor Wicksell would have used explicitly: the demand for money, M^d, is a decreasing function of the rate of interest, r. Recall that the variable which was accorded preeminence in determining the demand for nominal money balances in the quantity theory of money was the level of money income, PY. For a constant value of PY, the location of the demand for money function will be known.

In a state of full equilibrium the actual rate of interest which prevails will be such as to bring the desire to save and the desire to invest into equality with each other. This is the natural rate of interest, r_n. But this is not the end of the story since another requirement of equilibrium is that it should equate the desire to hold money with the existing supply of money. If the initial supply of money is M^{s1} and the demand for money

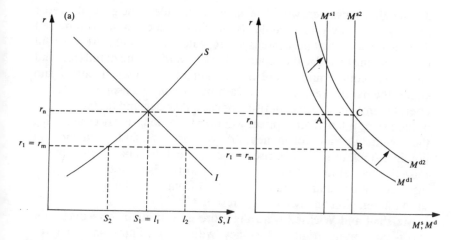

Figure 3.1 (a) Relationship of interest to saving and investment; (b) demand for money as function of rate of interest

function is M^{d1}, then the unique rate of interest which simultaneously establishes both real and monetary equilibrium is the natural interest rate, r_n.

The repercussions of an increase in the money supply brought about by a once and for all open market purchase are illustrated in Figure 3.1(b). There will be downward pressure on the rate of interest which is depicted by a move down the initial demand for money function M^{d1} from point A to point B. (Once again it must be borne in mind that Marshall and Wicksell would not employ the apparatus depicted in Figure 3.1(b), though this analysis is very much in accord with the spirit of their respective theories.) The market rate of interest, r_m, is pushed below the natural rate. From Figure 3.1(a) it is clear that the decline in the rate of interest from r_n to r_m will generate a rise in investment from I_1 to I_2. Moreover the fall in the rate of interest is also accompanied by a reduction in saving (saving falls to S_2) and by its mirror image, a rise in the demand for current consumption. Both of these repercussions – the rise in the demand for both investment goods and consumption goods – will open up what, in later Keynesian usage, came to be known as an inflationary gap. The aggregate demand for output as a whole, represented by the sum of desired consumption and desired investment, exceeds the maximum level of output that the economy is capable of producing. Either consumers or investors (or both) will be rationed in the market for commodities. (The various formulations of the concept of 'forced saving' tended to assume that capital accumulation would win the day and that consumers would be on the losing side.) The general level of prices and money wages would rise in consequence. Indeed, provided that the open market purchase is not repeated, there will exist powerful forces tending to nudge the economy back towards a state of full (real and monetary) equilibrium where the market rate of interest once again equals the natural rate. As in the cash-balance mechanism, these forces operate through the effect of rising prices on the demand for money. For as long as r_m is less than r_n prices will rise; for as long as prices are rising the nominal demand for money, M^d, will also rise; and, for a constant nominal stock of money, a rise in the nominal demand for money will raise the market rate of interest. In other words rising prices will tend to displace the demand for money function from its initial position, M^{d1}, until the function finally comes to rest at M^{d2}.

Marshall and Wicksell were therefore in a position to reconcile the short-run non-neutrality of money with its medium- and long-run neutrality by introducing the distinction between the market rate of interest, which the central bank can influence in the short run, and the natural rate of interest, which is the centre of gravity towards which the market rate will eventually tend. The mechanism which produces this centripetal tendency is a process of (temporary) price inflation or price deflation. Consequent variations in the demand for money will ensure that the market rate will eventually move back into equilibrium with the natural rate of interest.

The above analysis may be restated in terms of the Cambridge equation for the demand for money. The downward slope of the M^d functions in Figure 3.1(b) implies that the Marshallian k is not a constant in the short run, but is itself a function of the market rate of interest. In other words the Cambridge equation should be modified as follows:

$$M^d = k(r_m)PY^*$$

where $k'(r) < 0$: the lower the rate of interest, the higher the value of k, that is the higher the demand for money for a given level of money income.[12] However, owing to the fact that discrepancies between the market and natural rates of interest cannot persist into the medium and long run, in full equilibrium $r_m = r_n$. Moreover, since r_n is independently determined by productivity and thrift, it can be taken to be a datum for the reasons outlined in Chapter 2. Once the economy reverts to a state of rest, the Cambridge equation becomes

$$M^d = k(r_n)PY^*$$

---

[12]The same argument applies in reverse to V, the income velocity of circulation of money: the lower the rate of interest the higher is V since $V = 1/k$.

To summarize, although the classical writers recognized the effects of monetary policy on the market rate of interest, and hence on the optimal ratio of money to money income, these effects were evanescent. To the extent that r_n is a stable magnitude, which in turn requires that the saving and investment schedules are themselves stable, k and V may validly be regarded as parametric.

Friedman and Keynes on the Marshall–Wicksell mechanism

Largely as a result of the dominance of Keynesian monetary theory from 1936 onwards, the Marshall–Wicksell mechanism lay neglected for several decades. All earlier monetary theory was held to have been superseded by that milestone in the history of economics, Keynes's *General Theory*.[13] It was not until Milton Friedman[14] revived the Marshall–Wicksell approach to monetary theory and drew out its implications for the conduct of monetary policy that it regained some of the prominence which it certainly merited. Friedman's analysis is identical to the version of the Marshall–Wicksell mechanism outlined above in all but one respect. Whereas Figure 3.1 is couched in terms of once and for all changes in the stock of money, Friedman's analysis concentrates on the consequences of excessive rates of monetary expansion (dM^s/M^s) which are generated by misguided attempts by the central bank at maintaining interest rates at 'unnatural' levels. His analysis has been raised by one time derivative so that, instead of referring to the levels of nominal variables as above, Friedman refers to their rates of change.

The traditional role which had been assigned to monetary policy following Keynes's *General Theory* was, first, to smooth out potentially disruptive variations in the rate of interest which arise from the inherent volatility of the liquidity preference function (see Chapter 4); and, second, to maintain the general level of interest rates at 'low' levels so as to maintain a sufficient buoyancy of private investment. Low and stable interest rates were the order of the day for central banks working against a Keynesian backdrop.

Friedman (1968) delivered a withering denunciation of monetary

---

[13]There were notable exceptions. For example, Patinkin (1965) gives an excellent account of Wicksell's cumulative process.

[14]Friedman is one of those rare exceptions among modern monetarists in being thoroughly versed in the classical literature on monetary theory. Another notable exception is David Laidler.

policies conducted according to these principles. In particular he rejected any role for monetary policy in maintaining low interest rates. Low in relation to what? In relation to last year's interest rate? In relation to the interest rate prevailing ten years ago? There is, he claimed, only one criterion for judging whether the interest rate is high or low: a particular interest rate is high when it exceeds the natural interest rate and it is low when it falls below that rate. To speak of target interest rates without reference to the natural rate is theoretical nonsense. In terms of the conduct of monetary policy, the pursuit of low interest rate targets will not only fail in achieving its objective but will also produce serious inflationary side effects.

His argument runs as follows. Suppose the central bank, in thrall of its Keynesian advisers, decides to aim at a particular interest rate r_1 (see Figure 3.1(b)). The steps that the bank will take to achieve this objective will be to raise the supply of money. Initially the bank will be successful in reducing the interest rate from r_n to r_1, but once prices start to rise, the rate of interest will tend to creep back upwards towards r_n. If the bank remains committed to an interest rate target r_1, it will be obliged to increase the money supply still further, but once again the centripetal tendency of the market rate to converge on the natural rate will force the bank to increase the money supply at a rate which continually outstrips the rate of growth of output. From a process involving a piecemeal succession of step increases in the money supply, leading to a similar succession of price increases, emerges a full-blown inflationary process which, unless monetary policy changes direction, could lead to accelerating inflation and to the first glimpse of the fearful spectre of hyperinflation which lies in wait at the end of the tunnel.

Once the economy succumbs to the experience of inflation, certain other consequences will follow in its train. In particular a wedge will be driven between the nominal rate of interest, i, and the real rate of interest, r. Inspection of equation (3.2) reveals that a positive rate of inflation will entail a nominal interest rate in excess of the real rate, the difference between the two being the rate of inflation itself. Even if the central bank abandons its futile attempts to peg the real interest rate at r_1, but refuses to implement policies which will push the real interest rate above r_n, the economy will settle down to an inflationary equilibrium with $r_m = r_n$ and with $i = \mathrm{d}P/P + r_n$. Prices will be rising at a rate equal to the difference between the rate of monetary expansion and the rate of real economic growth.

The policy upshot of Friedman's analysis should be quite clear. The authorities should abandon all attempts to control a variable, the rate of interest, which is beyond their control. An active interest rate policy will always be frustrated by the tendency for the natural rate of interest to reassert itself. Moreover, since the natural rate of interest is intrinsically *unknowable*, even well-intentioned attempts to stabilize the rate of interest around a rate which is supposed to equal the natural rate are doomed to failure. The efforts of the central banks would be more profitably deployed in attempting to control the only variable which is within their power to control and whose magnitude is knowable: the role of monetary policy should be to monitor and control the rate of growth of the money supply. The monetary authorities should abandon interest rate targets in favour of money supply targets.

At this stage of the argument Friedman introduced a paradoxical contrast between his approach and that of the prevalent Keynesian conventional wisdom (remember that he was writing in 1968). It is normally assumed, he said, that low interest rates are a sign that monetary policies have been expansionary and that high rates of interest are a sign that monetary policies have been restrictive. Not so. High interest rates are the result of lax monetary policies and low interest rates are a result of tight monetary policies. The resolution of Friedman's paradox is quite simple: high *nominal* interest rates are the result of the high rate of inflation which results from attempting to use expansionary monetary policies to maintain low *real* interest rates.

Finally, it is interesting to note the unexpected similarities between Friedman's analysis and that contained in various passages of Keynes's *General Theory* which refer to full employment states. Unfortunately terminological differences tend to obscure these similarities since Keynes preferred to use the phrase 'the neutral rate of interest' where Marshall, Wicksell and Friedman used the phrase 'the natural rate of interest'. The 'neutral' rate of interest *à la* Keynes and the 'natural' rate *à la* Marshall turn out to be identical: 'the *neutral* rate of interest [is] the natural rate in the above sense which is consistent with *full* employment' (*General Theory*, p. 243, original italics). Keynes refers to the impossibility of the actual interest rate being below this neutral, full employment rate without producing demand inflationary consequences: '[The rate of interest] cannot be in equilibrium at a level *below* the level which corresponds to full employment; because at such a level a state of true inflation will be produced' (*General Theory*, p. 202, original italics). In other words, Keynes was counselling against misguided attempts by the monetary authorities to peg the rate of interest below the neutral rate on account of the inflationary consequences which would ineluctably follow. Since the neutral rate is that minimum interest rate consistent with full employment, no good can come from a monetary policy which aims to stimulate demand by reducing the interest rate still further. The only variable that can 'give' in such circumstances is the absolute price level. A diagrammatic representation of Keynes's state of 'true inflation' is given in Figure 4.17 in Chapter 4. However, in a state of unemployment equilibrium in which the rate of interest exceeds its neutral value Keynes argued that it was a proper objective of monetary policy to use those instruments at its disposal – including, obviously, the money supply – to coax the rate of interest downwards so as to raise private investment.

Monetarism and the quantity theory of money*

We shall see in Chapter 4 how the Keynesian revolution seriously undermined the analytical foundations of the quantity theory of money. For Keynesians, the quantity theory of money either had to be abandoned as totally useless or, less drastically, had to be radically modified to encompass the lasting effects of changes in the quantity of money on the level of real income. Throughout most of his career as a professional economist, Keynes had adhered to the basic tenets of the quantity theory, having been brought up in the quantity theory tradition by Marshall and Pigou. Indeed his influential *Tract on Monetary Reform* (1923) is nowadays widely hailed as a paragon of monetarist orthodoxy. He was therefore more inclined to be lenient on the quantity theory than most of his followers – witness his attempt at formulating a 'generalized quantity theory of money', discussed in the last section of Chapter 4.

As is almost inevitably the case, the vigorously expressed views of Keynes's more enthusiastic disciples were to carry the day. The money supply was dislodged from its position of prominence at the centre of macroeconomic debate and was ignominiously shunted into the comparative obscurity of specialist tracts on money and banking. For the vast majority of macroeconomists during the thirty years following the publication of Keynes's *General Theory*, alterations in the money supply were of no intrinsic interest. To the extent that variations in the money supply mattered at all they mattered only in so far as they accompanied changes in other, more important variables such as the rate of interest or the nominal exchange rate.

Nevertheless, despite the almost universal acceptance of Keynesian ideas in academic, political and journalistic circles after the Second World War, there was a small band of economists who kept the faith, refusing to succumb to what had, by then, become a new orthodoxy. Most conspicuous among the ranks of the Old Believers were the members of

---

*This section presumes some knowledge of Keynesian monetary economics. The reader may choose to skip this section and return to it once he has digested the contents of Chapter 4.

the Chicago School of monetary economics.[15] Milton Friedman (1956) has written eloquently of how the guttering embers of the quantity theory of money were rekindled and, eventually, revived by the Chicago 'oral tradition'.[16]

Friedman's justly celebrated essay, 'The quantity theory of money: a restatement', was a landmark in the development of macroeconomics since it cleared the ground for the eventual reinstatement of the quantity theory of money to its former position of pre-eminence in macroeconomics and monetary theory. A detailed account of the 'restatement' would take us far beyond the compass of this book.[17] However there are certain propositions which are of pivotal significance for the subsequent evolution of monetarist thought. One important proposition is the following:

> The quantity theory is in the first instance a theory of the demand for money. It is not a theory of output, or of money income, or of the price level. Any statement about these variables requires combining the quantity theory with some specifications about the conditions of supply of money and perhaps about other variables as well. (Friedman, 1956)

Judging from this commendably modest statement it would appear that the quantity theory is of only limited relevance to the formulation of a strategy for macroeconomic management since it is presented as but one building block within a larger edifice. But Friedman ventured further by claiming that a quantity theorist 'accepts the empirical hypothesis that the demand for money is highly stable'. Of course this should not be taken to imply that the velocity of circulation of money, V, or the Cambridge k, are 'numerically constant over time'. What it does imply is that the behaviour of V and k should be explicable in terms of variations of a small number of determining variables. The most obvious example of

---

[15]Mention should also be made of the Austrian School, and in particular F. A. von Hayek, who never accepted the validity of Keynesian economics and hence never accepted the Keynesian dismissal of the quantity theory.

[16]Don Patinkin, one of the most distinguished products of the economics department of the University of Chicago, has taken issue with Friedman's account of the supposedly widespread acceptance, oral or otherwise, of the quantity theory among faculty members in the post-1936 period. Patinkin cites his own lecture notes for the years 1942–45 in order to dispute, *inter alia*, Friedman's claim of intellectual continuity from around the mid-1920s down to 1956, the year in which Friedman's 'restatement' of the quantity theory was published. Perhaps rather tongue in cheek, Patinkin preferred to regard Friedman's essay, not as a 'restatement of the quantity theory of money', but rather as 'a most elegant and sophisticated statement of modern Keynesian monetary theory' (Patinkin, 1972, p. 108). Damnation by faint praise?

[17]Patinkin's 1972 essay is a healthy antidote to the plethora of sweeping generalizations which give the 'restatement' much of its 'flavour' (a favourite Friedmanite word).

predictable variations in V and k has already been touched upon in our simple account of the Marshall–Wicksell transmission mechanism where the demand for money depends upon only two variables, the rate of interest, r, and the level of money income, PY. In Figure 3.1 a knowledge of the level of money income enables us to locate the position of the M^d function in (r, M) space, while a knowledge of the rate of interest enables us to locate our position along this M^d function.

Nevertheless we are still a long way from the arena of ideological controversy. Almost all of the Keynesian economists who wrote on monetary matters accepted that the demand for money depended, *inter alia*, on the rate of interest and on the level of money income, though they also tended to share Keynes's apprehension that the demand for money might be highly unstable, being liable to sudden parametric shifts with each change of 'the state of the news'. Thus far, however, there appeared to be little to set the world on fire.

From the early 1960s onwards matters started to hot up as a result of a series of empirical studies which found significant correlations between changes in the money supply, M^s, and changes in money income, PY. It was at this stage that a vital shift of focus occurred which gave powerful impetus to the development of full-blown monetarism. The modest claims which Friedman had made on behalf of the quantity theory in his 1956 'restatement' ('the quantity theory is not a theory of output, or of money income, or of the price level') gave way to a series of unequivocally doctrinaire generalizations regarding the relationship between the quantity of money and the level of money income. These generalizations in turn gave rise to the re-emergence of the quantity theory of money as a theory of determinants of the absolute price level, playing the role that had previously been assigned to it by the classical writers, a role that lies at the very heart of modern monetarism.

The apparently significant correlations between left-hand side variables – normally the nominal money stock or its rate of change – and right-hand side variables – normally money income or its rate of change, various measures of the rate of interest, etc. – were almost universally interpreted as suggesting stable demand for money functions. This was an enormous interpretative leap since the only left-hand side variables which are ever directly observable are supply-side variables. It was, and to a large extent remains, an essential canon of monetarist faith that these correlations must be interpreted as demand for money functions.

Only a few isolated dissidents, most notably Nicholas Kaldor, pointed to a more realistic alternative explanation for this apparent econometric stability. Accepting for the sake of argument that the statistical evidence did in fact come down on the side of a set of strong correlations between certain measures of money and of money income, the statistical relations that were being estimated were not stable demand for money functions at all but rather stable *supply* of money functions. What Kaldor was suggesting was that changes in money income would, in certain circumstances, lead to changes in the supply of money. This can happen for a variety of reasons, but perhaps the most obvious case of such a causal nexus is when the central bank pursues interest rate targets.[18] Since an increase in money income can be expected, *ceteris paribus*, to raise interest rates, a pre-emptive increase in the money supply will serve to relieve upward pressure on interest rates. In other words, increase in money income will result in increases in the money supply: increases in the demand for money balances are being continually fed by increases in the supply of such balances. In essense the supply of money is demand determined. It does not have an independent life of its own: it is not exogenous.

Given that interest rate targets were operative throughout most of the post-war period, it is small wonder that a strong correlation between changes in money and changes in money income should have been manifest in regression equations for that period. For Kaldor the monetarist fallacy cropped up at the most elementary level of statistical testing: whereas in most areas of applied econometric research great care would be taken to accommodate the 'identification' problem, monetarists tended to brush such problems to one side by simply *assuming* that a demand-side relationship was being observed. Kaldor (1970) insisted that, for most of the period over which regression equations had been estimated, the supply of money had been an endogenous variable, that is a variable whose behaviour is linked to the behaviour, actual or anticipated, of other variables. In our simple example movements in the money supply are determined by movements in money national income via the potential effects of the latter on the rate of interest. To treat the money supply as exogenous by analogy with commodity money (e.g. gold) is tantamount to discounting the repercussions of two centuries of financial innovation and development.

What external factors may give rise to autonomous increases in money national income? One obvious factor is fairly uncontroversial: real economic growth. Exogenous increases in the Y component of PY may occur either as a result of capital formation or technical progress or both. In all events PY will rise, so too will the demand for money and, if the authorities take steps to offset potentially deleterious increases in the rate of interest, the money supply will be expanded.

---

[18] A similar argument applies when the central bank pursues targets for the nominal exchange rate.

But what about the P component of PY? What factors may account for the persistent tendency for the price level to rise over time? It is in response to this question that quite fundamental differences of opinion emerge between monetarists and what may be loosely called Keynesians.[19] British Keynesians, in particular, have tended to view an inflationary process as the outcome of the exercise of trades union power on both the microeconomic level and on the macroeconomic level. Various theories have been proposed which suggest that the rate of inflation may, at best, be only weakly related to the level of aggregate demand and may, at worst, be totally unrelated to aggregate demand. For example, the real wage resistance hypothesis, first formalized by Sir John Hicks, posits that trades unions will take steps to protect the real wages of their members in the face of unfavourable external developments such as a deterioration in the terms of trade brought about by a depreciation of the nominal exchange rate. Another hypothesis points to rivalry among different trades unions which leads to leapfrogging wage claims. These disparate, but potentially complementary, hypotheses have been grouped together as *cost–push* explanations of an inflationary process. Their common features are at once negative and nebulous. On the negative side they deny any role to monetary expansion in initiating an inflationary process. Any observed correlation between variations in the price level and variations in the money supply arises from the upward pressure on the demand for nominal money balances that is exerted by autonomous increases in P and hence in PY. Once again the objective of stabilizing interest rates obliges the central bank to accommodate autonomous, inflation-induced increases in money national income.

The nebulous aspect of the cost–push approach concerns its econometric testability: how can one possibly measure attitudinal variables such as the degree of militancy of trades unions or the intensity of the rivalry among trades unions? The various attempts at formally modelling such hypotheses empirically have stumbled at the first hurdle, namely, the almost insurmountable difficulty of devising a convincing, measurable variable with which to gauge the strength of cost–push pressures. Indeed, there are few hypotheses which are more calculated to provoke a sense of profound exasperation and contempt, even among quite moderate monetarists, than cost–push models of inflation. Laidler (1974) goes so far as to accuse those who adhere to cost–push explanations of inflation of practising 'bad economics'. Cost–push theorists retort by

---

[19]This is loose usage in the sense that Keynes himself had very little to say about the determinants of money wages and prices apart, of course, from opining that money wages tended to be downwardly rigid on account of a highly interdependent set of microeconomic labour supply functions: see Chapter 5.

rejecting what they regard as a spurious scientism, insisting that a hypothesis may still be correct even though it is formally untestable by standard econometric criteria. With a certain sense of *Schadenfreude* they also point out that recent experience, particularly in Western Europe, tends to bolster their scepticism on the connection between inflation and aggregate demand. Endemic inflationary pressures have persisted in these economies despite unprecedentedly high levels of unemployment. While monetarists and those of similar sympathies have been driven to devising theories to explain why the 'non-accelerating inflation rate of unemployment' (NAIRU) has shown such an alarming upward trend, cost–push theorists persist in the view that NAIRUs simply did not exist in the first place! The *a posteriori* search for explanations of rising NAIRUs is little more than a wasteful chase after a will o' the wisp.

Kaldor's dissident view concerning the direction of causation between money and money income has never commanded general acceptance among macroeconomists.[20] The unearthing of stable demand for money functions, combined with the belief that, given the political will, the supply of money could be controlled by the actions of the central bank, had policy implications which were at once wide ranging and quite disarmingly simple. The demand for nominal money balances, M^d, is, at a first approximation, a function of a small number of variables. Of paramount importance among these is the level of money income, PY. On the other hand the supply of nominal money balances, M^s, is, according to this view, under the direct control of the monetary authorities. The money supply is exogenous. A one-off increase in the money supply will stimulate desired monetary expenditures. In the short run output will rise, but in the medium run the whole of the increase in the money supply will be dissipated in the form of higher prices. In all events PY rises in proportion to the rise in M^s, this rise in money income being just sufficient to raise M^d to a level consistent with monetary equilibrium.

It should be clear from the above account that monetarists lay the blame for unacceptably high rates of inflation at the door of profligate central bankers and their misguided (Keynesian?) advisers. The cure for inflation should be equally clear: put into reverse those policies which

---

[20]More's the pity. If Kaldor's argument had been properly taken on board by applied econometricians they would have been spared a great deal of painful head scratching when they tried to explain why 'demand' for money functions appeared to have broken down from the early 1970s onwards. For an example of this reluctance to give a serious airing to the 'endogeneity' argument, see Judd and Scadding (1982). These authors work mercilessly on their scalps in a largely unsuccessful attempt to explain the recent monetary experience of the United States.

caused the problem in the first place. The rate of growth of the money supply should be brought down (gradually, counsels Friedman) until it is growing in line with the secular rate of growth of output, always bearing in mind that the income velocity of circulation of money may exhibit an upward trend as a result of, for example, financial innovation.

Although the primary focus of attention in this chapter has been the role of the quantity theory of money in pre-Keynesian macroeconomics, we have succumbed to the natural temptation of drawing preliminary comparisons between old and new macroeconomics. Admittedly modern monetarism can draw upon a far more complex literature[21] than the rather simple ideas of the classical writers. Nevertheless the similarity of approach between the old quantity theory of money and modern monetarism is really quite striking. Gone are Friedman's earlier reservations ('the quantity theory is not a theory of output, or of money income, or of the price level'). The quantity theory has resumed its old role as a theory of prices first and foremost. In this context it is instructive to examine how Friedman himself eventually conceived of the differences between monetarists on the one hand and Keynesians on the other. In his celebrated 'common model', Friedman (1974a) presented a set of equations which are essentially the equations for the *IS–LM* model of income-expenditure equilibrium. These equations are supposed to constitute the common core of both Keynesian and monetarist modes of analysis. This common core is, as it stands, indeterminate since there is one equation too few. Equivalently there is one variable too many. The system can only be made fully determinate by imposing restrictions on one of the variables, and it is at this point that the monetarist and Keynesian approaches diverge. Monetarists assume that real income is predetermined at its full employment, natural value Y^*, and hence, for monetarists, the primary focus of attention is the determinants of the absolute price level, P. By contrast Keynesians, being more concerned with the factors that determine the level of real income, Y, relegate the determinants of the absolute price level to a subsidiary order of importance. The Keynesian device for ensuring the full determinacy of the 'common model' is, according to Friedman, to assume that the price level is exogenously given. In symbols, monetarists assume that $Y = Y^*$ and concentrate on the determinants of P; Keynesians, on the other hand, assume that $P = P_0$, where P_0 is an arbitrarily fixed level of absolute prices, and concentrate on the determinants of Y. Friedman

---

[21]The formal analysis of, for example, Karl Brunner and Allan Meltzer's various models is, at times, almost impenetrable. These two authors, who almost always wrote together, originally coined the word 'monetarist' to cover a broad approach to monetary theory and policy.

recognized that this was only a first approximation to a satisfactory analytical separation between rival positions, but he insisted that these distinctions were broadly accurate.

This rather naïve taxonomic exercise met with predictably vocal dissent among Keynesians: if Keynesians really had assumed that the price level was exogenously fixed at P_0 they would have laid themselves open to the serious charge of indifference to price inflation. That the Keynesian school has wrongly come to be identified in popular debate with 'inflationism' speaks volumes for the success of the sustained monetarist onslaught on what had appeared to be an unassailable orthodoxy. The fact is, of course, that although Keynesians share the monetarists' concern about the evils of inflation, they do not regard inflation as the only macroeconomic problem which governments ought to tackle. In particular, Keynesians insist that, in certain circumstances, it is within the power of governments to take measures to alleviate excessively high levels of unemployment. The objective of maintaining acceptably low levels of unemployment and the objective of keeping the lid on inflationary pressures may come into conflict with each other (see Chapter 6 on Phillips curves, etc.). Nevertheless this potential for conflict between policy objectives does not imply that the authorities should abandon all macroeconomic attempts to mitigate the burden of general unemployment. This is in stark contrast with the monetarist view which sees no role for active employment policies: the level of unemployment will be 'ground out [at its natural level] by the Walrasian system of general equilibrium equations' (Friedman, 1968). Through monetarist eyes, the only valid focus of attention for policy makers is the rate of inflation, and the only appropriate instrument for bringing the rate of inflation down to acceptable levels is successive reductions in the rate of growth of the money supply. If only the problems of macroeconomic management were so simple!

Conclusions

We have seen in this chapter how there is a strong line of continuity running from that indispensable constituent part of the old classical macroeconomics, the quantity theory of money, through the refinements of that theory in the nineteenth and early twentieth centuries and down to the revival of a revamped quantity theory by Friedman and his monetarist followers. The advent of the new classical macroeconomics (see Chapter 7) was to mark the complete rehabilitation of the quantity theory at the very core of macroeconomic analysis. Monetarists, old and new, handle the effects of alterations in the money supply in remarkably similar fashion, though there may be differences of emphasis regarding the channels through which the 'transmission mechanism' operate. For Hume, as for Friedman, the initial repercussion of, for example, an increase in the money supply is a temporary stimulus to output and employment, prices rising in this initial stage less than proportionately to the rise in the money supply. In the longer run, however, the neutrality of money reasserts itself: output reverts to its full employment (natural) value, and prices rise equiproportionately to the increase in the money supply. Since money is neutral in all but the short run,[22] the classical dichotomy must be reinstated.

Monetarists have a marked penchant for charting the impressive genealogical credentials of their theories. After all, most of the great thinkers on economic matters have, at one time or another, embraced a version of the quantity theory of money, even the egregious Mr Keynes. This zeal to trace the intellectual lineage of monetarism is exemplified in the work of Milton Friedman. By the mid-1970s, when the monetarist star was very much in the ascendant, nagging doubts remained concerning the *mechanism* by which changes in the money supply affected changes in the price level in advanced capitalist economies, where the principal medium of exchange is what may be loosely termed 'bank' money as opposed to commodity money. This was a ticklish question at the time since there seemed to be no professional consensus as to the nature of the transmission mechanism. The suspicions of many sceptics were aroused by the tendency of some monetarists (for example, A. A. (now Sir Alan) Walters (1971)) to skirt this question, preferring instead to concentrate on the uncovering of statistical regularities. A rather crude scientism had by then come into vogue. The sceptics responded to the rather patchy treatment of the transmission mechanism by referring to the 'monetarist black box': the money supply went in on one side of the box and the price level (or the level of money income) came out at the other side, but the process by which an alteration in the former produced an alteration in the latter remained mysterious to the non-monetarist.

The origins of the 'black box' allegations are complex, but they lay partly in Friedman's (1969) celebrated, but unfortunate, analysis of the repercussions for aggregate spending and the price level of scattering ten-dollar notes from a helicopter. This model provoked widespread criticism. Is Friedman really asking us to believe, his critics asked, that the effects of, say, a single open market purchase are to be analyzed by analogy with such aerial beneficence?

Friedman was clearly stung by such criticisms. His riposte was to hark

---

[22]For many new classical macroeconomists, money is neutral even in the short run.

back to David Hume:

> I must say there are few things that annoy me more . . . than continual
> repetition of black box arguments. What is the mechanism? . . . If anybody
> asks what is the mechanism whereby an increase in the money supply brings
> about an increase in prices, what David Hume has to say answers that question
> about as well as anything else I know. I ask myself, what do we really know that
> he did not know, and there is only a very little. We know the numbers better;
> we can attach numerical magnitudes; and we are a bit more sophisticated about
> the dynamic process of decelerating and accelerating inflation than he was; but
> beyond that he had it all. (Friedman, 1974b)

I would hazard that few disinterested readers of his *Essays* would feel
sufficiently confident to conclude that, technical matters apart, Hume
'had it all', particularly with reference to economies where the stock of
gold does not constitute the predominant means of exchange.

Keynesian critics of monetarism have highlighted the dangers inherent
in maintaining an intellectual tradition to well beyond its sell-by date. The
classic statements of the quantity theory of money were formulated at a
time when the only universally accepted means of exchange was
commodity money, normally gold. In the days of Hume, Smith and, to a
lesser extent, Ricardo, it would have been hard to conceive of the
subsequent developments which were to take place in banking practice in
particular, and the financial environment in general. The fact that such
developments have taken place and will continue to take place requires
monetarists and Keynesians alike to undertake a continuous root and
branch rethink about how alterations in the money supply affect
economic activity.[23] To treat the money supply as we understand it at the
end of the twentieth century as exerting an influence directly analogous to
that of gold in the eighteenth century is highly misleading. For example,
the broad definition of money favoured by most monetarists principally
comprises bank deposits. It is straining credibility more than a little to
view increases in the total volume of bank deposits (or, on the other side
of the balance sheet, increases in the extent of bank credit) as having very
similar effects in a modern economy to those of increases in the supply of
gold in eighteenth-century England. Circumstances alter cases.

---

[23] I should not like to leave readers with the false impression that monetarists are
unworldly, innocent of the technicalities of monetary policy in advanced economies.
Nothing could be further from the case. Many have their fingers very much on the pulse of
day to day developments in a wide range of financial markets. Others have written learned
histories of the monetary experience of various countries: *vide* Friedman and Schwartz's
(1963) monumental *A Monetary History of the United States, 1867–1960*. Nevertheless,
despite the formidable scholarly output of the monetarists, the fact remains that, in public
discussion of their ideas, their rhetoric assumes an overtly polemical tone. Simplistic,
normally hydraulic, images are conjured up ('pumping new money into the system') in order
to win over the allegiance of the less sophisticated.

4

The Keynesian revolution

> The composition of this book has been for the author a long struggle of escape . . . a struggle of escape from habitual modes of thought and expression . . . The difficulty lies, not in the new ideas, but in escaping from the old ones, which ramify, for those brought up as most of us have been, into every corner of our minds.
>
> (J. M. Keynes, *General Theory*, p. viii)

The 'old ideas' which Keynes had such difficulty in shaking off were, of course, the constituent parts of the classical theory of the macroeconomy: the real theory of interest, the theory of labour market adjustment, and the quantity theory of money. Indeed, as Keynes himself conceded, the classical system made perfect sense once the fundamental premise upon which it was grounded was accepted from the outset: the proposition which lay at the heart of the strong version of Say's Law, namely, that there existed a stable equilibrium at full employment.

Despite the remarkable robustness of the classical model, the interwar period witnessed a growing dissatisfaction with its ability to explain persistent mass unemployment. It will be recalled from Chapter 2 that the classical writers laid the blame for the widespread unemployment of the period at the door of monopolistic elements in the labour market which prevented money wages from falling to their 'appropriate' level in relation to the stock of money. Nevertheless this explanation sounded increasingly hollow as each year of the Depression came and went. Enter, in 1936, *The General Theory of Employment, Interest and Money*.

Keynes rejected the classical view that, even in a perfectly competitive economy, spontaneous disturbances such as a fall in desired investment would be prevented from affecting the levels of income and employment as a result of smooth adjustments of relative prices which serve to maintain equilibrium at full employment. The two most important relative prices which were supposed to perform this equilibrating function in classical macroeconomics were the real wage rate and the real rate of interest. Keynes attempted to demonstrate how these two critical relative prices would not adjust in such a way as to maintain full employment. Moreover, he maintained that this 'failure' on the part of relative prices was not the result of the presence of monopolistic forces which impeded the process of relative price adjustment. In deriving his own theory of employment he made the assumption which was most favourable to the classical position, namely that of perfect competition. Nevertheless, despite this apparently uncongenial assumption, he claimed to have exposed the forces which could hold the economy in the grip of general unemployment for long periods of time.

In order to clear the ground for his own theory of employment, Keynes set out to undermine the twin supportive pillars of the classical edifice: the theory of interest and the theory of labour market adjustment. His critique and reformulation of the theory of interest will be dealt with in a later section of this chapter; the analysis of the labour market will be dealt with in Chapter 5. Nevertheless it is instructive to anticipate matters a little and take a bird's eye view of Keynes's theory, a theory which, with the benefit of hindsight, he was to regard as 'extremely simple and should be obvious' (*General Theory*, p. viii: henceforth page and chapter references to the *General Theory* will be denoted by the abbreviation *GT*).

The principle of effective demand

The idea that lies at the heart of the *General Theory* is the principle of effective demand which, at its barest, states that, in an economy which is not yet hitting up against any supply-side constraints, the level of output will be determined by the sum of the expenditure plans of different sections of society.[1] Almost the whole of the *General Theory* is given over to an analysis of the simplest case, that of a closed economy with no government but, curiously, with a central bank. There is therefore no analysis of the effects of variations in either government expenditure, G, or in the overall level of taxation, T, upon the level of national income. In

---

[1]Complications arise in an open economy since expenditure by domestic residents on goods produced abroad must be deducted from expenditure by foreigners on domestically produced goods.

this case desired real expenditure, E, can be divided simply into two constituent parts: desired real consumption expenditure, C, and desired real investment expenditure, I. Thus $E = C + I$. The principle of effective demand states that output will settle down at a unique level where the combined expenditure plans of consumers and investors are simultaneously realized. That is the *equilibrium* level of output satisfies the condition that $Y = E = C + I$. The most rudimentary expression of this principle is the familiar Keynesian cross diagram, alias the 45° diagram.[2]

We shall refer to the $E = C + I$ line as the *aggregate expenditure function*. This function is 'flatter' than the 45° line because of the leakage through saving: as income rises, consumption rises, but by less than the rise in income since saving also rises. Inspection of Figure 4.1 reveals that the equilibrium level of national income is Y_1, for only at this level will planned expenditure and income be equal to each other. On the other hand if the level of income happens to be Y_2, planned expenditure will only equal E_2. Some part of the output of the economy will be left unsold, thereby leading to an unwanted accumulation of inventories by firms (the rate of inventory accumulation is represented by the vertical distance BC). Sooner or later firms will cut back on the scale of production and employment and the economy will converge towards the equilibrium level of income, Y_1.

If the aggregate expenditure function shifts upwards either as a result of an improvement in business confidence leading to an increase in desired investment or as a result of a spontaneous rise in the propensity to consume, output and employment will rise by an amount sufficient to restore equality between desired expenditure and real income. The Keynesian model of the determination of national income is thus based on the income–expenditure method of analysis since it postulates that, if the initial state of the economy is one of less than full employment, income will be determined by aggregate desired expenditure.

In this most basic of models, a rise in income can only come about either through a rise in consumption or through a rise in investment. Keynes focused particular attention on the effects of changes in investment on the level of national income, introducing a modified version of R. F. Kahn's (1931) multiplier analysis. But the income–expenditure model can be extended in a variety of directions. Government expenditure can be included as an additional source of demand, similar in its effects to private investment; variations in the general level

---

[2]Readers who are unfamiliar with this diagram should consult any elementary textbook on economics. A simple account is also contained in Trevithick, 1983, Chapter 3.

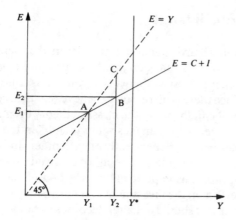

Figure 4.1 Keynesian cross diagram

of taxation will alter both consumption and investment expenditure; the open economy version of the model treats a rise in exports as a stimulus to demand and a rise in imports as a diminution of demand. Monetary policy may also be brought into the picture by making the rate of investment dependent upon the rate of interest which, in turn, is influenced by the monetary environment. Nevertheless, despite the complexities that can be introduced into full-blown Keynesian models, the essence of the income–expenditure method remains substantially intact.

It was Keynes's fundamental contention that there is no reason to believe that the equilibrium level of income – fortuitous accidents apart – will coincide with the full employment level of income, Y^*. Persistent general unemployment could therefore be attributed to an overall deficiency of aggregate demand relative to full-employment income. This deficiency of demand accounts for the discrepancy between Y_1 and Y^* in Figure 4.1. General unemployment, for which monopolistic forces in the labour market had previously been held to be culpable, came to be seen as the most alarming and conspicuous byproduct of a more radical phenomenon, a general deficiency of demand for output as a whole. The income–expenditure method turned Say's Law on its head:

> For the proposition that supply creates its own demand, I shall substitute the proposition that expenditure creates its own income, i.e. an income just sufficient to meet the expenditure. This, we shall find, is a more general proposition than the former. (*Collected Writings of John Maynard Keynes*, henceforward abbreviated to *CW*, Vol. XIX, pp. 80–81)

The Keynesian theory of interest

Keynes's starting-point in his investigation of the factors that determine the rate of interest was a spirited attack on the classical theory of interest (see *GT*, Chapter 14). Since classical theory rests on the assumption of full employment, and since there is no reason to believe that the economy actually is in a state of full employment, the classical theory of interest is indeterminate. Classical theory only makes sense if shifts in the saving and investment schedules occur independently of each other. In classical theory, a shift in the saving schedule as a result of changed preferences regarding present and future consumption patterns by households should not, in itself, have any effect on the investment schedule. And vice versa: a change in the desire to invest should not alter decisions by households as to how to arrange their consumption expenditure over time.

This approach would be perfectly reasonable,[3] said Keynes, if it were possible to fix the position of the saving schedule. However, since saving was a function of income as well as the rate of interest, i.e. $S = S(r,Y)$, one had to have prior knowledge of the level of income before one could locate the position of the saving schedule in (r, S) space. The classical writers were able to refer to a unique saving schedule by taking the level of income to be given at its full employment value. The saving schedule which they were in effect analyzing was the full employment saving schedule, $S^* = S(r, Y^*)$. But this schedule is but one among an infinite set of possible saving schedules in (r, S) space, each particular schedule being defined with respect to a specific level of income.

Consider the example illustrated in Figure 4.2. The initial saving and investment schedules are S' and I' respectively. We are assuming an initial state of unemployment equilibrium so that the saving schedule S' does not coincide with the full employment saving schedule $S^* = S(r,Y^*)$. What would happen if there were a sudden improvement in the state of business confidence which resulted in a rise in desired investment at all rates of interest? The investment schedule shifts from a position I' to a position I''. The classical theory of interest predicts that the rate of interest will rise from r_1 to r_2. Keynes's liquidity preference theory of interest, on the other hand, rules out such a change in the rate of interest (see the next paragraph but one). The principle of effective demand suggests that, in an underemployed economy, a rise in desired investment will raise the level of income by some multiple of the increase in investment (in the simplest case that multiple is equal to $1/1 - c$, where

---

[3]Reasonable but misguided since monetary forces in fact dominate real forces in the determination of the rate of interest.

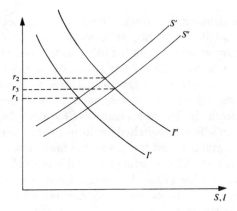

Figure 4.2 Interdependent saving and investment schedules

c is the marginal propensity to consume). Since s, the marginal propensity to save $(s = (1 - c))$, is positive, the rise in income will serve to shift the saving schedule to a position such as S''.[4]

The upshot of this objection to the classical theory of interest is thus that it is impossible to ascertain by how much a given change in the desire to invest will affect the rate of interest until the effect that such a change has upon the level of income has also been determined. Saving and investment schedules are not independent of each other. This proposition holds good even if the initial state is one of full employment: a fall in the desire to invest or a rise in the propensity to save will reduce national income, which in turn will cause the saving schedule to shift to the left.

The indeterminacy allegation, though powerful in highlighting the destructive force of abandoning the assumption of full employment, was not, in itself, world shattering. Indeed, if Keynes had stopped there, the classical writers could have disposed of his criticisms without difficulty. They could have hit back by asking: you assert that income alters as a result of a change in, for example, the desire to invest; we have always argued that the rate of interest, not the level of income, will bear the brunt of this parametric change; can you advance arguments – no assertions please – which may lead us to abandon our view?

So Keynes had to go very much further than merely point out that the classical theory of interest was indeterminate. And this he duly did. The classical theory of interest was not only indeterminate, continued

---

[4]We are not yet in a position to determine where the new saving schedule will be located and hence are not able to give a value to r_3, the new rate of interest. The full *IS–LM* system is required before we can find solutions for all of the major variables: see below.

Keynes, it was also fundamentally wrong. Classical theory neglected considerations of stock equilibrium in the market for financial assets. The liquidity preference theory of interest, on the other hand, concentrated on the role that preferences between existing stocks of financial assets played in determining the rate of interest. Saving and investment can, as a first approximation, be regarded as the flow demand for, and supply of, new financial assets respectively. The novel feature of Keynes's theory of interest was the manner in which he switched the focus of attention away from the *flow* supply of, and demand for, investible funds towards the supply of, and demand for, *stocks* of existing financial assets of differing degrees of liquidity. As Shackle (1967) has pointed out, the liquidity preference theory of interest is based on the dominance of the stock principle over the flow principle.

For simplicity of exposition let us assume that our elementary economy possesses only two financial assets, one liquid – money – and the other illiquid – bonds. We shall further assume that money yields no interest but that it is capital certain in the sense that it can be 'transformed' by the act of direct exchange into any other asset or commodity without any friction and without being subject to the risk of a capital loss. Bonds, on the other hand, despite their attractive characteristic of yielding a positive return, are neither capital certain nor liquid; in order to move out of bonds into some other asset or to purchase commodities the bond owner must first of all exchange his bonds for money, thereby incurring the risk of making a capital loss. The all round inconvenience of selling the bonds for money in order to buy goods or other assets must count as a minus point. To the extent that wealth holders regard illiquidity as an undesirable characteristic in a financial asset, they will have to be compensated by earning a yield on bonds which is sufficient to induce them to hold the existing stock of bonds. For this reason Keynes described the rate of interest as the reward for remaining illiquid; it is the reward for not holding one's wealth in the form of money. It was 'the reward for not hoarding'. (This phrase, which may strike the modern reader as rather curious, was charged with significance for Keynes's contemporaries, who had tended to regard the phenomenon of hoarding with alarm as it rendered part of the money stock 'inactive', thereby reducing the velocity of circulation of money.)

Keynes proposed two different explanations of the liquidity preference schedule which played such an important part in his monetary theory of interest. The first, better known version sees the liquidity preference schedule as the outcome of speculation among wealth holders concerning the future behaviour of bond prices and, hence, future behaviour of the rate of interest. We may label this the *speculative* version of liquidity preference theory. Many excellent accounts and critiques of this version are available[5] elsewhere, so only a very brief sketch will be given here. Individual wealth holders have a certain opinion regarding what constitutes a normal rate of interest. Different wealth holders have different opinions over what constitutes a normal rate of interest. If an individual speculator thinks that the current rate of interest is abnormally low, i.e. bond prices are abnormally high, he will move entirely out of bonds into money because of his belief that the next movement in the rate of interest will be in an upward direction. Similar behaviour characterizes an individual speculator who thinks that the current rate of interest is abnormally high: he will take steps to move out of money into bonds.[6] So the market for financial assets is composed of bulls and bears, the bulls having low liquidity preference and the bears having high liquidity preference. Some bulls will be more bullish than others and some bears will be more bearish than others because of a spread of opinion in the market as to what constitutes a normal rate of interest. Aggregation of these diverse opinions among wealth holders yields the familiar negatively sloping liquidity preference schedule depicted in Figure 4.3.

We have labelled this schedule M_A^d to emphasize that it is the *asset* demand for money as opposed to the transactions and precautionary demand for money. The negative slope of M_A^d is a reflection of the spread of opinion among speculators concerning the normal rate of interest. The wider the spread of opinion, the steeper will be the M_A^d schedule. Conversely, the greater the degree of consensus over what constitutes a normal rate of interest, the flatter the M_A^d schedule will be. Complete unanimity of opinion would imply a horizontal M_A^d schedule throughout its entire range.

According to the speculative version of liquidity preference theory, unanimity of opinion may eventually establish itself at some low, positive rate of interest. There may exist a price of bonds which is universally regarded as so high – and a corresponding rate of interest which is so low – that not even the most bullish of speculators believes that the next movement in the price of bonds is going to be upwards. This is the extreme case where, if there were the smallest sign of interest rates falling

---

[5]Tobin's (1958) path-breaking article on the theory of liquidity preference is the *locus classicus* for a discussion of the deficiencies of Keynes's speculative version. See also Chick (1983).
[6]As Tobin points out, in the speculative version of liquidity preference theory, wealth holders are 'plungers' – all or nothing speculators. They either hold the whole of their portfolios in the form of money or in the form of bonds but they do not hold a combination of bonds and money.

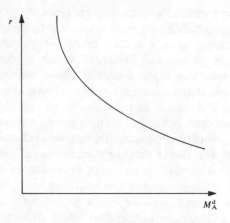

Figure 4.3   Asset demand for money schedule

further, all speculators would attempt to move out of bonds and into money. This is the case of *absolute liquidity preference*.

The speculative version of liquidity preference theory has been subjected to much criticism since it was first proposed in the *General Theory*. Most of it has come from Keynes's interpreters (e.g. Sir John Hicks, James Tobin) who have never been particularly happy with what Hicks called a 'bootstraps' theory of interest: balancing as it does the opinions of bulls and bears, the rate of interest will be what, on average, it is expected to be.

A more appealing, but less well-known, version of liquidity preference theory was proposed by Keynes in an article published in 1937 summarizing the salient features of the *General Theory* (*CW*, Vol. XIV, pp. 109–23). In this article he argued that the rate of interest was a measure of our uncertainty concerning the future: it is the gauge of our mistrust in what the future may hold in store for us. The holding of money is the means by which we avoid committing ourselves to a particular course of action from which we would find it difficult to extricate ourselves should the need arise. The greater our mistrust of what the future may contain, the more we put a premium on liquidity (i.e. the greater our asset demand for money): the rate of interest is the measure of that premium. In this version of liquidity preference theory, wealth holders need not be plungers (see footnote 6): they will hold part of their portfolios in liquid form and part in illiquid form. The onset of greater uncertainty regarding the future simply induces wealth holders to attempt to raise the proportion of their portfolios which comprise liquid assets. Furthermore, some wealth holders will attach greater importance to liquidity than others so that, once again, aggregation leads to the familiar downward sloping liquidity preference schedule. Increased uncertainty has shifted M_A^d upwards.

We are now in a position to construct an overall demand function for money. If, for simplicity, we assume that the transactions and precautionary demand for money, M_{TP}^d, is principally determined by the level of money income, as in the Cambridge formulation of the quantity theory of money, M_A^d may be added to M_{TP}^d to derive the total demand for money, M^d.

Following the classical writers, Keynes assumed that the money supply, M^s, was exogenously given by decisions of the central bank and could be represented diagrammatically by the vertical line in Figure 4.4. For given portfolio preferences by wealth holders as between money and bonds, and for a given level of money income, the position and shape of the demand for money function is fully determinate. This function, together with the exogenously fixed money supply, determines the rate of interest at r_1. For this reason Keynes referred to the rate of interest as a monetary phenomenon in that it is determined by the interaction between the demand for money and the supply of money. He pointed to the sharp contrast between his monetary theory of interest and its classical rival which stressed real phenomena. Keynes's liquidity preference theory of interest provided the answer to the classical economists who claimed that shifts in saving or investment schedules would evoke interest rate responses which would prevent quantity responses from occurring. This would *not* be the case if liquidity preference remained unchanged. Let us scrutinize Keynes's claim in greater detail.

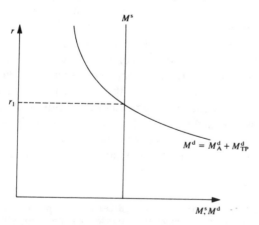

Figure 4.4 Overall demand for money function

Liquidity preference and the principle of effective demand

Early in the previous section we put words into the mouth of a fictitious classical economist who had asked Keynes the question: if the rate of desired investment were to fall, what reasons do you have for claiming that the level of income, not the rate of interest, would adjust so as to restore equilibrium between saving and investment? The easiest way to grasp the essence of Keynes's answer is to examine an economy which starts off in a state of full employment but which suddenly experiences a decline in the desire to invest. The full employment saving schedule (Figure 4.5(a)) is $S^* = S(r, Y^*)$ and this crosses the initial investment schedule I' at a rate of interest r_1. This is the classical natural rate of interest: Keynes was to name it the *neutral* rate of interest, by which he meant that unique rate of interest at which investment would equal *full employment* saving (see final section of Chapter 3). Moreover, the rate of interest r_1 not only maintains equilibrium between saving and invest-ment: it also maintains equality between the supply of and demand for money since from Figure 4.5(b) we see that r_1 is the single interest rate at which $M^{d1} = M^s$.

The decline in business confidence has the effect of shifting the position of the investment schedule to the left. In Figure 4.5(a) it shifts from I' to I''. If the rate of interest fell to r_2, as classical theory predicted it would, the fall in investment would be exactly matched by an equal rise in consumption and income would remain unchanged. However, according to liquidity preference theory, the rate of interest is, in the first instance, determined by the interaction between the demand for, and supply of, money. There is absolutely no reason to believe that the decline in the desire to invest will be accompanied by a change in asset preferences such that liquid assets are now less in demand than before.[7] Hence, initially at least, the demand for money schedule stays put at M^{d1}.

However the 'failure' of the rate of interest to fall to r_2 means that saving exceeds investment at a level of income Y^*. Such a disequilibrium is unsustainable and income starts to decline. The fall in Y produces two effects: (a) the saving schedule shifts to the left; (b) the demand for money schedule shifts downwards. (Remember that both functions have the level of income as an argument: $S = S(r, Y)$ and $M^d = kPY + M^d_A(r)$.) The leftward displacement of the saving schedule and the downward displacement of the demand for money schedule continue until a new rate

---

[7]If there is any connection between the investment decision and the portfolio allocation decision, it is likely to work in the wrong direction: increased pessimism all round is likely to increase liquidity preference and, if anything, raise the rate of interest instead of lowering it.

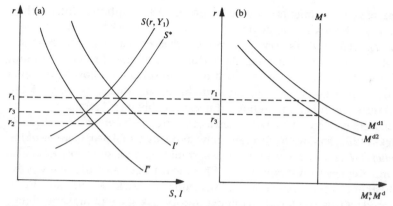

Figure 4.5   Effects of a decline in investment

of interest, r_3, is reached such that $r_2 < r_3 < r_1$. This new interest rate is similar to r_1 in that it simultaneously equates saving and investment on the one hand and the supply of, and demand for, money on the other, but there is one important difference: the level of income which is consistent with this rate of interest is below its full employment value.

It has been argued here that Keynes's theory of interest played a vital role in the formulation of the principle of effective demand. Without it the quantity adjustments outlined above could not have taken place. Unfortunately this is not the usual perception of its role. Many of Keynes's followers (e.g. Nicholas Kaldor) have argued that the quantity adjustments highlighted in the multiplier mechanism were free standing, independent of any particular theory of interest. Indeed Keynes himself claimed that the principle of effective demand had been formulated before he had worked out the details of his liquidity preference theory! Nevertheless the reader must ask himself what the status of the multiplier analysis would have been if the classical theory of interest had been right after all.

The Hicksian *IS–LM* model

It must be continually borne in mind when approaching the Keynesian model that it is a general model where almost all of the component parts are interconnected. Since the *raison d'être* of the *General Theory* was to explain why, in certain circumstances, general unemployment may be a persistent feature of a market economy, it cannot take refuge in that particular assumption which allowed the classical model to be split up into

separate compartments, namely the enabling assumption of full employment. As Patinkin, the doyen of modern Keynes scholars, has pointed
out 'the *General Theory* . . . can be regarded as the first practical
application of the Walrasian theory of general equilibrium' (Patinkin,
1976, p. 98).[8] The problem which now confronts us is how to come to
grips with a model of general equilibrium in which so many of the
variables and functional relationships are highly interdependent.

In a celebrated article published a year after the *General Theory*, J. R.
Hicks (1937) sought to elucidate some of the essential propositions of the
General Theory in a manner which would be accessible to those who
found Keynes's own exposition of his ideas rather abstruse and wordy.
(Other interpreters such as W. B. Reddaway, J. E. Meade and R. F.
Harrod had also undertaken this expository task at about the same time.)
Hicks's aim was an ambitious one: to portray in a single, two-dimensional
diagram many – though obviously not all – of the key relationships of the
General Theory. The outcome of his endeavours was to be what, until
recently, was the most widely used tool of analysis in macroeconomics,
the *IS–LM* model.

Hicks approached the formidable task of extracting the salient features
of a book 309 pages[9] in length by concentrating on two key sets of
relationship: (a) the connections between saving, investment, the level of
income and the rate of interest; (b) the connections between the demand
for and supply of money, the level of income and the rate of interest.
These two sets of relationship were to yield respectively the *IS* curve and
the *LM* curve. We shall follow the standard convention of assuming
initially that the price level is fixed[10] in order to enable us to isolate the
determinants of the level of real income. The 'fix-price' assumption was
regarded as reasonable in times of widespread unemployment when
changes in the level of demand could be expected to manifest themselves
more in changes in output than in changes in the general level of prices. It
clearly becomes less tenable the nearer the economy is to a state of full
employment. Since the *IS–LM* model is meticulously derived in most
intermediate textbooks on macroeconomics,[11] only a very cursory
account will be presented below.

---

[8]Walrasian? Both Keynes and Walras would have understandably been astounded to see
their ideas linked in this way. This author's preference would be to omit the modifier
'Walrasian' from an otherwise perceptive statement.

[9]If the final three chapters of notes are included, the *General Theory* comprises 384
pages.

[10]This assumption is obviously a source of disquiet to monetarists. If it were not
eventually relaxed their disquiet would be justified.

[11]See, for example, Dornbusch and Fischer (1978).

In order to gain an intuitive grasp of the significance of the *IS* curve, consider the following hypothetical question: what would happen to the level of income if, for reasons as yet unspecified, the rate of interest were to fall? The initial effect would be to raise the level of desired investment above the flow of saving, leading to an excess of injections into the circular flow of income over leakages from it. Income therefore starts to rise and, according to the Keynes–Kahn multiplier mechanism, the ultimate rise in income will be a determinate multiple, $1/1 - c\,(= 1/s)$, of the rise in investment. This process is illustrated in Figure 4.6. The direct relationship between saving and income is shown in the left-hand panel. Note that levels of income further to the left of the origin are higher than those nearer to the origin. Note also that, in order to avoid three-dimensional diagrams, the dependence of saving on the rate of interest has been suppressed. Both saving and investment are measured along the vertical axis, which is common to each panel. In the right-hand panel the inverse relationship between the level of desired investment and the rate of interest is depicted.

A fall in the rate of interest from r_1 to r_2 raises the desired rate of investment from I_1 to I_2. The rise in income, $\Delta Y = Y_2 - Y_1$, is a multiple, $1/s$, of the rise in investment, where s is the marginal propensity to save and $1/s$ is the multiplier. Moreover this rise in income generates a rise in saving, $\Delta S = S_2 - S_1$, just sufficient to fund the rise in investment. The process depicted in Figure 4.6 highlights one of the fundamental postulates of Keynesian economics, namely, that saving and investment are brought into equality with each other through variations in the level of income.

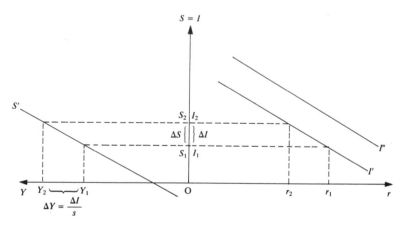

Figure 4.6 Effects of decline in interest rate on investment, saving and income

If this hypothetical experiment of linking reductions in the rate of interest to the consequent multiplier-induced increases in income were repeated for a large range of values of r, an *IS* curve would be traced out. The locus of pairs such as (r_1, Y_1) and (r_2, Y_2) in Figure 4.6 defines the *IS* curve in Figure 4.7. It should be noted that if there were a sudden improvement in business confidence such that entrepreneurs wish, on average, to invest more, there would be a rightward shift in the investment schedule (from I' to I'' in Figure 4.6) and a concomitant rightward shift in the *IS* schedule (from IS' to IS'' in Figure 4.7).

The intuition behind the derivation of the *LM* curve may be grasped by reversing the hypothetical question which was posed in the case of the *IS* curve: what will happen to the rate of interest if, for reasons as yet unspecified, the level of income rises? Consider the simplified account of the monetary framework of the *General Theory* given in an earlier section of this chapter. The rate of interest is determined by the interaction between the supply of, and the demand for, money, the latter being, in turn, a function of the rate of interest, r, and the level of money income, PY. For a constant price level, P_0, a rise in the level of real income raises the transactions and precautionary demand for money, M_{TP}^d, and thereby raises the overall demand for money, M^d. Since the supply of money, M^s, is taken as given by assumption, the income-induced rise in M^d serves to raise the rate of interest from r_1 to r_2. An example of this chain of causation is illustrated in Figure 4.8. The 'off-stage' rise in the level of real income from Y_1 to Y_2 shifts the demand for money function from $M^d(P_0 Y_1)$ to $M^d(P_0 Y_2)$ which, in turn, raises the rate of interest from r_1 to r_2. This positive relationship between the level of income and the rate of

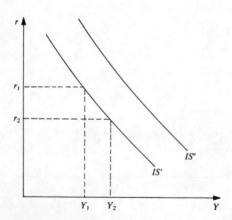

Figure 4.7 Two *IS* curves

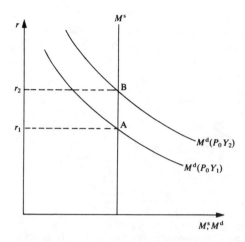

Figure 4.8   Derivation of the *LM* curve

interest is summarized in the *LM* curve which is a locus of pairs such as (r_1, Y_1) and (r_2, Y_2) in Figure 4.9.[12] Points A and B in Figure 4.8 correspond to points A' and B' in Figure 4.9.

A very simple linear example may help in understanding the theory that underpins the *LM* curve. It is a basic axiom of Keynesian monetary theory that the rate of interest moves rapidly to establish equilibrium between the supply of money and the demand for money. This being the case, the 's' and 'd' superscripts attached to both variables may be suppressed, being denoted by the common symbol, *M*. The condition for equilibrium in the money market thus becomes

$$M = kPY - \beta r \tag{4.1}$$

where β is a measure of the sensitivity of the demand for money to variations in the rate of interest. Rearranging this equilibrium relation we obtain

$$Y = M/kP + (\beta/kP)r \tag{4.2}$$

For given values of the money supply and the price level, this equation defines a one-to-one relationship between the rate of interest (the

---

[12]A rigorous diagrammatic derivation of the *LM* curve is rather complicated and space consuming. Most intermediate textbooks on macroeconomics provide a more extensive account of its derivation than is given here.

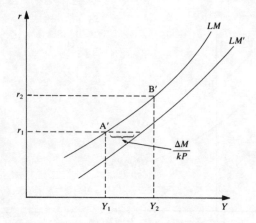

Figure 4.9   Expansionary monetary policy and the *LM* curve

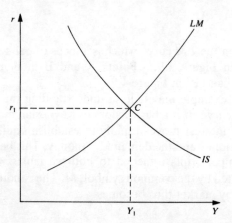

Figure 4.10   Income–expenditure equilibrium

dependent variable in the *LM* curve) and the level of income (the independent variable).[13]

The point of intersection of the *IS* curve with the *LM* curve determines a unique combination of the rate of interest and the level of real income compatible with income–expenditure equilibrium. At point C the level of

---

[13]The effect of an increase in the supply of money on the position of the *LM* curve should be fairly clear from this simple equation. The *LM* curve will shift to the right, the horizontal distance between the old and the new *LM* curves being $\Delta M/kP$ where ΔM measures the increase in the money supply.

income, Y_1, and the rate of interest, r_1, are such as to satisfy simultaneously two requirements of full equilibrium: they equate the desire to save with the desire to invest; and they equate the demand for money with the supply of money.

The rate of interest: both a real and monetary phenomenon?

At first glance the *IS–LM* system might appear to refute both the classical proposition that the rate of interest is exclusively a real phenomenon and to refute the rival Keynesian proposition that it is exclusively a monetary phenomenon. Since the rate of interest is just as likely to alter as a result of a shift in the *IS* curve as it is as a result of a shift in the *LM* curve, it is surely both a real and a monetary phenomenon. It is a real phenomenon in the sense that it reflects the influence of saving and investment as summarized in the slope and position of the *IS* curve; and it is also a monetary phenomenon in that it reflects the interaction between the supply of and the demand for money as summarized in the slope and position of the *LM* curve. This plausible, almost commonsensical compromise rapidly gained acceptance and was partly responsible for calming the turbulence produced by the 'liquidity preference versus loanable funds' debate.[14] The classical and Keynesian theories of interest appear both to have been vindicated, if only in part.

Nevertheless, although this compromise reinstated saving and investment to some extent, it assigned to them roles which were radically different from those assigned to them in the original classical model where they *directly* determined the rate of interest (see Figure 2.2 in Chapter 2). By contrast, in the *IS–LM* system the influence of saving and investment on the rate of interest is only indirect. For example, a rise in investment raises the rate of interest only to the extent (a) that it raises income; and (b) to the extent that the rise in income raises the rate of interest by raising the demand for money. Effect (a) is likely to be strong but effect (b) could be uncertain, depending on how interest elastic is the demand for money, i.e. upon the steepness of the *LM* curve. In all events it is clear that the above mentioned compromise concerning the real and monetary nature of the rate of interest is something of a fudge: real forces only affect the interest rate through their effect on the demand for money, which is surely a 'monetary phenomenon' if ever there was one.

---

[14] A good example of the consensus which emerged concerning the theory of interest is to be found in Alvin Hansen's influential handbook on the *General Theory: A Guide to Keynes* (1953).

When one considers the central role played by 'monetary phenomena' in explaining why output could deviate from its full employment value for long periods of time, it is small wonder that, in the years immediately preceding the publication of the *General Theory*, Keynes referred to his theory of activity as 'a monetary theory of production' (*CW*, vol. XIII, pp. 405 ff.).

Monetary policy in the *IS–LM* model

The *IS–LM* model is well suited to illustrating the short-run[15] effects of both monetary policy and fiscal policy on the level of aggregate demand. The use of these policies to influence the general level of output and employment in one direction or another is usually referred to as *demand management*. When the problem confronting the authorities is one of unemployment and underutilized resources, their attention quite naturally turns towards policies which will have the result of raising the level of effective demand, that is, towards expansionary monetary and fiscal policies. On the other hand when the relevant problem is one of 'overheating', leading to the possibility of a demand inflation, the authorities' attention will turn to contractionary policies.

For a given fiscal stance, an expansionary monetary policy will involve the central bank in undertaking open market purchases, thereby increasing the stock of money and simultaneously reducing the rate of interest. Within the *IS–LM* model it will produce a rightward shift in the *LM* curve (see footnote 12). The immediate effect of the open market purchase is to reduce the rate of interest from r_1 to r_2 at an unchanged level of income, Y_1. However, the fall in the rate of interest will stimulate investment and, through the multiplier relation, the level of income will increase. As income rises the overall demand for money will also rise. There will therefore be a tendency for the rate of interest to creep back upwards, ultimately settling down at an intermediate rate r_3. Having initially travelled from point A to point B in Figure 4.11, the economy will tend to a new position of income–expenditure equilibrium at point C. The equilibrium level of income will be Y_2.

Special note should be taken of the chain of cause and effect which this version of the monetary transmission mechanism entails. The open market purchase simultaneously raises the supply of money and reduces the rate of interest. In Keynes's words, 'The primary effect of a change in

---

[15]The long-run effects of monetary and fiscal policies are complex: the interested reader should consult Blinder and Solow (1973) for a stimulating treatment of these matters.

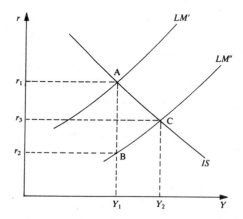

Figure 4.11   Monetary transmission mechanism

the quantity of money on the quantity of effective demand is through its influence on the rate of interest' (*GT*, p. 298). Those components of aggregate expenditure which are sensitive to variations in the rate of interest – private investment in the simplest case – are stimulated by the fall in interest rates and real incomes rise in consequence. In the Keynesian account of the monetary transmission mechanism it is the rate of interest which occupies centre stage: the supply of money plays merely a supporting role.

Two important limiting cases in which an expansionary monetary policy is completely impotent in raising the level of real income are illustrated in Figures 4.12(a) and 4.12(b). The first, depicted in 4.12(a), is the case in which the fall in the rate of interest from r_1 to r_2 fails to stimulate investment: the interest elasticity of investment is zero. An expansionary monetary policy, even if it succeeds in reducing the interest rate, fails to set the multiplier process in motion. The second case, depicted in Figure 4.12(b), is where the increase in the supply of money fails to exert the necessary downward pressure on the rate of interest since the latter has reached some critical minimum value r^*. In this case the *LM* curve is horizontal at this particular interest rate. The range over which the *LM* curve is horizontal is known as the liquidity trap: over this range there is said to be absolute liquidity preference. Even if the *IS* curve is non-vertical, i.e. it exhibits a significant interest elasticity, it has nothing to 'bite on' since the authorities are powerless to reduce the rate of interest. Once again the multiplier mechanism is grounded.

These two pathological cases have attracted a great deal of criticism from monetarists and others of a neoclassical inclination. Quite naturally

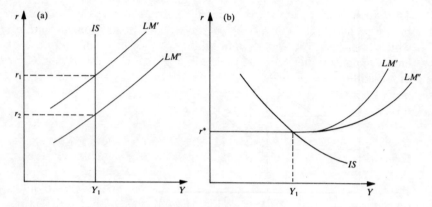

Figure 4.12 Impotence of monetary policy. (a) Zero interest elasticity of investment; (b) absolute liquidity preference

they see monetary policy as the most important instrument of demand management.[16] Keynesians, they claim, downgrade monetary policy by emphasizing the difficulties the authorities face in manipulating interest rates, particularly in a downward direction. And even if Keynesians concede that the authorities can alter interest rates after all, they always have the fallback position of arguing that interest rates do not have much effect on aggregate expenditure because of the supposed interest inelasticity of investment. These Keynesians are thus portrayed, in Leijonhufvud's (1968) stingingly dismissive phrase, as 'elasticity pessimists'.

This author is not competent to evaluate the extent to which these views were widespread among Keynesians. Some Keynesians, for example the contributors to the Oxford surveys of investment behaviour in the late 1930s, believed that the investment decision was the outcome of many factors but that the rate of interest did not figure prominently among them. Others, for example Nicholas Kaldor, feared that the liquidity trap was a distinct danger facing the British economy in the 1950s. However, most Keynesians never subscribed to either (still less both) of these extreme points of view. As for Keynes himself, he never even hinted that investment may have a zero interest elasticity (Figure

---

[16]Demand management is a rather inappropriate phrase in this context since it has connotations of attempting to guide real quantities (output, employment, etc.) in one direction or another. Monetarists and the new classical school deny that monetary or fiscal policies have any influence over real aggregates. Fiscal policy is useless as a macroeconomic instrument, while monetary policy, though powerful in its effects, only influences the price level in the medium/long run.

4.12(a)). The problem with investment lay not in its interest inelasticity but rather in the inherent volatility of the investment decision, a volatility which imparted corresponding instability to the levels of output and employment. On the other hand he did admit of the theoretical possibility of a liquidity trap (Figure 4.12(b)) but knew of no example of it in the past and did not regard it as imminent even in the distressed conditions of the 1930s.

It is easy to imagine how the results of a small number of empirical studies on investment, coupled with a few casual *obiter dicta* from the *General Theory*, came to be restated in terms of the *IS–LM* analysis as a vertical *IS* curve and a horizontal *LM* curve. 'What would happen if . . .' exercises, which examine the implications of extreme cases, can be quite revealing. However, what is quite beyond this author's range of comprehension is how these oddities, these hypothetical curiosa, should have come to be regarded in many circles as part and parcel of 'Keynesian economics'. But we digress.

Fiscal policy in the *IS–LM* model

The consequences of an expansionary fiscal policy may be analyzed along similar lines. An increase in government spending, ΔG, has effects analogous to those of a spontaneous increase in private investment. An increase in government expenditure shifts the *IS* curve from *IS'* to *IS"* in Figure 4.13. The horizontal distance between *IS'* and *IS"* is equal to $\Delta G/s$. In the absence of any repercussions of the rate of interest, the rise in income is given by the simple multiplier formula. However, apart from

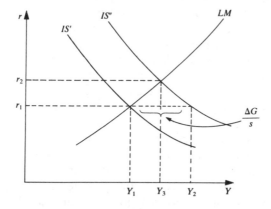

Figure 4.13   General crowding out hypothesis

the extreme case of the liquidity trap, it cannot be assumed that the rate of interest will remain constant at r_1: the rise in the demand for money which accompanies the rise in income will tend to raise the rate of interest which will, in turn, tend to reduce private investment. Hence, instead of rising from Y_1 to Y_2, the level of income settles down at Y_3 $(Y_1 < Y_3 < Y_2)$ because of the dampening effect on private investment of the induced rise in the rate of interest from r_1 to r_2. In symbols, $\Delta Y = Y_3 - Y_1 = \Delta G/s + \Delta I/s$ where $\Delta G/s$ is obviously positive but where $\Delta I/s$ is negative. This is the most widely recognized version of the *crowding out* hypothesis.

Inspection of Figure 4.13 reveals that, in general, an increase in government spending will not be matched by an equal fall in private investment so that income will rise as a result of the fiscal stimulus, though the rise will be less than is suggested by the simple multiplier formula. The extent to which private investment is crowded out depends (a) upon the extent to which the rate of interest rises as income rises, which, in turn, depends upon the income and interest elasticities of the demand for money; and (b) upon the extent to which private investment responds to variations in the rate of interest. The information required to gauge the strength of effect (a) is contained in the slope of the *LM* curve while the corresponding information for effect (b) is contained in the slope of the *IS* curve. Clearly if the *LM* curve were a horizontal line there would be no rise in the rate of interest and hence no negative feedback on private investment. Similarly, even if the rate of interest did rise as a result of the rise in income, private investment will not fall if the interest elasticity of investment is zero. In this case the *IS* curve will be a vertical line. These two extreme cases of zero crowding out are illustrated in Figures 4.14(a) and 4.14(b). That eccentric sept of the Keynesian clan, the dreaded 'elasticity pessimists', are purported to believe that these two pathological cases describe the world we live in (see previous section).

Now that we are in hot pursuit of theoretical abnormalities, we may as well go to the other extreme and ask the polar opposite question: under what circumstances will there be complete, 100% crowding out? That is to say, under what circumstances will $\Delta G/s = -\Delta I/s$? The most obvious case of 100% crowding out occurs when the *LM* curve is vertical, i.e. where the interest elasticity of the demand for money is zero. The vertical *LM* curve is shown in Figure 4.15(a) while the demand for money function which it implies is shown in Figure 4.15(b).

In Keynesian monetary theory a rise in income causes, in the first instance, an excess demand for money, but the consequent rise in the rate of interest tends to choke off the asset demand for money so that the total demand for money once again equals the predetermined supply of money. The demand for money not only jointly determines the rate of interest along with the supply of money, it also 'yields' to it (see Figure

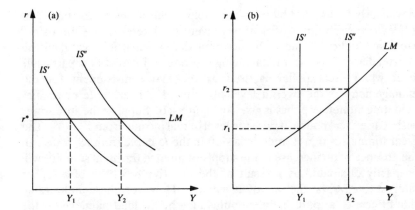

Figure 4.14 Zero crowding out

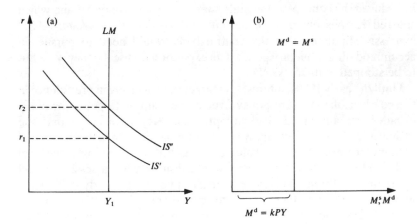

Figure 4.15 Complete crowding out

4.4). However, if this 'yielding' characteristic of the demand for money is negligible, as many monetarists have claimed in the past, then the relevant demand for money function will be a vertical line which will, in equilibrium, coincide with the M^s line (see Figure 4.15(b)). This is the case where the total demand for money bears a strict, immutable relation of proportionality to money income, that is, where $M^d = kPY$.

The type of crowding out discussed above may be labelled *monetary* crowding out since it originates in variations in the demand for money in relation to a fixed supply of money. The danger of monetary crowding out may clearly be averted by the simple expedient of raising the supply of money by an amount sufficient to prevent the interest rate from rising. Monetary policy is said to be *accommodating* when it is assigned the intermediate objective of stabilizing the rate of interest at a particular level while fiscal policy is used as the major instrument for the management of the overall level of demand. An example of accommodating monetary policy is given in Figure 4.16. Suppose the authorities wish to use fiscal policy to raise the level of real income from Y_1 to Y_2. The fiscal stimulus is represented by a shift in the *IS* curve from *IS'* to *IS'''*. In the absence of an increase in the supply of money, the fiscal stimulus will be partly dissipated as a result of the negative feedback of a higher interest rate, r_1, on the rate of investment. However, these undesirable side effects of a 'pure' fiscal stimulus may be avoided painlessly if the central bank increases the supply of money by an amount sufficient to shift the *LM* curve to a position *LM'''*, thereby effectively pegging the rate of interest at a target level r_T. Indeed, in the original article which introduced the concept of the multiplier into macroeconomics and which spurred Keynes on to write the *General Theory*, R. F. Kahn (1931) expressly stipulated that the central bank would need to pursue an accommodating monetary policy if an expansionary fiscal policy were not to be stopped in its tracks.[17]

Until the early 1970s, interest rate targets had been given precedence in the conduct of monetary policy over money supply targets. For many decades the authorities had accepted the Keynesian view that the magnitude of the money supply was of little significance in itself. A range of monetary indicators – the volume of liquidity in the economy, the level and structure of interest rate, etc. – were consulted when assessing overall monetary conditions. This came to an abrupt end in the early 1970s when many governments abandoned attempts to smooth out fluctuations in interest rates and opted instead to pursue policies aimed at holding the rate of growth of 'the' money supply within particular well-defined ranges. Very recently we have witnessed a revival of concern over interest rates and a corresponding decline in the importance attached to money supply targets. This is particularly conspicuous in the United Kingdom where monetarism had been a cornerstone of macroeconomic policy for well over a decade. Less and less is heard of money supply targets (they have nearly always been exceeded in practice), concern over interest rates

---

[17]'It is, however, important to realise that the intelligent co-operation of the banking system is being taken for granted . . . If the increased circulation of notes and increased demand for working capital that may result from increased employment are made the occasion for the restriction of credit, then any attempt to increase employment may be rendered nugatory.' (Kahn, 1931, pp. 174–5)

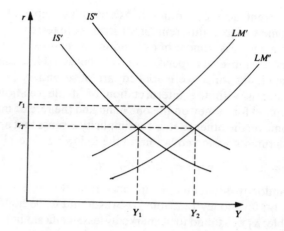

Figure 4.16   Accommodating monetary policy

having almost entirely displaced them in the debates over the direction of monetary policy. It will be interesting to see how much further this trend will continue.

Monetary accommodation and the estimation of demand for money functions

It would be inappropriate in a chapter on the Keynesian revolution to probe too deeply into the anatomy of monetarism. Nevertheless, the preceding discussion of the role which Keynesians have traditionally assigned to money supply policy, namely, that of accommodating changes in the demand for money which would otherwise jeopardize interest rate targets, has a direct bearing upon the interpretation of econometric studies which purport to demonstrate the existence of stable demand for money functions. In his 1956 'restatement' of the quantity theory of money, Friedman specified a long string of variables that could be expected to determine the demand for nominal money balances. Some of these variables were either intrinsically unobservable or were very difficult to measure with any reasonable degree of accuracy (for example, the ratio of human to non-human capital). In practice, therefore, monetarists have narrowed down the list of determining variables. Various measures of the rate of interest enter on the right-hand side of regression equations, as do various measures of money income. Occasionally P and Y are separated out; occasionally permanent income is substituted for current income; at other times a wealth variable takes the place of the income variable; different lag structures are tested; the data are subjected to a wide assortment of estimation procedures.

For our purposes the exact specification of the variables, and the econometric techniques which were applied, are of secondary interest. Our concern here is with the interpretation of stable relationships between the demand for money on the one hand and the rate of interest and money income on the other. Let us for simplicity assume that applied econometricians run regression equations of the following general form:

$$\log M_t = \alpha_0 + \alpha_1 \log r_t + \alpha_2 \log (PY)_t + u_t \tag{4.3}$$

where u_t is a randomly distributed disturbance term. From the earliest studies of demand for money functions, α_2 was found to be highly significant and stable; α_1 was found to be markedly less significant but, in the light of what is claimed below, this should not be surprising. Since the M_t variable was almost universally interpreted as the demand for nominal money balances, the coefficient α_2 was similarly interpreted as the money income elasticity of the demand for money. The monetarist viewpoint derives much of its empirical strength from this discovery that α_2 was highly significant and stable.

But is there any other explanation for the stability of α_2? The slope of a particular *LM* curve is a diagrammatic representation of a demand for money function in (Y, r) space. It is constructed on the assumption that the money supply is exogenously given, that the rate of interest responds with almost infinite speed to establish monetary equilibrium, and that the price level is given. We saw earlier how the slope of the *LM* curve would depend upon the interest and income elasticities of the demand for money, in our example α_1 and α_2 respectively. (Note that, since α_1 and α_2 are elasticities, they differ from the coefficients k and β in equations (4.1) and (4.2).)

As we saw in the final section of Chapter 3, many British Keynesians believe that what follows provides a reasonably accurate thumbnail sketch of how monetary policy was conducted down to the early 1970s. Inflationary pressures are the result of a variety of cost–push factors which serve to raise money wages, and hence prices, independently of the level of aggregate demand. The insensitivity of money wages to market pressures, and their tendency to assume a life of their own, particularly in an upward direction, gave rise to the view that inflation was an autonomous process. This view should not, of course, be taken to extremes. At very high levels of demand, for example, a pure demand-led inflation will be superimposed upon, and will probably dominate, the autonomous components of an inflationary process. *Per contra*, when aggregate demand is at very low levels and unemployment is abnormally high, there may be some, though probably weak, tendency for money wage claims to be moderated. In between these two extremes, however, it was felt that increases in the general level of money wages were largely unrelated to the pressure of aggregate demand. Moreover, the absolute price level would tend to rise in line with increases in money wages, appropriately adjusted for productivity growth, because of the mark up pricing hypothesis: prices were assumed to be determined as a mark up over variable costs of production, the most important of such costs comprising money wages.

The repercussions of a cost–push inflationary process can be illustrated quite simply within the framework of the *IS–LM* model. In Figure 4.17 the initial money supply, the initial price level and the initial level of real income are M_0, P_0 and Y_0 respectively. Let us now assume that autonomous cost–push pressures result in a rise in the price level from P_0 to P_1. This will raise the nominal demand for money. If the nominal supply of money is held constant at M_0, the liquidity preference theory of interest predicts that the interest rate will be higher for all levels of real income. This is represented diagrammatically as a north-westerly displacement of the *LM* curve to a position $LM(M_0/P_1)$. In the absence of monetary accommodation, the rate of interest would rise to r_1 and the level of real income would fall to Y_1.

However, according to the groundrules which were operative down to the early 1970s in most Western economies, the upward pressure on the rate of interest would be resisted. Since interest rates were being targeted

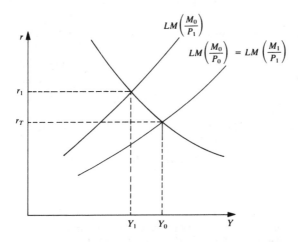

Figure 4.17   Cost–push inflation and monetary accommodation

during this period, the central bank would take steps to adjust the money supply by an amount sufficient to prevent the interest rate from rising above r_T, the target interest rate. The money supply is thus increased from M_0 to M_1 and, since the ratio M/P fixes the position of the LM curve, a cost-inflationary process is not allowed to influence those variables which lay at the core of macroeconomic management at the time, the rate of interest and the level of real income. Monetary accommodation would ensure that the LM curve would remain anchored in its original position in (r, Y) space.

Another way of illustrating the same phenomenon is to consider the effects of accommodating monetary policy not in (r, Y) space, but in (r, PY) space. It is assumed as before that the authorities are pursuing an interest rate target, r_T, and that the fiscal stance is unchanged. In other words monetary and fiscal policies are being combined in such a way as to maintain an interest rate r_T and a level of real income Y_0. If we also assume that the authorities are completely successful in achieving their objective of preventing the interest rate from deviating from r_T, and hence of preventing real income from deviating from Y_0, then the only combinations of r and PY which will ever be observed empirically will lie along the horizontal line passing through points A, B and C.[18] Each increase in P raises PY_0, and each rise in PY_0 calls forth a validating increase in the money supply.

What are the implications of the highly stylized account which has just been presented? The most conspicuous implication is empirical: any statistical association which may be unearthed between M_t and variables such as r_t and $(PY)_t$ in equations similar to equation (4.3) cannot be taken to signify the existence of a stable demand for money function. Whatever the parameters which attach to the 'true' demand for money function, the estimated coefficients α_1 and α_2 cannot be interpreted as interest and money income elasticities of the demand for money. Indeed, to the extent that a policy of targeting the interest rate is highly successful, deviations of the interest rate from target will be correspondingly small and the estimated coefficient α_1 will be biased towards zero.[19] Under a regime of successful monetary accommodation it will never be possible to observe points along a given LM curve: only points such as A, B and C in Figure 4.18 can ever be observed. The equation for the LM curve contains all of the characteristic parameters of the 'true' demand for money

---

[18]This analysis becomes seriously defective once a full-blown inflationary process has emerged. The experience of inflation and the build up of inflationary expectations require a very strict distinction to be drawn between nominal and real interest rates.

[19]A similar point is made in a different context by Blinder and Solow (1973).

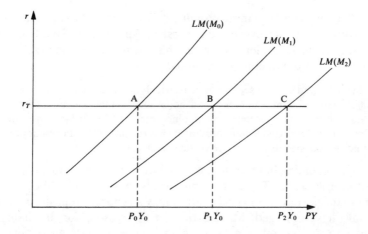

Figure 4.18 Cost–push inflation and accommodating monetary policy

function, in particular the 'true' interest and money income coefficients of the demand for money. The inability to estimate a 'true' *LM* curve reflects an equivalent inability to estimate a 'true' demand for money function. Both of these cognate economic relationships are lurking in the wings waiting for the director's call, but the call never comes. Only a change of scriptwriter and director will give them the prominence accorded to them in monetarist theory.

These observations gain added relevance when the question of the stability of the demand for money function is brought into the picture. Let us suppose for the sake of argument that the demand for money function is unstable: the *LM* curve is prone to sudden shifts as a result of alterations in the state of liquidity preference. If no action were taken by the central bank to neutralize the volatility of liquidity preference, the rate of interest would be similarly volatile. One of the justifications which Keynesians had advanced for a policy of monetary accommodation was that these unnecessarily harmful fluctuations in interest rates could be ironed out by appropriate action by the central bank: a sudden increase in liquidity preference would be offset by an expansion in the money supply, while a sudden decline in liquidity preference would lead to a contraction in the money supply. Hence, even though the demand for money function is inherently unstable, the damaging consequences of such instability are not allowed to manifest themselves. Once again we are not in a position to observe a 'true', though unstable, demand for money function.

Monetarists have long been aware of these objections but they remain largely impervious to them. Consider the position taken by David

Laidler, probably the most prominent British monetarist. At a symposium on monetarism organized under the auspices of the Royal Economic Society in 1980, Laidler gave a clear résumé of the conventional opinion among applied monetary economists:

> In the United States it seems now to be widely accepted that the correlation between the quantity of money and money income that long runs of time series data display is not just the result of coincidence, but does in fact constitute evidence of a causative relationship that has run primarily from money to money income rather than vice versa. (Laidler, 1981, p. 7)

Head counting in order to assess the weight of professional opinion is notoriously hazardous: if the same canvass of opinion had been carried out in the heyday of Keynesian orthodoxy an entirely opposite consensus would have emerged. More seriously, the reasons for dismissing the reverse causative relationship running from money income to money are not given.[20] Such peremptory treatment of alternative hypotheses is a regrettable characteristic of much of the monetarist literature.

James Tobin, the most eminent of the American Keynesians, was clearly not a party to this consensus. Tobin painted a rather more muted, less cut and dried picture when, at the same symposium, he stated: 'However stable "the" money demand function may be, equating it to money supply cannot describe the whole economy if the function contains more than one endogenous variable.' He concluded: 'The question whether money causes money income or income money or both is still undecided' (Tobin, 1981).

Few economic relationships have been subjected to more exhaustive econometric scrutiny than 'demand' for money functions. The fact that these studies have failed to allay the doubts and reservations of a significant minority of economists points to something fundamentally awry in the specification of the complete model. The monetarist preference for small-scale, normally reduced form, regression exercises leaves many questions unanswered, particularly concerning the processes by which changes in the money supply are generated. I suspect that the question of causation cannot be satisfactorily resolved one way or another without a deeper understanding of the characteristics of the policy makers' reaction function. *Why* do central banks increase the

---

[20]Econometric tests of the direction of causation between variables often rely on the *post hoc ergo propter hoc* principle: if changes in the money stock were found systematically to precede changes in money income, this would – or so it was thought – provide strong *prima facie* evidence in favour of treating the money supply as the exogenous variable. I treat all such tests with a great deal of circumspection: much more needs to be known of the 'policy makers' reaction function' before any reliable inferences can be drawn from timing relationships between variables.

money supply? Are there, as we have suggested, ulterior objectives of monetary policy to which monetary targets must yield in practice, even when the public stance of policy is ostensibly to monitor and control growth in the money supply? To treat the money supply as if it fell like manna from Threadneedle Street, resulting in agents 'finding themselves' with excessive money balances, is surely inappropriate to the monetary analysis of modern economies. Attempts formally to model the policy makers' reaction function would go a long way to remedying the interpretative difficulties which continue to snap at the heels of researchers in this field.

Finally we must return to the vexed question of the relevance of empirically estimated equations such as equation (4.3) for curbing a cost–push inflation. Despite being anathema to most monetarists, cost–push theories of inflation have commanded widespread adherence in less committed circles, particularly in Britain. What may be rather loosely termed the 'institutionalist school' lays the blame for cost–push pressures at the door of certain defects in the process of collective bargaining and recommended policies which would aim at keeping the lid on inflationary wage demands. Various forms of incomes policies were widely canvassed with this end in view.

Laidler (1974) was prepared to accept – but only for the sake of argument – that a cost–push inflation, backed up by a policy of monetary accommodation, could describe an actual inflationary process. Whereas for the institutionalist school the roots of the problem were to be found in the deficiencies of the industrial relations system, for Laidler these were mere epiphenomena: the far more fundamental problem resided in the compliance of the monetary authorities which took the form of a willingness to underwrite the repercussions of upward pressure on money wages. But, continued Laidler, what would happen if the brakes were put on the rate of monetary expansion so that monetary policy ceased to be accommodating? If the statistical correlation between money and money income exemplified in equation (4.3) remained stable after the change in policy regime, one or both of two effects would ensue: the rate of inflation would fall and/or the levels of real income and employment would fall. To the extent that cost–push pressures remained firmly ingrained in the industrial relations practices of the economy, the levels of real income and employment would bear the entire brunt of this tightening of monetary policy. On the other hand, to the extent that falling levels of output and employment serve to diminish cost–push pressures, the rate of inflation would tend to fall. Trades union leaders, faced with the dilemma of trading off higher pay against lower employment, might eventually moderate their wage demands. If, on the other hand, they remain committed to their bad old ways, the persistence of autonomous upward pressure on money wages and price will lead to ever higher levels of unemployment.[21] Laidler believed that the force of monetary tightness would succeed in outfacing trades union intransigence and that trades union behaviour would alter in the light of changed circumstances. Recognition by trades union leaders that the central bank was no longer willing to pick up the tab for unreasonable wage claims would introduce a new sense of market realism into pay bargaining.

We have seen how monetarists reject the very idea of cost–push inflation since they perceive it to be grounded in irrational, non-optimizing behaviour. Those of a more eclectic disposition admit of the possibility of autonomous trades union pressure on money wages and prices but accept that the strength of such pressure will abate as output and employment fall after the introduction of money supply targets. Implicitly they subscribe to the concept of a non-accelerating inflation rate of unemployment, NAIRU. For these writers (e.g. Peter Jay, 1974) the level of unemployment is caught between the hammer of cost–push pressure and the anvil of monetary tightness. Only at NAIRU do these two forces reach a precarious equilibrium.

One interesting aspect of this debate, which has flourished in one guise or another from the mid-1970s onwards, concerns the status of the money supply–money income relationship which had been observed down to the early 1970s. It was taken for granted that, though new parameter values may emerge with the passage of time, the stable relationship between money and money income would survive the change of policy regime. Lucas (1976) has delivered a forceful reminder of the perils of assuming that the statistical regularities which had prevailed under one policy regime would carry over after the economy had undergone a change of policy regime. It is therefore methodologically invalid to infer that stat-istical correlations between money and money income which had been observed over periods when the money supply was largely an endogenous variable would persist into periods in which the money supply was largely an exogenous variable. The switch from targeting interest rates, letting the money supply be a free variable, to targeting the money supply, letting interest rates be free variables, will introduce an enormous discontinuity into the money–money income relationship. Moreover the

---

[21]The Thatcher government which was ousted from office in November 1990 appeared to have reached a conclusion rather similar to this, but having abandoned monetarism *stricto sensu* suggested a somewhat different mechanism. The slogan 'excessive wage demands price workers out of jobs' was bruited widely abroad, having assumed an almost axiomatic status in certain circles. What the adherents to this view seemed to have in mind is some simple partial equilibrium model of supply and demand where external forces determine price, in this case money wages, above its equilibrium, market clearing level.

problem of discontinuity may be more serious than mere changes in parameter values (e.g. discrete alterations in α_1 and α_2 in equation (4.3)): it is conceivable that the relationship between money and money income may break down completely, disappearing out of sight. If this turns out to be the case then the central plank will have been cut from under the platform of monetarism. Once confidence has been shaken in the rudimentary empiricism which monetarists have traditionally favoured,[22] *a posteriori* conjectures on the reasons behind the breakdown of 'demand' for money functions (discussion of the effects of financial innovation on the velocity of circulation of money is enjoying a certain vogue at the moment) will ring increasingly hollow, particularly when one recalls the sharp definitional focus of the original monetarist position of which Friedman (1968) and Friedman (1974a) are exemplars.

Crowding out, the Treasury view and classical economics revisited

It is important to distinguish monetary crowding out from the version of the crowding out hypothesis articulated in the stylized version of the Treasury view which we presented in Chapter 2. The Treasury view was based on the assumption that the position of the saving schedule was fixed solely by preferences of households as between consumption now and consumption at some indefinite date in the future. By implication it assumed that, in a stationary economy, changes in the level of income would not shift the saving schedule, as they did in the Keynesian system.

The critical premise which gave rise to this conclusion was the assumption of a saving function which was invariant with respect to the level of income. But the *IS–LM* system is based on no such premise. Each point along the *IS* curve corresponds to a *different* saving schedule in (r, S) space. For example, the two saving schedules depicted in Figure 4.2 correspond to different points along the Keynesian saving schedule in the left-hand panel of Figure 4.6. Indeed the very idea of a downward sloping *IS* curve is devoid of meaning with the strict interpretation of classical theory. Obviously the *propensities* to save and invest were allowed to alter as a result of exogenous changes in tastes and technology. The natural interest rate was allowed to vary accordingly. Nevertheless, none of these changes in propensities could alter the level of income. In other words, if one were to undertake the singularly unrewarding task of trying

---

[22]This is the famous 'methodology of positive economics'. For the original and most persuasive statement of this methodology, see Friedman (1953).

to squeeze an *IS* relationship out of the classical system, it would be a vertical line meeting the horizontal axis at some predetermined level of income which, if the labour market were working without monopolistic interference, would correspond to full employment output, Y^*. An increase in government spending will produce a movement up this vertical line from, say, point A to point B, but fiscal policy is powerless to shift this relationship to the right. Moreover there is no point drawing an *LM* curve within this framework since the rate of interest is, in all but the short run, a real phenomenon.

This interpretation of the classical system stands in marked contrast to other stylized accounts of the 'classical' case in terms of the *IS–LM* system. The 'classical' case is supposed to be the one depicted in Figure 4.15, in which the *LM* curve is a vertical line but in which the *IS* curve is downward sloping and capable of being shifted by fiscal policy. In our interpretation of the classical case in Figure 4.19 none of these statements holds true: there is no *LM* curve, vertical or otherwise, except perhaps in the short run; the *IS* is vertical; and fiscal policy cannot alter the position of the *IS* curve. The only variable which is capable of altering the position of the *IS* curve is the real-wage rate. If the market clearing real-wage rate, w^*, prevails, the level of income will be Y^* and the *IS* curve will touch the Y axis at Y^*. If the real-wage rate were to rise to w_1 such that $w_1 > w^*$, income will fall to Y_1 and the *IS* curve will shift to the left. This is depicted in Figure 4.19.

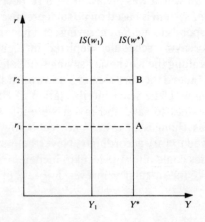

Figure 4.19 *IS* relationship in classical system

Does private investment crowd itself out? A backwards glance at a forgotten debate

We have now encountered two distinct mechanisms through which an increase in government expenditure crowds out an equivalent flow of private expenditure. For the modern monetarists, crowding out will be 100% if the interest elasticity of the demand for money is zero. This is the case of the vertical *LM* curve depicted in Figure 4.15. For the much older Treasury view, crowding out would *always* be 100%, on account of the fixity of the saving schedule. The reader is referred back to Figure 2.3 in Chapter 2. The inappropriateness of the *IS–LM* paradigm for illustrating the classical position is shown in that remarkably unrevealing diagram, Figure 4.19.

We shall see in this section how both versions of the crowding out hypothesis can be turned on their respective heads. Over the years, the crowding out debate has been conducted exclusively in the context of the macroeconomic effects of changes in government spending, *G*. Now exactly the same modes of analysis may be applied to other disturbances. The most obvious candidate for further scrutiny is changes in *ex ante* private investment. After all, in most short-run macroeconomic models, investment and government spending are treated interchangeably, often being lumped together as some composite variable *I* + *G*. In the Hicksian model, the *IS* curve may shift to the right as a result of one of three factors: (a) government spending increases; (b) *ex ante* private investment may rise; (c) the saving schedule may shift downwards in the left-hand panel of Figure 4.6. We have already dealt extensively with (a); we shall omit discussion of (c), i.e. we shall assume that saving and consumption functions do not undergo parametric shifts. What of (b)? What are the repercussions on the level of real income of a spontaneous increase in the desire to invest?

In the case of monetary crowding out the answer is at once blindingly obvious and entirely counterintuitive. The rise in private investment will *crowd itself out*. To see how this result is arrived at, all the reader need do is to refer back to Figure 4.15 once again, but this time to picture the shift of the *IS* curve from *IS'* to *IS''* as being the result of a sudden improvement in business confidence which raises the investment plans of entrepreneurs. The rate of interest rises just as it did in the case of the rise in government spending. More specifically, it rises by an amount sufficient to choke off the tendency for the rise in the *desire* to invest to have any effect on the *actual* flow of investment. The whole of the increase in the desire to invest is dissipated in the form, not of a rise in real income as Kahn's multiplier analysis suggested, but of a rise in the rate of interest from r_1 to r_2.

I know of no monetarist who has embraced this perverse conclusion. A rise in desired private investment is nearly always regarded as a good thing in its own right, irrespective of what is supposed to be happening to the money supply. Nevertheless, the strict logic of the monetarist position must force them to acknowledge that changes in the I component of $I + G$ are just as ineffective in altering the overall level of economic activity as changes in the G component. One is left wondering if the singling out of government spending for special attention in preference to private investment has its origins in a more general political hostility to increased state involvement in the economy. It is well known that many, though by no means all, monetarists show sympathy with libertarian ideas in economics. While in principle one can maintain a clear distinction between monetarism and libertarianism, in practice there is quite a considerable degree of overlapping membership. Is it pure coincidence that those who subscribe to the crowding out hypothesis also tend to be antipathetic to government intervention *per se*?

And how stands the Treasury view in the light of what has been said above? It may come as something of a surprise to the reader to discover that Keynes exposed exactly the same analytical muddle over the relative merits of public investment programmes over private entrepreneurial initiative more than sixty years ago. In his famous pamphlet written in support of the Liberal Party's programme for economic recovery, *Can Lloyd George Do It?*,[23] Keynes attacked the Treasury view head on:

> If it were announced that some of our leading captains of industry had decided to launch out boldly, and were to sink capital in new industrial plant to the tune, between them, of £100 millions, we should all expect to see a great improvement in employment. And, of course, we should be right. But, if the argument we are dealing with [the Treasury view] were sound, we should be wrong. We should have to conclude that these enterprising business men were merely diverting capital from other uses, and that no real gain to employment could occur. (*CW*, Vol. IX, pp. 115–16)

Keynes was rejecting a special case of the Treasury view illustrated in Figure 2.4 of Chapter 2. This is the case where the interest elasticity of saving was zero, so that each increase in government spending would be matched dollar for dollar by decreases in private investment. But surely, insisted Keynes, exactly the same argument can be applied to the situation where the initiating force is a spontaneous rise in private investment. Consider Figure 4.20, which is a slightly amended version of Figure 2.4.

---

[23]This pamphlet was jointly written with H. D. (later Sir Hubert) Henderson.

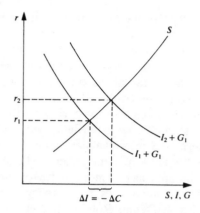

Figure 4.20   Private investment crowds itself out

Initially the demand for investible funds is given by the $I_1 + G_1$ schedule but, as a result of a spontaneous improvement in the state of business confidence, the investment schedule shifts to the right. Since government spending remains at G_1 by hypothesis, the $I + G$ schedule shifts to a position $I_2 + G_1$. The outcome suggested by intuition and common sense, namely an enhancement of output and employment, is ruled out of court by the logic behind the Treasury view. Once again the rate of interest rises from r_1 to r_2, that is, by an amount just sufficient to stifle the potentially beneficial effects of the improvement in business confidence. Few erstwhile adherents to the embryonic crowding out hypothesis were prepared to countenance such a devastating conclusion. Little more was heard of the Treasury view after 1929.

Keynes's riposte to the analytical inconsistencies which lay at the core of the Treasury view has already been treated earlier in this chapter, so a mere two-sentence recapitulation will suffice. The classical error consisted in regarding the saving and investment functions as independent entities even in conditions of unemployment and idle capacity. For Keynes, an increase in the desire to invest would shift the saving schedule bodily to the right along the lines suggested by Kahn's multiplier analysis and, in so doing, render the classical modes of analysis so cumbersome as to become almost totally useless.

Keynes's generalized quantity theory of money: price and output changes

Keynes was keenly aware of the magnetic pull that the quantity theory of money continued to exert on the minds of his contemporaries. This theory of prices had, after all, commanded the allegiance – not always unqualified, as we saw in Chapter 3 – of most serious writers on economic matters for well over two centuries and, even in the depressed conditions of the 1930s, it provided an alternative, more familiar frame of reference for evaluating the novelty of Keynes's monetary theory. In order to highlight the contrast between his approach to monetary theory and that of his classical predecessors and contemporaries, Keynes sought to recast his theory in the mould of what Sir Dennis Robertson later called the 'ancient ceremony' of the quantity theory. His objective was to show how the simple quantity theory of money was merely a special case of a more comprehensive theory of prices, a theory which he referred to as the *generalized* quantity theory of money (*GT*, p. 285).

In the previous sections of this chapter we assumed that the price level was exogenously fixed at P_0. This convenient assumption enabled us to infer a one to one correspondence between changes in the desired level of money expenditure and changes in the desired level of real expenditure. Let the desired level of money expenditure be denoted by E', where $E' = PE$. In the fix-price case, since $E' = P_0E$, a change in E' will be translated into an equiproportionate change in E and hence in Y.

Generality of analysis now requires the relaxation of the restrictive assumption that the price level is a datum. A given change in E' will, by definition, be divided between a change in real expenditure and a change in the price level. The formulation of the generalized quantity theory of money may therefore be split into two parts: (a) an examination of the effects of an increase in the quantity of money on E'; (b) an examination of how the increase in E' is divided between an increase in real expenditure (and hence real income) and an increase in the price level.

Part (a) has been dealt with in the preceding sections. The briefest thumbnail sketch of the chain of cause, effect and feedback runs as follows: an increase in the supply of money reduces the rate of interest, which raises the level of desired investment, which, via the multiplier, raises aggregate money expenditure, which raises production and hence money income, which raises the demand for money, which raises the rate of interest somewhat, etc., etc. Since the system is assumed to be stable, the economy converges to a new equilibrium at a higher level of money expenditure and money income. In the fix-price case illustrated in Figure 4.11, $E_2 = Y_2$ and $E'_2 = P_0Y_2$. The elasticity of money expenditure with respect to the money supply will depend upon the interest and income elasticities of the demand for money, upon the interest elasticity of investment expenditure, and upon the magnitude of the multiplier.

But what about part (b) of our inquiry? What factors will determine the division of the change in E' between a change in Y and a change in P? Two important elasticities must be defined: e_Y, which measures the elasticity of output with respect to money expenditure (in symbols, $e_Y = E'/Y.\Delta Y/\Delta E'$); and e_P, which measures the elasticity of the price level with respect to money expenditure (in symbols, $e_P = E'/P.\Delta P/\Delta E'$). By virtue of the equilibrium condition that $E' = PY$, it follows that e_Y and e_P sum to unity: $e_Y + e_P = 1$.

In the fix-price case which was examined extensively in the previous sections of this chapter, $e_P = 0$ by hypothesis so that $e_Y = 1$: increases in the level of desired money expenditure are converted in their entirety into increases in real income. At the other extreme is the case where an increase in desired money expenditure exhausts itself entirely in the form of a higher price level ($e_P = 1$) and has no effect whatsoever on real income ($e_Y = 0$). The latter response is an obvious characteristic of an economy at full employment, the case illustrated in Figure 4.21. An increase in the supply of money from M_1 to M_2 initially shifts the LM curve from a position $LM(M_1/P_1)$ to a position $LM(M_2/P_1)$. If e_Y were unity and e_P were zero, real income would rise to Y_1. However, since the initial state of the economy is assumed to be one of full employment, real income cannot rise above Y^*: Y_1 is a physically unattainable level of real income. An inflationary gap has therefore been opened up since initially the money value of desired expenditure exceeds the money value of national income, $P_1 Y^*$. The consequent rise in prices serves to eliminate this inflationary gap by shifting the LM curve back towards its initial

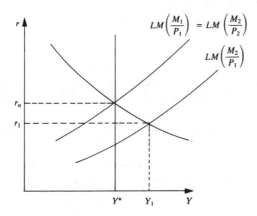

Figure 4.21   Increase in money supply at full employment

position. Prices will rise and the *real* money supply, M^s/P, will fall for as long as E' exceeds PY^*. Ultimately the real money supply reverts to its initial value, that is, $(M_1/P_1) = (M_2/P_2)$. The rate of interest rises back to r_n, Keynes's neutral rate of interest.

Hence the central prediction of the quantity theory of money, that there will be an equiproportional relationship between changes in the money supply and changes in the price level, only holds good in the special case of a fully employed economy. The simple[24] quantity theory *assumes* that $e_Y = 0$ and that $e_P = 1$, whereas the generalized quantity theory proposed by Keynes makes no such assumption. Intuitively one would expect that e_Y would be much larger than e_P when there was widespread unemployment; that e_P would rise as unemployment fell; that e_P would eventually 'overtake' e_Y as the level of activity rose beyond some critical point; and that e_P would tend to unity as full employment was approached.

Concluding remarks

This chapter has touched on a wide range of disparate theories which have formed the basis of the Keynesian theory of output and employment. The Keynesian model provides a *Weltanschauung* which two generations of economists have found at once intuitively plausible and realistic. Elaborations of the *IS–LM* apparatus have formed the backbone of highly complex econometric models which have proved to be indispensable tools for economic forecasting.

But perhaps the Keynesian revolution has fallen victim to its own success. So undisputed was the hegemony of Keynesian ideas, and so total was the eclipse of the classical model, that the whole area of macroeconomics appeared to be a closed book. If Keynes had not

---

[24]It is not only crude versions of the quantity theory of money which make this assumption. We saw at the end of Chapter 3 how Friedman (1974a) proposed a 'common model' which was intended to sort out the differences between Keynesians and modern quantity theorists. The common model which he examined was essentially the set of equations from which the *IS–LM* system is derived. He pointed out that the *IS–LM* system is underdetermined: it is one equation short. Keynesians, he claimed, provide the missing equation by assuming that the price level is fixed and that income is variable, whereas quantity theorists view things in reverse, fixing the level of real income at Y^* and allowing the price level to vary. Another way of stating Friedman's distinction is that Keynesians believe that $e_Y = 1$ while quantity theorists believe that $e_P = 1$. Of course, whatever Friedman and his followers might believe, Keynesians believe nothing of the sort: if output and employment are abnormally low, e_Y will be quite high, but if output and employment are near their full employment values, e_Y will be very low. To repeat, circumstances alter cases.

provided all of the answers, he had certainly given a powerful sense of direction to a productive research programme in many diverse areas of macroeconomics.[25] A sense of hubristic self-confidence was palpable down to the mid-1960s. Nemesis was to come in the form of the vigorous monetarist counterattack on what had become a tired, rather complacent conventional wisdom. The monetarist backlash bore many of the hallmarks of the Keynesian revolution thirty years earlier, most obviously in the simplistic misrepresentation, amounting almost to caricature, of the rival position. At times the Keynesian–monetarist debate appeared to be teetering on the brink of a rather unseemly dogfight, with each side attaching to the other side opinions which they had never espoused in the first place. Three interconnected allegations were levelled at the Keynesian School: (a) that they unjustifiably downgraded monetary policy (by which was meant money supply policy) to a subordinate role; (b) that they were indifferent to inflation; and (c) that their theories were devoid of adequate foundations in microeconomics.

Allegation (a) only holds water in a very narrow sense. Keynesians reject the applicability of the simple form of the quantity theory of money, with its relationship of proportionality between changes in the money supply and changes in the price level. Broadly speaking, increases in the supply of high-powered money[26] can come about through one of three routes: through open market purchases of bonds by the central bank; through budget deficits which are not fully funded by the sale of bonds to the public, i.e. through budget deficits which are financed in part by borrowing from the banking system; and through monetary inflows across the foreign exchanges. The *General Theory* model applied only to a closed economy, so that the last route is ruled out by hypothesis. Moreover, since there was no explicit treatment of fiscal policy in the *General Theory*, the monetary repercussions of budget deficits were not formally analyzed: this rules out the second route.[27] The only remaining way in which the money supply could increase was as a result of open market purchases. For Keynesians the channels through which an open market purchase stimulates aggregate demand flow from its initial effect on the rate of interest. Depending upon how much the interest rate falls,

---

[25]For example the justified unease with the closed economy model of the *General Theory* prompted extensive research, most conspicuously by James Meade, into the application of Keynesian methods to problems of balance of payments adjustment.

[26]According to Friedman and Schwartz's theory of the 'proximate determinants of the money supply', alterations in the supply of high-powered money led to a multiple increase in the total supply of money, however broadly that aggregate is defined.

[27]This may strike the reader as surprising since Keynesians have often had the label 'fiscalist' attached to them. Throughout the *General Theory* the only form of macroeconomic intervention which was explicitly analyzed was *monetary* intervention.

the ultimate effect on the price level works through a string of elasticities, the most important among which is e_Y, the elasticity of output with respect to money expenditure. The 'narrow sense' in which the monetarist allegation is valid is the very special case of a fully employed economy where $e_Y = 0$ by definition.

Allegation (b), that of indifference to inflation, is more difficult to rebut. Despite writing extensively on the problem of inflation throughout most of his career as an economist, Keynes had very little to say on the subject in the *General Theory*, the main focus of which was the determinants of the levels of real income and employment. A very convenient expository device was to assume that the level of money wages was a datum, though Keynes repeatedly insisted that nothing of importance turned on this restriction and that his analysis would survive intact even when money wages were allowed to alter. Nevertheless, Keynes's preoccupation with the factors which would influence the levels of real income and employment gave rise to the view that his was 'the economics of depression' (Hicks's (1937) phrase). The applicability of Keynesian methods of analysis to economies where money wages and prices are not exogenously given was called into question in the 1960s, a decade in which inflationary pressures began to mount. Keynes himself had always been acutely aware of an important lacuna in his model: 'We are, as I have said, one equation short' (*GT*, p. 276). The missing equation is one which determines the level or the rate of growth of money wages and hence prices. We shall return to this important topic in Chapter 6 where Phillips curves and their progeny are discussed.

But perhaps the most damning charge is contained in allegation (c): however useful its applicability to real world problems, Keynesian economics is profoundly flawed in that it is based on a series of conjectures which can find no basis in neoclassical choice theory. The consumption function has been singled out for special criticism in this respect. To economists of a neoclassical cast of mind, persistent excess demand or supply in any market points to some form of malfunction which is preventing the price mechanism from operating smoothly. More specifically, if there is general excess supply in the labour market, why do prices not move to eliminate this disequilibrium. Are agents – workers, employers, producers, consumers, savers, investors, etc. – not optimizing, or are the outcomes of their attempts at optimization being partly conditioned by the intrusion of external forces which act as additional constraints side by side with the traditional budget constraints? This reduces to the even more rudimentary question: what is supposed to be happening to prices in a Keynesian recession?

At the core of neoclassical economics lies a vision of an economy where the self-seeking of individuals entails the maximization of some objective function. Thus firms are assumed to maximize profits and households to maximize utility. For the neoclassical school this view of *Homo œconomicus* must form the basis of any theory of rational economic behaviour, whether microeconomic or macroeconomic. Moreover, since the groundrules for optimization are laid down and operate at the microeconomic level first and foremost, the construction of a coherent macroeconomic theory must take as its starting-point a convincing set of theories of microeconomic behaviour. The neoclassical writers draw on the pioneering analysis of Vilfredo Pareto (1848–1923) who pointed to a set of optimal outcomes where no one could gain from trade without diminishing the utility of someone else. For example, if I swap four of my apples for three of your pears, and if I am better off and you are at least no worse off as a result of that trade, there will be a general improvement in welfare. The initial, pre-swap state was therefore suboptimal since there was still scope for mutually advantageous trade: you may be no better off, but at least you are no worse off, and I am definitely better off as a result of trading four apples for three pears. The final, Pareto-optimal state, will be one in which all opportunities for mutually advantageous trade have been exhausted.

A state of excess supply in a particular market therefore implies that there is scope for mutually beneficial trade between buyer and seller. In a competitive economy such a state of affairs can only be transitory. Rational, optimizing agents, perceiving the benefits of a revision of trading arrangements among themselves, will take steps to exploit this opportunity to achieve a Pareto-improvement of welfare. In general prices as well as quantities traded can be expected to alter to eliminate excess supply.

A consistently articulated *general* theory of economic behaviour must therefore be able to carry over these precepts of rationality to the highly aggregated plane of macroeconomics. Is it possible to explain the phenomenon of general unemployment – persistent excess supply in the labour market – without sacrificing the paradigm of rational, optimizing economic man? We shall attempt to provide a tentative answer to this knotty question in Chapter 5.

5

Keynes and the labour market

We saw in Chapter 2 how the classical economists rested their belief in the inherent tendency towards a state of full employment upon an analysis of the functioning of the labour market which has proved to be both durable and compelling. The new classical macroeconomics, which we shall examine in greater detail in Chapter 7, can, to a considerable extent, be viewed as a return to pre-Keynesian methods of analysis, particularly in their treatment of the operation of the labour market. Pigou's *Unemployment* (1913) and *The Theory of Unemployment* (1933) have made a striking, if largely unacknowledged, comeback in the writings of Lucas, Sargent and Wallace. An understanding of Keynes's critique of the classical theory of labour market adjustment is therefore an essential prerequisite for a fuller evaluation of the contribution of the new classical macroeconomics to our understanding of the workings of a market economy. It will be seen that many of the disputes between Keynesians and monetarists/new classicals find their origins in quite fundamental prognostic disagreements concerning the response of the labour market to a state of general excess supply.

The classical view restated

The sanguine view of the classical writers that deviations from the normal state of full employment could be regarded as temporary 'lapses from full employment' (Pigou's phrase) was based upon a very simple disequilibrium adjustment mechanism derived from Marshallian partial equilibrium analysis. According to Marshall, when supply exceeded demand in any market, the forces of competition would exert downward pressure on the price peculiar to that market. A fall in price of sufficient magnitude would ultimately ensure that the initial excess supply would be eliminated.

This approach has considerable intuitive appeal when it is applied to the markets for apples or second-hand cars, and even when it is applied to *individual* labour markets. However, the classical writers tended to transfer the same principles of adjustment from the microeconomic to the macroeconomic plane, though their applicability at this level of aggregation is altogether more problematical, as Keynes was to point out. Since the demand for labour is a decreasing function of the real wage rate and the supply of labour is (perhaps) an increasing function of the real wage rate, they argued that the origins of general unemployment could be traced to the maintenance of a real wage rate, w_1, which exceeded the market clearing real wage rate, w^*. Given this diagnosis, the remedy for unemployment was patently clear: real wages should fall. Moreover in a competitive market economy the requisite fall in real wages from w_1 to w^* would occur spontaneously. The unemployed would vie with the employed by offering their labour services at lower wages. Provided that labour is homogeneous in quality, employers would have the incentive to hire the cheaper labour. The process of undercutting the existing wage rate would continue until all of those willing to work had been absorbed into employment.

The economic experience of the interwar period, particularly in Britain, posed weighty questions concerning the origins of general

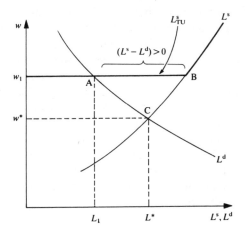

Figure 5.1 Unemployment and the trades union labour supply function

unemployment. It was clear to the classical writers that there were tens of thousands of workers who were unemployed and who were prepared to work at the going (real or money) wage rate. The general level of wages exceeded the marginal disutility of employment.

So what forces impeded the real wage rate from falling so as to bring into employment those willing to work at the going wage rate? If the going wage rate was 'wrong', as it appeared to be, what stood in the way of its downward revision? The answer appeared to be obvious: the refusal of those workers in employment to accept wage cuts, coupled with the inability, for institutional reasons, of unemployed workers to undercut the general level of wages, resulted in a strong tendency to wage rigidity. The 'institutional' barriers to price competition between employed and unemployed workers had arisen, of course, as a result of the pervasive powers of the trades union movement. Unions were viewed as monopolistic combinations of labour which catered mainly for the interests of those of their members who were in employment at the expense of the unemployed. In effect the competitive labour supply function had been supplanted over most of its range by what may be called the 'trades union labour supply function', L_{TU}^s, illustrated by the bold lines in Figure 5.1. The function L_{TU}^s includes part of the competitive labour supply function, i.e. that segment of L^s above and to the right of point B, but renders inoperative the remaining part, i.e. that segment of L^s below and to the left of point B. Workers who are willing to work at less than the wage stipulated by trades unions (w_1 in Figure 5.1) will be excluded from active participation in the labour market for as long as these powerful combinations maintain their stranglehold as monopoly suppliers of labour.

In the above account the distinction between changes in money wages and changes in real wages has been deliberately blurred. With rare exceptions the classical economists took it for granted that a reduction in the money-wage rate would be translated into the all important reduction in the real-wage rate which was required by marginal productivity theory. The reasons for this puzzling association of money wage changes and real-wage changes in classical theory are not altogether clear, though we speculated in Chapter 2 that the influence of the quantity theory of money probably played an important part since it anchored the price level to the quantity of money in circulation, releasing the money-wage bargain to determine real wages. A fallacy of composition, involving the illegitimate transfer of microeconomic methods of analysis to macroeconomics, also appears to have added to the confusion.

Real and money wages in the *General Theory*: what is involuntary unemployment?

> Until recently no economists doubted that an all-round reduction in the rate of money wages might be expected to increase, and an all round enhancement to diminish, the volume of employment. (A. C. Pigou, 1937, the opening sentence of his Presidential Address to the Royal Economic Society)

It is well known that Keynes opposed money-wage cuts as a cure for unemployment, but the reasons for his opposition have been widely misunderstood. Indeed, the Keynesian model has often been accused of neglecting the labour market altogether, and in particular of neglecting optimizing behaviour in the labour market. The irrational spectre of money illusion is often seen to lie behind the complex façade of income–expenditure models derived from the *IS–LM* system. It is arguable that the recent resuscitation of classical ideas is a reaction against the alleged Keynesian neglect of optimizing behaviour in general and against rather mechanical[1] income–expenditure models in particular. From those brought up to regard the *IS–LM* system as the last word in representing *the* Keynesian system, such a virulent reaction is hardly surprising. Keynes's theory of labour market adjustment has fallen victim to widespread ignorance and neglect. We shall attempt to redress the balance in this section.

Piecing together Keynes's labour market analysis is not an easy task since the fragments are promiscuously scattered throughout the pages of the *General Theory*. In addition there is, as yet, no consensus of opinion among Keynes scholars over his treatment of the labour market so that what is presented here must be regarded as the personal view of the author.

Much to the unease of many of his followers, Keynes retained the underlying behavioural relationships of the neoclassical model. He thus accepted the marginal productivity theory of the demand for labour and its corollary that a fall in the real wage rate is a necessary condition for a rise in employment. On the supply side he also accepted the notion that there would exist some relationship between the willingness to work and the real wage rate. If workers are to supply more labour they may require a reward in the form of a higher real wage rate in order to compensate them for the higher marginal disutility of employment. A state of general excess supply in the labour market could therefore be depicted in a manner which the classical economists would instantly recognize and find acceptable. Hence in Figure 5.1 the extent of general unemployment

---

[1] *Ad hoc* is a frequently used buzz phrase in this context.

could be measured by the horizontal distance AB, this level of unemployment being *associated* with a real wage rate w_1. (For reasons that will become clear later, the L^s_{TU} schedule is irrelevant in the Keynesian system.)

The really fundamental point of dispute between Keynes's analysis of the labour market and that of his classical predecessors lay, not in the depiction of a *state* of general unemployment, but in his rejection of the classical theory of *disequilibrium adjustment*. The analytical core which Keynes shared with Pigou did not extend to their respective prognoses of how an economy responds to excess supply in the labour market. Keynes claimed that, even if the labour market were competitive, the real wage rate would not fall in the presence of a substantial excess supply of labour. Excess supply would exert downward pressure on the money wage rate only: the level of real wages would remain largely unaffected by a steady reduction in the level of money wages which a state of persistent excess supply would entail. It is the money wage alone which is determined by the bargains struck between workers and employers. The real wage rate is not a variable which can be directly negotiated in the bargaining process. Even though workers would be willing to offer their labour services at a lower real wage rate, and even though employers would be willing to hire more workers at a lower real wage rate, neither party to the bargaining process is capable of exerting downward pressure on this all important relative price. Keynes summarized the fallacy that lay at the heart of the classical theory of labour market adjustment:

> The traditional theory [of employment] maintains, in short, *that the wage bargains between the entrepreneurs and the workers determine the real wage*; so that, assuming free competition amongst employers and no restrictive combinations amongst workers, the latter can, if they wish, bring their real wages into conformity with the marginal disutility of employment offered by the employers at that wage. If this is not true, then there is no longer any reason to expect a tendency towards equality between the real wage and the marginal disutility of labour. (*GT*, p. 11, original italics)

The impotence of the two parties to the wage bargain to bring about a reduction in the real wage rate is what makes Keynesian unemployment *in*voluntary. Workers would prefer to be at point C rather than point A in Figure 5.1, while employers would be maximizing profit at point C as well as point A. Despite the scope for a Pareto-improvement in welfare if the real wage were reduced to w^*, the means of achieving such an improvement are absent in a money using economy. The possibility of mutually advantageous trade which standard competitive theory would associate with point A is devoid of operational significance, not through any unwillingness on the part of workers or employers to exploit such an opportunity, but through their impotence to affect the only price that matters in this market, the real wage rate.

Keynes asserted that the real wage rate is determined, not by bargains between workers and employers, but by 'certain other forces' (*GT*, p. 13). Let us assume that the economy inherits a real wage rate w_1. If there are no institutional or other barriers to the working of market forces, the general excess supply of labour associated with this real wage should lead to a decline in the level of money wages. Keynes maintained that such a reduction would lead to a more or less equiproportionate reduction in the general level of prices. He based this proposition on what he regarded as thoroughly orthodox Marshallian microeconomics which held that, in a perfectly competitive economy, the price of a commodity would equal its marginal cost of production.[2] Since labour is far and away the most important cost of production in the short run, a reduction in money wages will lower the marginal costs facing the representative firm which, on the assumption of marginal cost pricing, will lead to a fall in the price of output. The process of price deflation is 'balanced' in the sense that the money wage, the level of marginal costs, and the price level will all decline equiproportionately.[3] Obviously a process of balanced deflation would entail no alteration of the real wage rate.

This very simple line of argument is illustrated in Figure 5.2. Real national income is measured on the horizontal axis and the price level and the marginal cost of production are measured on the vertical axis. Since the problem in hand is one of excess supply in the labour market, the actual level of income, Y_1, will be less than its full employment value, Y^*. In these circumstances elementary competitive theory suggests that money wages will fall. Consider a step decline in the level of money wages from W_1 to W_2. This will result in a downward displacement of the marginal cost curve from $MC(W_1)$ to $MC(W_2)$. From the 'expected price equals marginal cost' principle the price level will decline from P_1 to P_2. The real wage rate will remain unchanged, that is $W_1/P_1 = W_2/P_2$, if marginal costs comprise only labour costs, a situation Keynes considered to be likely in the short run.

What forces fix the level of real income at Y_1? Keynes's answer is straightforward: effective demand. But this answer begs a further question: are there any circumstances in which an all round reduction of

---

[2]The 'expected price equals marginal cost' principle permeates the analysis of the *General Theory* and is most clearly stated in Chapter 21.

[3]The force of this proposition is in no way vitiated by allowing for other variable inputs in the short run provided that these inputs are also produced by labour under the same competitive conditions as Keynes assumed for the production of final output.

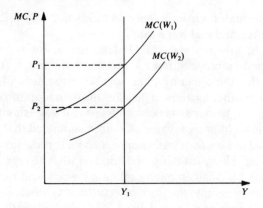

Figure 5.2   Money wages and the absolute price level

money wages and prices will stimulate the real value of desired expenditure and real national income?

Aggregate demand and money wages: the neoclassical synthesis

In Chapter 19 of the *General Theory*, the chapter entitled 'Changes in money-wages', Keynes confronted head on the question of the relationship between aggregate demand and the levels of money wages and prices. He listed several possible links between the various components of aggregate expenditure on the one hand, and the levels of prices and money wages on the other. To cut a long story short,[4] he concluded that most of these effects were ambiguous but that there was one effect which could, in principle, be quite powerful in raising the level of real expenditure and income: for a constant nominal stock of money, a fall in the price level will raise the real money stock which may, in turn, exert significant downward pressure on the rate of interest. To the extent that aggregate expenditure – and in particular private investment expenditure – is stimulated by lower interest rates, real income will rise in consequence. The nexus linking changes in the price level to changes in real income via the rate of interest is known as the *Keynes effect*.

The Keynes effect is illustrated in Figure 5.3. The nominal stock of money, M_1, is assumed to remain unchanged in the face of balanced

---

[4]For a fuller treatment of these and related matters, see Chick, 1983, Chapter 7.

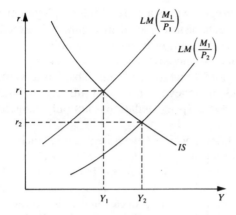

Figure 5.3   The Keynes effect

deflation. The fall in the price level from P_1 to P_2 raises the real money stock from M_1/P_1 to M_1/P_2 and reduces the rate of interest from r_1 to r_2. The resultant increase in investment expenditure raises real income from Y_1 to Y_2. Obviously this indirect mechanism by which real income rises as the price level falls could continue for as long as (a) the rate of interest continues to fall; and (b) the rate of investment continues to respond to these interest rate reductions. In other words, provided that the liquidity trap is not reached and that investment remains sufficiently responsive to interest rate reductions, falling prices could conceivably establish levels of expenditure and real income which correspond to their full employment values, E^* and Y^* respectively.

Nevertheless, the path to full employment through balanced deflation is likely to be fraught with hazards. Many unforeseen dangers may be lurking in the wings. For example, the enhanced possibility of bankruptcy and default arising from failure to meet contracts fixed in money terms could have quite severe knock on effects for the whole financial system. Firms and institutions which are otherwise financially sound could be hard hit by a protracted run of debt defaults. The inability of debtors to honour their financial obligations to creditors could lead to a general financial crisis not dissimilar to the endemic banking crises of the early nineteenth century. Many pre-Keynesian quantity theorists – most notably Irving Fisher – would have shuddered at the prospect of a prolonged bout of price deflation: the financial system might not be able to bear the strain.

Moreover, even if these undesirable side effects of deflation could be disregarded and the progress towards a state of full employment did in fact correspond to the mechanism depicted in Figure 5.3, exactly the same result could be more expeditiously achieved simply by increasing the nominal money supply. An increase in the real money supply can be brought about by the far more direct route of central bank intervention to increase the nominal stock of money by an amount sufficient to attain full employment. Reliance on wage–price deflation is not only dangerous, it is wholly unnecessary.

But there was one mechanism which Keynes neglected to include in his list of the effects of wage–price deflation and which was to play an important part in the revival of the classical belief in the inherent tendency towards a state of full employment. This is the celebrated (and often misunderstood) *real-balance effect*, occasionally also known as the *Pigou effect*. At the heart of the real-balance effect lies the hypothesis that desired consumption expenditure depends not only upon the level of income and the rate of interest but also upon the real net worth of the private sector: that is $C = C(r, Y, NW/P)$ where NW/P is the nominal value of private sector net worth deflated by the price level. Even during periods of falling prices, some components of NW will remain fixed in nominal terms so that, unless other components of NW fall more rapidly than the price level, reductions in P will raise NW/P which, in turn, will stimulate consumption expenditure.

The most obvious – and probably the most trivial – example of the real-balance effect is the impact of falling prices on the real value of bank notes in the hands of the private sector. If one possessed a \$100 bill, and if the price level fell ten thousandfold overnight, one would wake up next morning to find oneself effectively a millionaire. So obviously these non-interest bearing, non-redeemable liabilities of the government (fiat money) are included in NW.

But the real-balance effect may also operate on a wider array of assets which constitute the net worth of the private sector, though there has always been controversy over the range of assets to which it is supposed to apply. For example it is generally accepted that, since the real-balance effect concerns the *net* wealth of the private sector, indebtedness arising from *within* the private sector should be excluded from the definition of NW. It follows that the money supply should not be regarded as part of NW since by far its largest component are bank deposits, a magnitude technically referred to as 'inside money': the assets of depositors are matched by the liabilities of bank creditors.

And what about government interest bearing liabilities (bonds for short)? Do they figure in the definition of 'outside money'? Unfortunately a consensus view has yet to emerge on this question. It used to be thought that bonds should be included in a definition of the net worth of the private sector, but this has been challenged by R. J. Barro (1974), who has argued that bonds should not be regarded as part of the net worth of the private sector since the non-monetary liabilities of the government are a burden on this generation and on future generations. Sooner or later this burden will have to be faced up to in the form of higher taxation either now or in the future. Tax payers react to a rise in government spending funded through the sale of bonds by saving more now to meet future tax liabilities. Barro is making the perfectly valid point that when the government incurs debt by issuing bonds it is acting as a mere go between on behalf of the private sector: the private sector is becoming more indebted *to itself* through the financial intermediation of the government.

Despite the power of Barro's 'equivalence theorem', it seems reasonable to acknowledge at least some role for government bonds in the definition of *NW* in addition to fiat money. To the extent that the government, the major issuer of those assets which make up the private sector's net worth, does not alter its spending and taxation policies in response to a rising real value of its outstanding liabilities, aggregate spending will rise as the price level falls.

It will be recalled that the Keynes effect critically relies first upon the response of the rate of interest to wage–price deflation and secondly upon the response of investment to lower interest rates. In contrast, the real-balance effect exerts a direct influence on the level of spending independently of what happens to the rate of interest. It does not therefore run the risk of encountering those barriers which prevent the Keynes effect from operating, namely absolute liquidity preference and/or an investment function which is interest inelastic. The real balance effect may be represented diagrammatically as a rightward shift in the *IS* curve. The combined operation of the Keynes effect and the real-balance effect is illustrated in Figure 5.4. It should be noted that the real-balance effect operates even in the degenerate cases depicted in Figures 4.12(a) and 4.12(b): even if the *IS* curve is vertical and the *LM* curve is horizontal, the real-balance effect will nevertheless raise demand and hence output and employment.

Both the Keynes effect and the real-balance effect were to form the essential ingredients of the professional consensus which emerged in the years following the publication of the *General Theory* known as the *neoclassical synthesis*. According to this synthesis, Keynesian unemployment was a phenomenon which was primarily attributable to downwardly sticky money wages and prices, the obvious implication being that general unemployment would never arise if money wages and prices were perfectly flexible downwards as well as upwards.

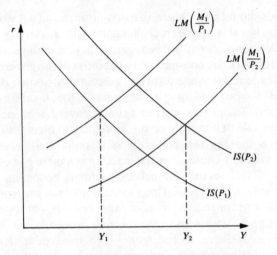

Figure 5.4 Keynes effect and real-balance effect

This is, of course, identical to the conclusion reached by Pigou in his *Theory of Unemployment*:

> With perfectly free competition there will always be a strong tendency toward full employment. Such unemployment as exists at any time is due wholly to the frictional resistances [which] prevent wage and price adjustments being made instantaneously.

In other words rigidities and frictions in the response of money wages and prices to a state of general excess supply provide a practical justification for demand management policies. These policies should be particularly aimed at adjusting the ratio of the nominal stock of money to the absolute price level since, following Modigliani (1944), the origins of general excess supply can be traced to a 'misalignment' between the money stock and the levels of money wages and prices.

Nevertheless, even with highly flexible wages and prices, the supposedly therapeutic properties of money wage reductions should be viewed with great circumspection. Professor Patinkin, who was largely responsible for the rigorous formulation of the real-balance effect, has always urged caution in regarding price deflation as an acceptable alternative route for the attainment of full employment. For a start the required reduction in the price level may have to be very large indeed before it has a significant impact on aggregate spending. Secondly, even though static analysis of the sort featured in Figures 5.3 and 5.4 may point to the stimulating effect of price reductions, dynamic considerations such as the effects of bankruptcy and default during the *process* of price deflation may serve to tighten the grip of recession rather than loosen it. We have already noted Fisher's concern about the financial instability that a process of money wage–price deflation could bring in its train. Finally, evidence from what was arguably the most traumatic period for capitalism, the post-1929 Depression in the United States, does not lend support to the real-balance hypothesis: 'For the 1929–32 period as a whole there was an increase in real balances of 42 per cent, and a decrease in real income of 40 per cent' (Patinkin, 1951).[5] Patinkin's point is that the comparison of positions of static equilibrium, one equilibrium being characterized by a considerably lower price level than the other, may be of very limited practical relevance. Indeed, these comparisons could be dangerous if they are accorded too great a prominence in an analysis of the impact of money wage–price deflation on employment.

Throughout most of the post-war period acceptance of the neoclassical synthesis by the economics profession was confined to the plane of pure theory. The Keynes effect and the real-balance effect were regarded as so weak and uncertain in practice that they rarely, if ever, featured in debates on economic policy matters. The abstract musings of macroeconomists did not encroach on the hard world of economic decision making. There was a widespread acceptance of the Keynesian view that far less painful alternatives to money wage cuts were available in the form of demand management policies. Moreover, despite its 'classical' predictions, the neoclassical synthesis was firmly grounded methodologically in the principle of effective demand: the classical money wage–real wage–employment nexus had been completely abandoned in favour of the money wage–price level–aggregate demand–employment nexus. However, in this latter nexus, the relation between the real wage rate and the level of aggregate demand – a relation which was accorded great prominence in the *General Theory* – was to become obscured almost to the point of invisibility. For four decades it was supposed that Hicks's *IS–LM* model contained all of the basic ingredients of the *General Theory* approach to the theory of employment. Interest rates apart, the price-theoretic aspects of Keynes's great work were ignored.

Aggregate demand and the real wage rate

The involuntary nature of Keynesian unemployment arises, as we saw earlier, from the inability of either workers or employers directly to exert the downward pressure on the real wage rate that was required by the

---

[5]Other evidence seems to be rather more generous to the real-balance effect: see Patinkin (1965).

marginal productivity theory of the demand for labour. Keynes accepted that an increase in employment would need to be underpinned by a reduction in the real wage rate but rejected the view that the forces of competition would automatically achieve this end. Thus he wrote 'The *general* level of real wages depends on the other forces of the economic system' (*GT*, p. 14, original italics).

What are these mysterious 'other forces' which are supposed to determine the real wage rate? They effectively reduce to just one force: the level of effective demand. But in what way do variations in effective demand alter the real wage rate? There would, at first sight, appear to be no connection between these two variables.

In order to simplify exposition we shall assume that the level of money wages is given[6] at W_0 so that we are able to fix the position of the aggregate marginal cost curve in Figure 5.5(b).

Suppose there is a rise in aggregate demand brought about by an expansionary fiscal policy. This is represented in Figure 5.5(a) by a rightward shift in the *IS* curve from IS_1 to IS_2. From Figure 5.5(b) we see that the rise in output raises marginal cost and hence raises the price level of output. Since the money wage rate is, by hypothesis, assumed to be constant at W_0, the real wage rate falls from W_0/P_1 to W_0/P_2 in Figure 5.5(c). The amount by which the real wage rate will have to fall is mirrored in the amount by which prices will have to rise since the aggregate marginal cost curve in 5.5(b) is derived from the marginal physical product curve of labour. Moreover, since any given *LM* curve is defined with respect to a particular real stock of money, the rise in the price level shifts the *LM* curve in a north-westerly direction from a position $LM(M_1/P_1)$ to $LM(M_1/P_2)$.[7] By means of this simple model, Keynes was able to accommodate the marginal productivity theory of the demand for labour within his income–expenditure theory of employment, something of a *tour de force*.

The above brief account throws into sharp relief the essential differences between the Keynesian and classical theories of labour market adjustment. In classical theory a spontaneous fall in the real wage rate is the initiating force tending to raise employment and output. In Keynesian theory the direction of causation is reversed: the fall in the real

---

[6] The same assumption was made in the first eighteen chapters of the *General Theory*, and for the same reason: holding money wages constant is an extremely helpful aid to exposition. In Chapter 19 Keynes let go of this convenient illustrative device so as to demonstrate how the principle of effective demand survived the relaxation of the assumption of given money wages.

[7] The second-round effect on the *LM* curve of a step increase in the price level which results from an expansion in demand is usually ignored in most expositions of the *IS–LM* model in which the price level is taken to be exogenously given.

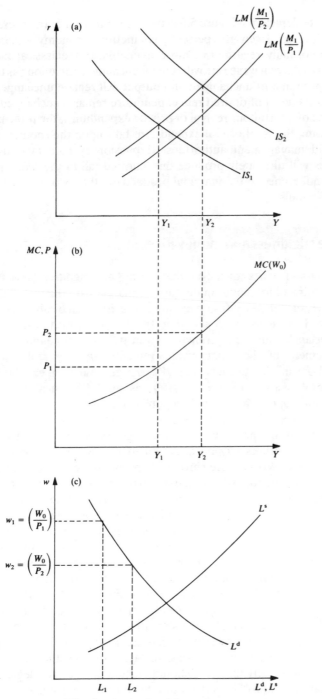

Figure 5.5 Effective demand and the real-wage rate

wage rate depicted in Figure 5.5 is the *consequence*, not the *cause*, of the rise in output. Even in a perfectly competitive economy – the state of affairs normally regarded as most amenable to neoclassical modes of analysis – the real wage rate will remain unchanged for as long as the level of output remains unchanged; and output will remain unchanged for as long as the level of desired real expenditure remains unchanged. In the absence of a fortuitous revival of private expenditure, the principal onus for raising the level of real expenditure falls upon the shoulders of the demand management authorities. Expansionary monetary and fiscal policies will ultimately produce the required fall in the real wage rate which adherence to the marginal productivity theory of the demand for labour entails.

Wage stickiness and money illusion

It is now widely acknowledged that Keynes accepted the classical theory of the demand for labour in the form of marginal productivity theory. In contrast, turbulent confusion has always surrounded his theory of labour supply. It is usually argued that the feature which distinguishes a Keynesian labour supply function from its classical counterpart is the replacement of the money wage rate, W, for the real wage rate, $w = W/P$, in the former. The 'Keynesian' function can be written $L^s = \phi(W)$ rather than $L^s = \psi(w)$, as in the classical model. One implication of the Keynesian function is that, since $\phi' > 0$, an increase in money wages will raise the supply of labour *irrespective* of what is happening to the price level. Money wage increases are valued in their own right: workers pay no attention to the purchasing power of the money wage. Workers are chronically prone to money illusion: if prices rise in the same proportion to the rise in the money wage, leaving the real wage rate unchanged, workers none the less supply more labour.

Leontief (1936) was the first of Keynes's critics to attack what he perceived to be a theory of labour supply grounded in irrational behaviour by workers. The $L^s = \phi(W)$ formulation of the theory of labour supply violates the classical homogeneity postulate which states that a scalar multiplication of all nominal quantities should leave real quantities, and the functional relationships that underlie them, unchanged. A doubling of both the money-wage rate and the price level should not alter the supply of labour. In an uncharacteristically confused reply to Leontief's powerful criticisms, Keynes (*CW*, XIV, p. 109) appears to concede that he was, in fact, rejecting the postulate that demand and supply functions should be homogeneous of degree zero in nominal quantities. His justification for this apparent rejection was not theoretical at all: it was based on what he claimed was the 'abundant evidence of experience'. (The manner in which 'evidence of experience', abundant or otherwise, can cast light on the validity of the classical homogeneity postulate remains a mystery to this author.)

It would be inappropriate to delve more deeply into the history of economic thought.[8] However, we might pause to speculate how the above formulation of the Keynesian labour supply function came about. In the author's view the main reason for the emergence of the $\phi(W)$ formulation lies in a confusion of observed fact for theoretical postulate. It was Keynes's view that, in practice, the money wage rate was downwardly rigid. This observation did appear to conform with the actual behaviour of money wages in the interwar period, particularly in Britain. Unfortunately this purely empirical observation was remarked on at length in several passages of the *General Theory*, giving the false impression that it had some wider theoretical significance. It was there-fore natural for Keynes's interpreters to infer that the supply curve of labour was horizontal at an arbitrarily given money wage rate for all levels of employment up to full employment: after all, an implication of the unwillingness of workers to accept a wage cut is that they are refusing to supply their labour at a lower money wage. This view is expressed diagrammatically in Figure 5.6.

This interpretation of the *General Theory* labour supply function seems initially quite plausible, but the further one pursues Keynes's chain of reasoning, the more apparent it becomes that he had something altogether different from the $\phi(W)$ formulation in mind. We saw earlier in this chapter how the assumption of given money wages was not an intrinsic part of Keynes's theory: 'The essential character of the argument is precisely the same whether or not money-wages, etc., are liable to change' (*GT*, p. 27). Chapter 19 of the *General Theory* is devoted in its entirety to an exploration of the different routes through which reduc-tions in money wages may affect the level of employment. It is true that, for a variety of reasons to do with the structure of wage bargaining in Britain, Keynes did not consider it very likely that money wages would fall, even in the presence of substantial unemployment. But this was an empirical observation which concerned the economic circumstances of a particular country at a particular period of time: it had nothing whatever to do with his *general* theory of employment. It has nevertheless given rise to such widespread misunderstanding in subsequent interpretations of his model that Keynes would have done better to exclude all discussion of money wage rigidity from the main body of the *General Theory*.

---

[8]Readers who wish to pursue the matter further might care to consult Patinkin (1976) and Trevithick (1976).

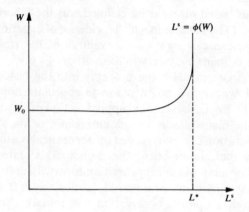

Figure 5.6 'Money illusion' labour supply function

Further evidence against the $\phi(W)$ formulation of the labour supply function is provided by an examination of the definition of involuntary unemployment given on page 15 of the *General Theory*:

> *Men are involuntarily unemployed if, in the event of a small rise in the price of wage-goods relatively to the money-wage, both the aggregate supply of labour willing to work for the current money-wage and the aggregate demand for it at that wage would be greater than the existing volume of employment.*

This extraordinarily convoluted definition, the whole of which is in italics, must have been responsible for deterring thousands of readers from proceeding beyond page 15 of the *General Theory*, but it does make sense. Consider Figure 5.7. The hypothetical experiment which Keynes is undertaking is an examination of the consequences of a fall in the real wage rate brought about through a rise in the general price level, P (what he refers to as 'the price of wage-goods') in relation to the money wage, W. The initial real wage rate is $w_0 = W_0/P_0$ and the corresponding 'existing volume of employment' is L_0. The fall in the real wage rate to $w_1(= W_0/P_1)$ raises the demand for labour to L^{d1} and (perhaps) reduces the supply of labour to L^{s1}. Since $L^{s1} > L^{d1} > L_0$, both the demand for and supply of labour still exceed L_0, the existing volume of employment, despite the reduction in the real wage. In other words involuntary unemployment is still present in the labour market, though its extent is less than it was initially.

Once again the phenomenon that makes this sort of unemployment involuntary is the inability of workers and employers directly to lower the real-wage rate to w^*. In Keynes's hypothetical experiment the reduction

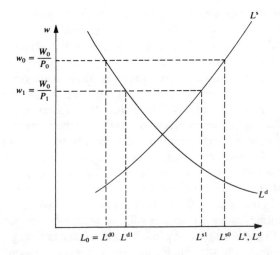

Figure 5.7 Keynes's definition of involuntary unemployment

in the real wage rate is brought about through a rise in the price level, which, in turn, is brought about through an increase in aggregate demand, though this is not made explicit in the definition (see Figure 5.4).

Keynes on the sources of money wage stickiness

In the above account workers passively accept a reduction in their real wage rate from w_0 to w_1 brought about through increases in the price level. However there are many passages in the *General Theory* in which Keynes asserted that, *even if* a similar reduction in w could be brought about via the route of money wage cuts (and we have suggested above that money wage cuts will *not* have this effect), workers would be unwilling to allow their money wages to fall. Workers are unworried by the erosion of W/P resulting from increases in P, but they will strenuously resist the same erosion of W/P resulting from reductions in W. At first blush this would appear to be yet another manifestation of the irrational phenomenon of money illusion affecting the supply of labour. So what was Keynes driving at?

Despite what we said earlier about the inefficacy of money wage cuts in reducing the real wage, let us, purely for the sake of argument, allow that reductions in W and equiproportionate increases in P have the same impact in lowering the real wage. Why do workers prefer to take real wage cuts in the form of price rises?

If money wage negotiations took place at a highly centralized level, with trades union leaders bargaining over the *general* level of wages, workers should be indifferent as between reductions in W and increases in P in effecting a given reduction in the real wage rate. This is a requirement of rational behaviour. But wage negotiations are very rarely conducted at such a high level of aggregation: wage bargaining is a fragmented, decentralized process. Moreover, the industrial relations climate in most Western economies sets great store by the preservation of a particular pattern of wage differentials between different categories of labour. (Witness the number of 'comparability' pay claims which have little to do with the tightness of labour markets.) The accepted pattern of wage differentials need not be absolutely rigid, but, for as long as the supply of labour in one market depends *inter alia* upon wages payable in other markets, money wage reductions will not readily be forthcoming. Workers will go to great lengths 'to protect their *relative* real wage' (*GT*, p. 14, original italics): 'the struggle for money-wages is . . . essentially a struggle to maintain a high *relative* wage . . . ' (*GT*, p. 252, original italics). Since a process of individual wage reductions in such circumstances is bound to be ragged and discontinuous, it will be hedged about with uncertainty and apprehension. Even though workers are prepared to accept a general reduction in the level of real wages, they are unwilling to take the first step of accepting money wage cuts in case other workers with whom they regard themselves as comparable fail to follow suit. Workers are caught up in a form of 'prisoners' dilemma'. The dominating strategy is non-cooperative: an individual group of workers has a clear interest in standing firm in resisting money wage cuts even though workers *en masse* may be better off if a cooperative strategy were pursued. Game-theoretic considerations point to a conflict between collective and individual rationality.[9] Collective rationality may require a reduction in W which, in turn, requires reductions in $(W_1, \ldots, W_i, \ldots, W_n)$ where W_i is the money wage rate in the ith labour market. However, considerations of individual rationality induce workers in the ith market to reject any move to revise W_i downwards. Similar resistance in the remaining $(n-1)$ labour markets renders the general level of money wages downwardly inflexible.

This divergence between collective and individual rationality is not encountered when the means by which the real wage is reduced is via an increase in the absolute price level. An increase in P is across the board, affecting all groups of workers equally and posing no threat to the

---

[9]'Individual' in this context should be taken to refer to the suppliers of labour in a particular labour market.

structure of established wage differentials. It is therefore individually rational for workers to resist money wage reductions but to accept an erosion of their real wage rate through price increases. Workers are not behaving irrationally since all workers are in the same boat when prices rise.

Real wages and employment: was Keynes wrong?

[The first postulate of classical economics] means that, with a given organisation, equipment and technique, real wages and the volume of output (and hence employment) are uniquely correlated, so that, in general, an increase in employment can only occur to the accompaniment of a decline in the rate of real wages. Thus I am not disputing this vital fact which classical economists have (rightly) asserted as indefeasible. (*GT*, p. 17)

But how indefeasible is the classical assertion which Keynes was so ready to accept? In the years following the publication of the *General Theory*, doubts started to be expressed about Keynes's favourable attitude towards the classical theory of the demand for labour. Had Keynes gone too far down the road of attempting to accommodate many of the central tenets of classical economics within the framework of his own theory of employment? Criticism was particularly levelled at the basic prediction of marginal productivity theory that movements in real wages and movements in employment should be inversely correlated. More technically movements in real wages should be *countercyclical*, with real wages falling in the upswing of the cycle and rising in the downswing.

The relationship of real wages to the phase of the trade cycle was subjected to empirical scrutiny in two celebrated papers, one by J. G. Dunlop (1938) using British data, and the other by L. Tarshis (1939) using American data. The results of both investigations suggested that, far from moving countercyclically, real wages moved procyclically: increases in output and employment appeared to be correlated with increases in the real wage rate. In a long reply to Dunlop and Tarshis, Keynes (1939) listed a number of possible explanations for the apparently procyclical behaviour of real wages. One explanation from this list is of particular interest: if the economy is in an unusually deep recession, firms may be operating at levels of output at which the marginal cost of production is *falling*. Moreover if the point of minimum marginal cost has not yet been reached, it follows *a fortiori* that the point of minimum average cost has not been reached either. This is illustrated in Figure 5.8.

For all levels of output up to Y_3, marginal cost is falling. Hence an increase in output from Y_1 to Y_2 will reduce the price level from P_1 to P_2

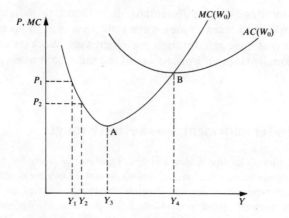

Figure 5.8 Procyclical behaviour of real wages

while the level of money wages remains unchanged at W_0. The real wage rate obviously rises as a result of an expansion of output over this range.

Keynes was nevertheless very cautious in accepting the phenomenon of diminishing marginal costs as a general characteristic even of an economy experiencing substantial levels of unemployment. He insisted that 'the critical point of upturn' (point A in Figure 5.8) would occur at a level of output 'which is highly relevant for practical purposes'. Hence a 'sharply different theory [of the behaviour of real wages] . . . becomes applicable after the turning point has been reached.' Circumstances alter cases: in deep recessions the economy is likely to be to the left of point A whereas in milder recessions the economy is more likely to be to the right of point A.

Nevertheless serious problems remain with Keynes's simple theory of the firm. In his reply to Tarshis and Dunlop, Keynes referred almost exclusively to the *marginal* cost curve of the representative firm, neglecting the relationship between average and marginal cost. If the normal U-shaped average cost curve is included in the analysis – as it is in Figure 5.8 – certain rather disturbing possibilities are opened up. In particular at levels of output below Y_4, the representative firm will be making a loss by equating price with marginal cost. Such a situation cannot persist for long since firms would go out of business. Points such as point A cannot describe the behaviour of firms in anything longer than the very short run. This problem would not arise with the assumption of *average* cost pricing but other, potentially more intractable problems would then have to be tackled, in particular how such behaviour could be reconciled with the idea that firms are profit maximizing organizations. Perhaps there was more than a grain of truth in the remark of one of his closest colleagues that Keynes 'had never spent the twenty minutes necessary to understand the theory of value'.

Real wages and employment: Patinkin's early contribution

On that rather unsatisfactory agnostic note matters rested for many years until Don Patinkin published his classic work, *Money, Interest and Prices*.[10] The grave doubts that had been cast upon the validity of marginal productivity theory in the late 1930s – doubts which Keynes himself had come to share, albeit reluctantly – had made very little impression on the literature. The main reason for this was, of course, the dominance of the *IS–LM* model – a model in which the real-wage rate does not figure at all – in the teaching of macroeconomics.

Patinkin's book was to focus attention once again on the reaction of real wages to changes in the level of employment. Patinkin argued that, in times of demand deficient unemployment, the marginal productivity theory of the demand for labour was, quite simply, irrelevant. Consider the assumptions which are required before we can regard the marginal productivity of labour curve as the actual demand curve for labour. First, the size of the capital stock is fixed, an assumption which is characteristic of all short-run analysis and which is wholly unexceptionable. The second, more questionable assumption is that, even in the short run, capital and labour are combined in variable proportions, that is, that a movement down the marginal productivity of labour curve will imply the employment of more workers with a given number of machines. On the other hand a more appropriate short-run assumption is that labour and capital are combined in fixed proportions: x men, no more and no less, are required to work y machines. The short-run capital–labour ratio (y/x in this example) is technologically fixed. The assumption of a variable capital–labour ratio implied by marginal productivity theory is more acceptable in long-run analysis such as formal models of economic growth, but it is likely to be inapplicable in short-run analysis.

These two assumptions together imply that, under the stipulated conditions of perfect competition, the capital stock will always be fully utilized irrespective of the extent of unemployment in the labour market. The capital stock, unlike the labour force, will always be fully employed. However, Patinkin pointed out that, during a Keynesian recession, underutilized capacity is typically observed side by side with unemployed

---

[10]First edition 1955, second edition 1965. All subsequent references will be to the second edition.

labour: capacity utilization will fall and unemployment will rise as aggregate demand falls.

Consider the case depicted in Figure 5.9 where the economy starts in a position of full employment at point A. Suppose the level of aggregate demand were suddenly to fall, for example as a result of a decline in planned investment. According to the analysis of the *General Theory*, the level of employment will fall from L^* to L_1 and the real wage rate will rise from w^* to w_1. At point B workers have been pushed off their labour supply function but employers remain on their labour demand function, albeit at a different point. The capital stock will be just as fully utilized at point B as at point A, but fewer men will be required to operate the fixed number of machines. Firms, unlike households, are assumed to be continuously in neoclassical equilibrium: given the value of the real wage rate, they produce just the right (profit maximizing) volume of output.

However, once we abandon the assumption that the capital stock can never be underutilized we are forced to recognize that the 'off stage' decline in aggregate demand will not only push workers off their 'ideal' labour supply function, L^s: it will also push employers off their 'ideal' labour demand function, L^d. (Clower (1965) has called L^s and L^d the *notional* labour supply and demand functions respectively.) The *effective*[11] demand for labour function, L^{dE}, is the vertical line BD, the notional function L^d being of significance only for purposes of comparing the constrained behaviour of firms with their preferred behaviour. The fact that the marginal productivity principle is redundant in conditions of general unemployment

> expresses the involuntariness with which firms, no less than workers, must be acting during periods of unemployment . . . For just as the latter are then not receiving as much employment as they would normally like at the prevailing real wage rate, so the former are not providing as much as they would normally like. Both firms and workers are being coerced by the same *force majeure* of insufficient demand in the commodity market. Both are being prevented from achieving their optimal model of behaviour. (Patinkin, 1965, p. 322)

In other words workers would *like* to be on the L^s curve and employers would *like* to be on the L^d curve but, following the decline in aggregate demand, neither workers nor employers are capable of achieving these objectives.

But what happens to the real wage rate following a fall in aggregate demand? The short answer is: we do not know. It could rise (e.g. towards w_1) as Keynes believed, it could fall (e.g. towards w_2) as Dunlop and Tarshis believed, or it could conceivably remain unchanged at its market

---

[11]This is, once again, a distinction derived from Clower (1965).

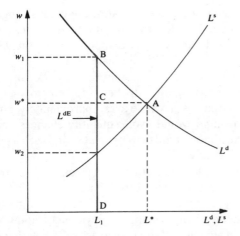

Figure 5.9 General underutilization of factor resources

clearing level w^*. By implication it is impossible to postulate any definite inverse correlation between changes in the real wage rate and changes in employment. Keynes's later scepticism on the precise nature of this connection seems to have been amply justified.

Having lain unnoticed for a number of years, Patinkin's insights have recently been elaborated and refined in the works of Robert Clower and in the writings of what may loosely be called the French Keynesian School, the most prominent member of which is Edmond Malinvaud (see Malinvaud, 1980 and 1985). The notion of quantity rationing figures prominently in the works of these authors. For example, they characterize a state of Keynesian unemployment as one in which workers cannot, in the aggregate, reach the L^s curve in Figure 5.9 and in which employers, since they cannot sell all of the output that they would like to produce, cannot reach the L^d curve. The constrained or effective demand curve for labour is L^{dE} in Figure 5.9. Workers are said to be rationed in the labour market and firms are said to be rationed in the commodity market. Workers and employers have been plunged by extrinsic forces into a suboptimal state in which neither group wishes to remain but from which they are powerless to extricate themselves. No amount of 'mutually advantageous trading' will come to their rescue.

Concluding remarks

It is often claimed that one of the most conspicuous shortcomings of Keynesian macroeconomics lies in its lack of a coherent theory of aggregate supply. According to this view, against the great strengths of Keynes's principle of effective demand should be set the evident weaknesses of his supply-side analysis. The application of the *IS–LM* apparatus was often uncritical and indiscriminate. An implicit assumption appeared to be lurking in the background of the Hicksian model, namely, that at levels of activity significantly below full employment, the elasticity of supply of output as a whole was approximately infinity. Changes in aggregate demand would evoke quantity changes and not price changes. Only in the region of full employment would such a pattern of response cease to be operative.

The passive reaction of aggregate supply to changes in aggregate demand was usually formalized in the 'reverse-*L*' supply function derived from a similar labour supply function in Figure 5.6. According to the $\phi(W)$ labour supply function, changes in the employment of labour which flow from prior changes in aggregate demand will not call forth changes in money wages when the initial state is one of less than full employment.[12] In these circumstances the levels of output and employment are entirely demand determined. The behaviour of relative prices, and in particular the reaction of the real wage rate to excess supply in the labour market, gains no mention at all since the principal focus of attention is the response (or more accurately the lack of response) of absolute prices to changes in the level of aggregate demand. Paradoxically the 'neoclassical' part of the neoclassical synthesis has surprisingly little to say about relative prices: the route back to full employment is through the downward revision of *absolute* prices. The mechanism through which the real wage rate adjusts to variations in aggregate demand in Keynes's labour market analysis is ignored altogether.

This proved to be a fateful oversight since one of the most devastating criticisms to be levelled at Keynesian macroeconomics in recent years has been that it has such shaky foundations in microeconomics. Stripped of the elaborate language of general equilibrium theory, what this criticism usually boils down to is a very simple question: if there is general excess supply in the labour market, what forces prevent the real wage rate from being adjusted downwards? The *IS–LM* model is deafeningly silent on this question since the only relative price which figures in it is the rate of interest. The fact that the *General Theory* model contains extensive, though fragmentary, analysis of the relationship between real wages and

---

[12]The 'reverse-*L*' labour supply function, $\phi(W)$, has been roundly criticized in the preceding sections. The introduction of this function into macroeconomic models was an articulation of the prevalent assumption of downward money wage stickiness. We have suggested that Keynes's labour supply function is in almost all respects identical to its neoclassical counterpart, embodying hypothetical comparisons of various real wage rates with the marginal disutility of employment.

employment is almost universally overlooked in expositions of the Keynesian system. It is hoped that this chapter goes some way to redressing the balance: relative prices *do* matter in the *General Theory*, though they do not adjust in the manner suggested by the classical writers and by their monetarist/new classical descendants.

Nevertheless there is one area in which the Keynesian model leaves much to be desired in its treatment of aggregate supply. This concerns the division of a given change in aggregate demand between price responses and output responses. For example, will an increase in aggregate demand manifest itself principally in the form of an increase in output, as the naïve *IS–LM* model suggests, or in the form of an increase in prices, as the equally naïve quantity theory of money suggests? If the result is a mixture of the two sorts of response, in what proportion will they be combined? Not only is the *IS–LM* system incapable of answering this type of question, even the *General Theory* gives us few clues apart from the somewhat cursory treatment of the two elasticities, e_P and e_Y, in Keynes's generalized quantity theory of money. These problems assume major proportions when allowance is made for the possible dependence of the level and rate of change of money wages on the level of aggregate demand. Enter the Phillips curve.

6

Inflation and the labour market

In the first 25 years after the Second World War the Keynesian approach to macroeconomic theory and policy came to dominate academic and governmental thinking in most Western economies. So complete was the ascendancy of Keynesian ideas that the antecedent classical modes of analysis were abandoned by all but a few diehard sceptics. A neutered, lever pulling version of the *General Theory* emerged, finding its characteristic expression in the various manipulations which the *IS–LM* system had made possible. The classical system had left so few remaining traces that the vast majority of students of economics could be forgiven for believing that, before Keynes, there *was* no macroeconomics. Keynes's struggle to break free from the classical economics with which he was so profoundly imbued, and his recurrent comparisons with what he regarded as the most powerful, though flawed, alternative approach to macroeconomic matters, were almost totally ignored. A hydraulic representation of his system dominated in which the historical evolution and context of Keynes's ideas could find no place. The year 1936 was Year Zero for macroeconomics. [1]

Keynesian economics, with its consumption function, investment function, liquidity preference schedule and the like, seemed the ideal testing ground for the application of rigorous statistical methods. The econometric counterpart of the much elaborated *IS–LM* system was the vast array of empirical models of the economy which have enjoyed undisputed popularity until recent years. The fact that Keynes had severe

---

[1] For the vast majority who subscribed to this consensus, 1937, the year in which Hicks introduced *IS–LM* analysis, is probably more significant.

reservations, occasionally bordering on outright hostility,[2] towards the applicability of econometric methods to macroeconomics was swept to one side. Econometricians searched for empirical regularities, eventually producing Keynesian models of quite staggering complexity. The heyday of scientific economics had arrived at last.

But there was one conspicuous blot on this otherwise rosy landscape. For all of its evident strengths, Keynesian economics did not stand comparison with classical theory in one vital respect: it was incapable of explaining the determinants of the levels of absolute price and money wages. Despite its acknowledged faults, classical economics did at least constitute a complete system in the sense that, if one accepted its fundamental presumption of full employment, the magnitudes of all of the remaining macroeconomic variables could be determined. In particular, recourse to the quantity theory of money enabled the classical writers to pin down the absolute price level and this, together with a knowledge of the full-employment real wage rate, w^*, made the money wage rate a determinate variable. Broadly speaking, since M^s fixed P, and since (W/P) was determined at its full employment value, $(W/P)^*$, through the forces of competition in the labour market, the equilibrium value of W could be ascertained.

No such claim for completeness could be made on behalf of the Keynesian model since its *raison d'être* was the abandonment of the enabling assumption of full employment in order to explain the phenomenon of general unemployment. Most representations of this model adroitly sidestepped the indeterminacy problem by assuming that the level of money wages was an institutionally determined datum. (Critics of the Keynesian approach often pointed an accusatory finger at this assumption, claiming that it removed wage theory from the hands of economists and handed it over to sociologists. Given the thinly disguised mutual suspicion which traditionally exists between economists and sociologists, it is scarcely surprising that most mainstream economists were deeply unhappy at what they regarded as an unjustified yielding of territory to an altogether less rigorous discipline.) A coda was appended to the equations of the *IS–LM* system in the form of the restriction that $W = W_0$ where W_0 is an exogenously given value for the money wage. From being underdetermined, the Keynesian model was made fully determinate by means of what many non-Keynesians regarded as a rather devious sleight of hand.

In general Keynesians recognized that changes in W could occur from

---

[2]The interchange between Keynes and that pioneer of econometrics, Jan Tinbergen, is particularly illuminating from the point of view of empirical methodology. See *CW*, Vol. XIV, pp. 285–9 and pp. 306–20.

time to time, but the factors influencing these changes were extrinsic to the equations of the income–expenditure model. In other words, the determination of the general level of money wages, and hence the absolute price level, was left dangling in the air, unexplained by the model. Keynes himself was keenly aware of this important lacuna in respect of his treatment of money wages: 'we are, as I have said, one equation short' (*GT*, p. 276).

As things turned out this theoretically suspect approach appeared to have been vindicated in practice by the economic experience of the post-war period. Apart from the inflation associated with the Korean War, this period was marked by a combination of unprecedentedly low unemployment rates with price levels which were admittedly creeping upwards, but at rates which were so modest that they were regarded as tolerable. The conjunction of low inflation and low unemployment came as a very pleasant surprise to those Keynesians who had feared that a policy commitment by governments to the goal of full employment would create an environment in which organized labour would press for ever higher levels of money wages. No precise functional relationship was posited between the level of aggregate demand and the pressure on money-wages: it was simply feared that a stated and credible commitment to the objective of full employment might foster an atmosphere in the wage bargaining process in which money wages could run out of control. The celebrated 'problem of money wages', which had so preoccupied Keynes and, subsequently, Joan Robinson, Richard Kahn, James Meade and Michal Kalecki, resulted from what they suspected would be a changed perception by organized labour of the policy responses of the monetary and fiscal authorities in the wake of the Keynesian revolution. The days were long since gone when governments were prepared simply to ride out the turbulence of periodic recessions. The advent of policy activism implied an adherence to policy rules radically different from those which had been applied previously. This would lead, or so it was widely feared, to a change in labour market behaviour. (A very similar point was made more rigorously three decades later in a provocative and potentially devastating critique of econometric policy evaluation by one of the leading lights of the new classical macroeconomics, R. E. Lucas (1976).)

Moreover, the unemployment rates with which post-war creeping inflations were associated were well below the rates which even the most sanguine of Keynesians would have regarded as feasible minima. Keynes's *lowest* estimate for the minimum unemployment rate for interwar Britain was of the order of 5% (see R. F. Kahn, 1975). Others, for example James Meade (1938), were more pessimistic: he considered the minimum unemployment rate for Britain in the same period to be in the region of 11%. As things turned out, however, the unemployment rate in Britain in the 1950s and 1960s only rarely exceeded 2%, there being no tangible evidence of an acceleration of inflation until after 1967. Apart from a few lone voices (see, for example, R. F. Kahn's evidence to the Radcliffe Committee in 1958), most economists tended to shunt the problem of inflation to the nether recesses of their minds, concentrating instead upon other, more pressing problems such as the difficulties of reconciling a high level of employment with balance of payments equilibrium.[3]

On that rather complacement note matters rested until 1958, the year in which A. W. Phillips of the London School of Economics published a paper[4] which proved to be a landmark in the evolution of macroeconomic ideas. Few articles can have made such a great and immediate impact on both the theoretical and practical planes. Phillips had already become something of a celebrity after his construction – he was an engineer by training – of an ingenious machine which demonstrated the functioning of the macroeconomy by using various dyed liquids to represent different income and expenditure flows and the factors which influenced these flows. With all of its interconnecting tubes, rarely can the concept of a leakage from the circular flow of income have assumed such a liquid manifestation! Phillips's machine was the apotheosis of what came later to be known, rather disparagingly, as 'hydraulic Keynesianism' (see Coddington, 1983).

Phillips had no master plan or grand theoretical design in mind when he undertook his celebrated study of the relationship between money wage inflation and unemployment in the United Kingdom for the period 1861 to 1957. His paper was intended to be a tentative, exploratory investigation of British data and little else besides. Nevertheless his results were quite remarkable. There appeared to be a determinate, stable, inverse relationship between the rate of change of money wages and the unemployment rate which had continued to hold good for almost a century. The shape of the inverse relationship is depicted in Figure 6.1. The annual rate of change of money wages, dW/W, is measured along the vertical axis and the unemployment rate, U, expressed as a percentage of the total workforce, is measured along the horizontal axis. The non-linear relationship has two asymptotes: (a) as the unemployment rate falls towards 0.8%, the rate of change of money wages tends to infinity; (b) as the unemployment rate rises towards 100%, the rate of change of money

---

[3]This observation is particularly relevant for Britain during this period where bouts of 'stop' in 'stop-go' policies coincided, not with high rates of inflation, but with balance of payments crises.

[4]It has been referred to as 'the paper that launched a thousand PhD. theses'.

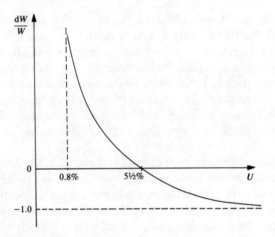

Figure 6.1   The Phillips curve

wages tends to a lower bound of -1.0%. The curve crosses the U-axis at an unemployment rate of 5.5%. Taking into account productivity growth, Phillips estimated that the unemployment rate which was required to produce a zero rate of price increase was around 2.5%.

Although Phillips hazarded some theoretical conjectures concerning the relationship he had uncovered, it was left to others, most notably R. G. Lipsey (1960), to provide the analytical underpinning for this astonishing statistical regularity. Lipsey's starting-point was the application of Samuelson's 'correspondence principle' to the disequilibrium dynamics of a micro labour market. Consider the supply and demand conditions in the ith labour market (Figure 6.2).

The money wage rate is measured along the vertical axis, W^{i*} being the market clearing wage; W^{i1} and W^{i2} are two arbitrarily given initial wage rates. Along the horizontal axis are measured the supply of and demand for labour in the ith market, L^{is} and L^{id} respectively. The question which Lipsey then posed was: if there is initial disequilibrium in the ith labour market, at what rate will money wages change? The answer which he proffered was equally simple: if the labour market is competitive, wages will change at a rate determined by both the sign and the extent of the initial disequilibrium. For example, in Figure 6.2, two initial disequilibrium states are depicted. The sign of the disequilibrium states is the same in both cases (positive, indicating the presence of excess demand) but they differ in the extent of the initial disequilibrium. At an initial wage W^{i1}, the extent of the disequilibrium, measured by the ratio $X^i = (L^{id} - L^{is})/L^{is}$, is greater than at an initial wage W^{i2}. The correspondence principle states that we should expect wages to be rising more

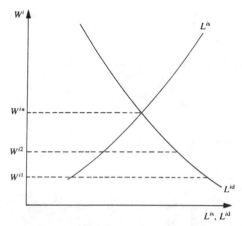

Figure 6.2 Samuelson's correspondence principle and the micro labour market

rapidly the larger is X^i. Thus $dW^i/W^i = \omega(X^i)$. Since X^i is larger at an initial wage W^{i1} than at W^{i2}, wages will be rising more rapidly if the starting-point is W^{i1}. As W^i approaches W^{i*}, both X^i and dW^i/W^i vanish.

One possible pattern of dynamic adjustment is illustrated in Figure 6.3. The rate of change of money wages is measured along the vertical axis and the excess demand variable, X^i, is measured along the horizontal axis. If the ith labour market initially experiences excess demand ($X^i = X^{i1} > 0$) money wages will rise at a rate $(dW^i/W^i)^1$. On the other hand, if the initial state is one of excess supply ($X^i = X^{i2} < 0$) money-wages will fall at a rate $(dW^i/W^i)^2$.

The ith labour market is but one of n micro labour markets. If all of the remaining $(n-1)$ markets respond in a manner similar to the one outlined above, aggregation across labour markets will yield a determinate relationship between the overall rate of change of money wages, dW/W, and an index of aggregate excess demand for labour, X_L, where X_L is defined as the ratio $(L^d - L^s)/L^s$. Aggregating the microeconomic relationship $dW^i/W^i = \omega(X^i)$ over all n labour markets yields the macroeconomic relationship $dW/W = \Omega(X_L)$.

The problem which the Phillips–Lipsey model then had to confront was one of measurability: X_L is not a directly observable magnitude. For example, one may suspect that the labour market is overheating, i.e. that $X_L > 0$, but without further quantitative information it is impossible to gauge the extent of the problem. Phillips hit upon a plausible resolution of this difficulty by isolating a directly measurable proxy variable for the pressure of demand in the economy in general and in the labour market in particular: the unemployment rate, U. Although X_L is an unobservable

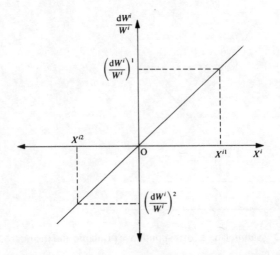

Figure 6.3   Dynamic adjustment of the micro labour market

magnitude, it is reasonable to suppose that it varies inversely with the unemployment rate. In other words we should expect there to be a one to one inverse relationship, probably non-linear, of the form $U = \Phi(X_L)$ where $\Phi'(X_L) < 0$ and, probably, $\Phi''(X_L) > 0$. Moreover, since $dW/W = \Omega(X_L)$, $dW/W = \Omega(\Phi^{-1}(U)) = g(U)$. From the restrictions placed on $\Omega()$ and $\Phi()$ was to emerge the familiar Phillips curve: $dW/W = g(U)$.

The transition from a theory of money wage determination to a theory of price inflation is quite straightforward. If we follow standard practice in assuming that prices are fixed as a mark up over variable costs and that the rate of productivity growth is exogenous, a modified Phillips curve of the form $dP/P = f(U)$ emerges. The choice of whether to use the money wage version, $g(U)$, or the price version, $f(U)$, of the Phillips curve depends upon the nature of the problem being examined.

Lipsey appeared to have provided a theory of the determinants of money wage changes and, by integration, of the time path for the money wage rate which the economic profession found so convincing that it went virtually unchallenged for several years. True, a minority of Keynesian economists in Britain continued to doubt the empirical validity of the Phillips curve, placing greater emphasis on cost–push forces which worked independently of the level of demand. For them the Phillips curve was a statistical mirage, a *trompe l'oeil*. But for other Keynesians, particularly in the United States, the Phillips curve furnished the last equation of the Keynesian model, supplanting once and for all that notorious intruder, the condition $W = W_0$. Its arrival, long overdue, was greeted with great enthusiasm in these circles.

Indeed, the Phillips curve did seem to conform with much of what Keynes had written on inflation in the years after the *General Theory*, the most illuminating example of which is the pamphlet *How to Pay for the War* (1940). In this pamphlet and elsewhere,[5] Keynes proposed the *inflationary gap* theory of inflation: upward pressure on money wages and prices would be felt with increasing severity as the pressure of demand approached and eventually exceeded full employment output, Y^*. Excess demand in the labour market, measured by Lipsey's X_L index, will generally be matched by excess demand in the goods market, X_G, defined as the ratio $(Y_e - Y^*)/Y^*$, where Y_e is the equilibrium level of income.[6] Both X_L and X_G will vary in tandem with each other.[7]

Thus Lipsey's postulated relationship between the rate of change of money wages and excess demand in the labour market not only possessed appealing microeconomic credentials, it also seemed to accord with much of what Keynes had written on the subject of inflation. We have already noted Keynes's anxiety over his system being 'one equation short' in the sense that there was nothing to anchor the level of money wages and the absolute price level. The relation $dW/W = \Omega(X_L)$, the theoretical basis of the Phillips curve, was interpreted as this 'missing equation' which finally closed the Keynesian model. Since a knowledge of dW/W could be used to trace the time path of money wages, $W(t)$, and since the magnitudes of X_L and its twin X_G could be explained by reference to the income–expenditure model, the Keynesian system was no longer underdetermined: the number of variables equalled the number of independent equations. The relationship between aggregate demand and money wages was therefore two-way: the level of money wages influenced aggregate demand through a combination of the Keynes effect and the real-balance effect; and aggregate demand influenced the time path of money wages through the relation $dW/W = \Omega(X_L)$. Keynesian economics no longer had to resort to the *deus ex machina* of postulating a 'sociologically determined' level of money wages. An audible sigh of relief rose from the ranks of mainstream macroeconomists.

---

[5]For an extensive treatment of Keynes's wartime writings on inflation, see Trevithick (1975).

[6]Remember that Y_e is that hypothetical level of income at which income and desired expenditure would be in equilibrium. In a depressed economy, Y_e is attainable, but in a severely overheated economy it is not.

[7]In more recent macroeconomic models (e.g. Malinvaud, 1985) excess demand in the goods market need not be associated with excess demand in the labour market. It is conceivable that $X_G > 0$ while $X_L < 0$.

The Phillips curve and economic policy

It was not long after the unearthing of the Phillips curve that economists and, later, policy makers came to grasp the full force of what they thought to be its implications for the conduct of demand management by the monetary and fiscal authorities. Following the pioneering work of Samuelson and Solow (1960), the Phillips curve came to be regarded as a trade off relation in that it clearly demonstrated the inflationary consequences of pursuing particular demand management strategies. Expansionary monetary and fiscal policies could only be bought at the expense of higher inflation rates. By contrast, contractionary policies would reap the benefits of lower inflation, but at the cost of higher unemployment. Policy makers were faced with a dilemma: they had to trade off a 'good' (high employment) against a 'bad' (inflation). The Phillips curve was regarded as an inescapable constraint on policy action which the authorities could only ignore at their peril.

The decision problem which confronted policy makers was given formal expression by Lipsey (1962). When Samuelson and Solow wrote of trading off inflation against unemployment, what they were implicitly postulating was a policy makers' social welfare function, $\Psi(dP/P, U)$, from which could be derived social indifference curves. These curves were concave to the origin: the nearer the curve was to the origin the higher the level of social welfare. Three examples of such indifference curves are illustrated by AA', BB' and CC' in Figure 6.4. In this simple model the Phillips curve assumes a role analogous to that of the budget constraint in traditional price theory: it is the ineluctable constraint which must be incorporated into the maximization procedure. The problem to be solved is thus:

$$\max \Psi \ (dP/P, \ U) \text{ subject to } dP/P = f(U)$$

The outcome of this thoroughly conventional static optimization procedure is, of course, a tangency solution at point T which yields a socially optimal pair $((dP/P)_{opt}, U_{opt})$.

In this way the Phillips curve came to be regarded as a 'menu for policy choice'. It was a list of options from which policy makers were compelled to make a decision. Moreover, once the choice had been made, the preferred combination of inflation and unemployment was not only feasible now but was *sustainable into the indefinite future*. In effect U_{opt} became the target unemployment rate while $(dP/P)_{opt}$ was the unpleasant, but inevitable, concomitant of this target rate. This conclusion was the *fons et origo* of the barrage of criticism which was to be heaped on the notion of a stable trade off relation in the wake of Milton Friedman's

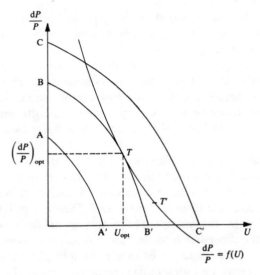

Figure 6.4 Trading off inflation against unemployment

Presidential Address to the American Economic Association in 1967 (see below).

Full employment and the target unemployment rate

At first blush the analysis outlined above possesses considerable intuitive appeal, but the further one delves into the arguments that lie at its core, the more profoundly disturbing are its conclusions. Although it was never stated so baldly, one implication of the Samuelson–Solow and Lipsey approach is that, since U_{opt} is the target rate of unemployment, it is, in essence, the full employment rate of unemployment: it is that unemployment rate which the authorities regard as attainable, sustainable and, taking the good with the bad, 'correct'.

But the analytical ramifications of this model are wide ranging and, in many respects, alarming. The target unemployment rate, U_{opt}, is the outcome of a set of normative political preferences which is expressed with rather spurious precision in the social welfare function $\Psi(dP/P, U)$. But suppose there is change of government and that the newly elected political party puts greater store by the containment of inflationary pressure, being prepared by implication to tolerate a higher unemployment rate than the previous government. In effect the form of the social welfare function will alter with the change of government and, in terms of

Figure 6.4, a new tangency solution at, say, T' will become relevant. What was formerly the target unemployment rate has been abandoned in favour of a new, higher rate.

It follows that U_{opt} is not an objective number generated by considerations of overall balance in the labour market: its value turns critically on the political preferences of governments which are supposed to be in a position *to define for themselves* what unemployment rate will correspond to full employment and to be capable of action to achieve their newly defined objective.

Naturally, neoclassical economists will stand aghast at what they regard as an unwarranted political intrusion into the realm of positive economics. They will not be alone. Keynesians – at least that branch of the family which continues to read the *General Theory* – will also be profoundly disturbed that the concept of full employment has become the object of unwelcome normative inroads. One has only to reflect on the enumeration of the varied properties of a state of full employment in the *General Theory* to realize that something is seriously wrong. One of the few areas of common ground which both Keynes and Friedman occupy centres on the definition of a state of overall full employment: full employment prevails when the aggregate supply of labour, L^s, equals the aggregate demand for labour, L^d, at a unique, market clearing real wage rate, w^*. It is that single level of employment where the marginal physical product of labour is brought into equality with the marginal disutility of employment at one and only one real wage rate: the marginal physical product of labour $= w^* =$ the marginal disutility of employment. Any unemployment which remains once this state of overall labour market balance has been achieved is frictional and structural in origin and is, by definition, invariant with respect to the level of aggregate demand. From the point of view of demand management, therefore, frictional and structural unemployment is an irreducible minimum unemployment rate.[8] Governments should not be deluded into thinking that they can arrogate to themselves powers that they do not and cannot possess.

The Phillips curve: trade off or disequilibrium adjustment mechanism?

We have just dealt at some length with the interpretation of the Phillips curve as a trade off, as a 'menu for policy choice'. But how consistent is

---

[8]Obviously supply-side policies may reduce frictional and structural unemployment by, for example, improving the provision of information and training and encouraging mobility within the labour market. Such policies are normally regarded as being outside the frame of reference of macroeconomics.

this view of the Phillips curve with Lipsey's previous theoretical underpinning of the relation which we outlined earlier in this chapter? How does Lipsey (1962) square with Lipsey (1960)?

Consider the original money wage version of the Phillips curve depicted in Figure 6.5. According to Lipsey, money wages rise at a rate in excess of the rate of growth of productivity (q) when there is an excess demand for labour ($X_L > 0$) which, in turn, implies that the unemployment rate is below U_0. But rising money wages serve to reduce the discrepancy between L^d and L^s (see Figure 6.2), with the result that unemployment rises. The process of money-wage inflation reduces by successive degrees the magnitude of X_L until it eventually vanishes. The relation $dW/W = g(U)$ is therefore a mechanism which illustrates how the labour market responds out of equilibrium. It shows how money wage adjustments lead to a convergence on a unique, stable unemployment rate, U_0, which corresponds to a condition of zero excess demand in the labour market. In other words $g(U)$ is simply a disequilibrium adjustment mechanism. The arrows along the $g(U)$ function in Figure 6.5 indicate the direction in which wage inflation and unemployment move, for arbitrarily given initial values for dW/W and U, towards their centre of gravity, the pair (q, U_0).

If this interpretation of the $g(U)$ function is correct, that is, if $g(U)$ is in reality a disequilibrium adjustment mechanism, then it cannot be treated at one and the same time as a trade off relation. Policy makers are not in a position to choose points along $g(U)$ since wage inflation and unemployment are always on the move towards q and U_0 respectively. What the 'Phillips curve as adjustment mechanism' approach suggests is that there

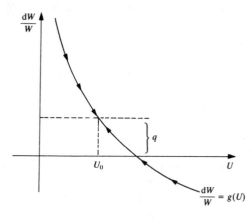

Figure 6.5 Money wage version of the Phillips curve

are competitive forces at work serving to eliminate initial excess demand, positive or negative, in the labour market. Wage inflation may well be the consequence of excess demand in the labour market, but it is also the means by which excess demand is eventually squeezed out of the system. Moreover the approach should work in reverse: if the initial state is one of excess supply in the labour market ($X_L < 0$ and $U > U_0$), money wage adjustments should nudge the economy back to a position of overall full employment at U_0. The reaction function $g(U)$ then merely becomes a formalization of what Pigou and other classical writers had been saying all along, namely, that downward revisions of the money wage rate would eradicate the phenomenon of general unemployment. Readers will not need to be reminded of Keynes's objections to *that* theory of labour market adjustment!

Reaction: the expectations-augmented Phillips curve

If ever there was an ideal candidate for econometric testing, it was the Phillips curve. Phillips's original exercise had many features which were attractive to applied econometricians: the initial empirical work had been rather haphazard, leaving many important hypotheses untested; the estimation techniques were simple; it was a reduced form equation, a collapsed version of a larger structural model, leading to the possibility of biases; in addition to the omission of many potentially significant explanatory variables, much refinement needed to be performed on the time series data. In brief, it was a fertile testing ground for those wishing to demonstrate prowess in their mastery of econometric technique.

But, overshadowing all purely technical considerations, the Phillips curve had one attraction which made it even more irresistible: its subject matter was 'important'. Not only did it furnish the missing equation of the Keynesian system, it had also assumed a role of paramount significance in the formulation of macroeconomic policy. Governments had to be persuaded that they were in a position to run their eyes down a list of options so as to gauge the inflationary consequences of a particular package of demand management policies. Economists were being involved in the process of economic decision making in a manner which had been unknown previously, and most of them found this admission to the counsels of the influential and powerful to be very congenial.

The 1960s were the years of jaunty self-confidence among economists, and the reasons for this were not difficult to fathom. Keynes had isolated the factors determining the levels of output and employment and had pointed to policies which could be implemented to achieve a state of full employment. Others, most notably James Meade, had taken the all important step of opening up the Keynesian model so as to take account of and explain international trade and capital flows. Then the neoclassical synthesis had restored the price mechanism to its position of prominence in matters touching on the allocation and (perhaps) the distribution of resources. Since monetary and fiscal policies had been assigned the role of guaranteeing the maintenance of full employment, the traditional neoclassical preoccupation with efficiency in the face of scarcity could come back into its own. And, to add the final touch, Phillips's insight had filled the only remaining gap by proposing, albeit in skeletal form, an empirical model of inflation which was to be theoretically fleshed out by Lipsey. Milton Friedman's widely reported remark that 'We are all Keynesians now' was an exaggeration, even for the time, but it did convey the *Zeitgeist* of the 1960s.

The mood of self-assured hubris among economists of this period was shaken to its very foundations in the later years of the 1960s. Nemesis came in the form of a blistering rebuttal of policy activism in Milton Freidman's Presidential Address to the American Economic Association (see Freidman, 1968). If Phillips's paper had been the landmark of empirical research in macroeconomics in the post-war period, Friedman's paper, published ten years later, enjoyed a similar status in the theory of macroeconomic policy. The main thrust of Friedman's paper was to displace what he regarded as an ill-informed and misguided optimism among post-war Keynesians concerning the ability of governments to intervene in the economy to achieve particular policy objectives. He singled out for special criticism two specific objectives which had figured so prominently in the application of Keynesian ideas: (a) the notion that the proper focus of attention for monetary policy was the attainment of targets for the rate of interest as opposed to targets for the supply of money; (b) that demand management policies could be adjusted in such a way as to achieve a target combination of inflation and unemployment which was sustainable indefinitely. We have already examined Friedman's criticisms of proposition (a) in Chapter 3. We shall now concentrate our attention on his criticism of proposition (b), the hypothesis that there exists a stable trade off relation between inflation and unemployment.

For Friedman, models which portrayed policy makers as having the power to choose from among differing combinations of inflation and unemployment were fantastic and potentially tragic exercises in self-delusion. Such room for manœuvre as existed in choosing between these two evils was only present in the very short run. In the longer run a policy choice which involved positive inflation[9] would lead to an acceleration in

---

[9]More precisely a rate of inflation in excess of the *expected* rate of inflation.

the rate of inflation. There only existed a trade off between the unemployment rate and the *rate of increase* in the rate of inflation. We shall refer to this as the 'accelerationist' hypothesis.

Friedman's argument was very simple and held considerable intuitive appeal. Take the case of a hypothetical economy which had had no experience of inflation in its recent history so that the rate of inflation which was expected to take place over the foreseeable future was zero. In symbols, $(dP/P)^e = 0$, where $(dP/P)^e$ is the expected rate of inflation. According to the price inflation version of the Phillips curve, we must of necessity infer that the economy had been operating at a level of demand which was consistent with an unemployment rate U^* in Figure 6.6. At point A, $U = U^*$ and $dP/P = (dP/P)^e$: the unemployment rate is at its natural value, U^*, and the actual and the expected rates of inflation are equal to each other, both taking the value zero in our example.

Let us now suppose that our government falls under the influence of economists who advise it to treat $dP/P = f(U)$ as a trade off relation in the manner outlined above. Suppose that the government, guided by these false prophets, decides that it is prepared to trade off a positive rate of inflation for a lower unemployment rate. It uses the monetary and fiscal instruments at its disposal to expand the economy with the aim of reducing the employment rate to, say, U_1. In other words it chooses to move up the Phillips curve from point A to a point such as point B which corresponds to its new perception of the 'optimal' unemployment inflation pair $(U_1, (dP/P)_1)$.

In its initial stages, this shift of policy priorities will appear to be vindicated by events: unemployment will be lower and inflation higher

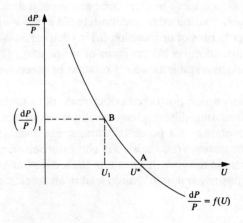

Figure 6.6 A shift in policy priorities: lower unemployment bought at cost of higher inflation

than before. But Friedman argued that matters do not rest there. Far from it, for the precondition which enabled the authorities to move the economy from point A to point B will begin to break down: the expected rate of inflation will not remain at zero. The experience of a positive rate of inflation will lead agents (workers, employers, borrowers, lenders, etc.) to abandon their former belief that prices would remain stable: agents will adjust their behaviour to these changed circumstances. To take one example, how will workers respond to the realization that the rate of inflation is not zero, as they had expected it to be, but is in fact positive? Previously their real and money wages had grown at a rate q, the rate of productivity growth. Unless they adjust their money wage claims so as to protect its real value from erosion through price increases their real wages will no longer grow in line with the growth in productivity as before. Workers therefore have an incentive to revise their expectation of inflation upwards and to lodge claims for money wage increases which fully reflect the extent of this revision.

Friedman then proposed two hypotheses, one general and the other specific, governing agents' behaviour in inflationary circumstances. The general proposition was that inflationary expectations would be revised upwards when the actual, realized rate of inflation exceeded the expected rate of inflation. The specific proposition was derived from the general and was put forward more tentatively: the *rate* at which the expected rate of inflation was revised upwards would be determined by the magnitude of the discrepancy between the actual and expected rates of inflation. In symbols, $(dP/P)^e$ rises when $dP/P > (dP/P)^e$ – the general hypothesis – and $d/dt(dP/P) = \phi((dP/P) - (dP/P)^e)$ – the specific hypothesis. When expectations are revised in accordance with the specific hypothesis, behaviour is said to be adaptive. The parameter ϕ measures the speed with which expectations adapt to past errors in predicting the rate of inflation. The adaptive expectations hypothesis had come to earlier prominence in Philip Cagan's (1956) path breaking study of the monetary dynamics of the European hyperinflations which followed the Great War. Friedman applied it to the altogether more modest inflationary experience of the late 1960s.

Nevertheless we are still left with the nagging question: under what circumstances will the actual rate of inflation exceed the expected rate of inflation?[10] Inspection of Figure 6.6 provides an instant pointer to the answer: when policy makers attempt to hold the unemployment rate at a level below its natural rate, U^*. In effect the Phillips curve depicted in Figure 6.6 is but one out of an infinite set of short-run Phillips curves, each

---

[10]The analysis carries over, *mutatis mutandis*, to the case where the expected rate of inflation exceeds the natural rate.

curve corresponding to a different expected rate of inflation. Two short-run trade off relations, one corresponding to an expected rate of inflation $(dP/P)^e_1$ and the other to a higher expected rate of inflation $(dP/P)^e_2$, are illustrated in Figure 6.7. The relation which Friedman proposed has entered the literature with the rather cumbersome title 'the expectations-augmented Phillips curve'. It postulates that the actual rate of inflation which prevails at any moment in time may be decomposed into two constituent parts: (a) an expectational component, measured by the variable $(dP/P)^e$, (b) an excess demand component, measured, as in the Phillips–Lipsey model, by the magnitude of $f(U)$. The natural unemployment rate is that unique rate, U^*, at which the excess demand component, $f(U)$, is exactly zero. Moreover, once the precise mathematical form of $f(U)$ has been unearthed by econometric testing, it is simplicity itself to arrive at an estimate of U^* – one has merely to evaluate the root of $f(U) = 0$.

Obviously positive inflation may remain a feature of this hypothetical economy even if it is operating at the natural unemployment rate (i.e. $f(U) = 0$) owing to the persistence of inflationary expectations. In this case the economy will be in an inflationary equilibrium. Any rate of inflation, positive, zero or negative, is compatible with U^* since the only necessary condition for an inflationary equilibrium is that inflationary expectations be fully realized, i.e. that $dP/P = (dP/P)^e$. The implicit assumption of the naïve Phillips curve was that the expected rate of inflation was zero. Phillips's omission of a price expectations term[11] from his original study may have been warranted in practice owing to the low rates of inflation which were experienced from the Great War onwards; but when it comes to analyzing inflationary processes in general it is invalid. The expected rate of inflation is not only an essential determinant of the actual rate of inflation, it is also endogenous to the system, being itself the outcome of past errors in predicting the rate of inflation.

Another way of approaching the accelerationist hypothesis is to rearrange slightly the equation for the expectations-augmented Phillips curve. Let $(dP/P) - (dP/P)^e$ denote the unanticipated rate of inflation, that is, that part of the rate of inflation which agents have failed to anticipate fully. On rearrangement this yields

$$(dP/P) - (dP/P)^e = f(U)$$

Bearing in mind the adaptive expectations hypothesis, it follows that

$$d/dt(dP/P)^e = \phi f(U)$$

---

[11] In fairness Phillips did include the rate of price change as one of his explanatory variables but attached little importance to it.

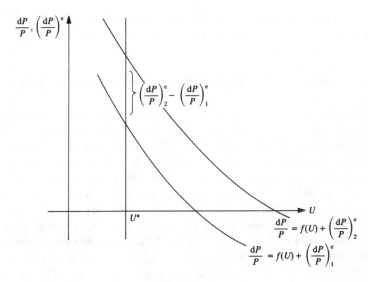

Figure 6.7 Short-run trade off relations

In other words, a trade off of sorts does exist after all: it is a trade off between the unemployment rate and the *rate of change* of the actual and expected rates of inflation. Friedman (1968) concludes:

> [T]here is always a temporary trade-off between inflation and unemployment; there is no permanent trade-off. The temporary trade-off comes not from inflation per se, but from unanticipated inflation, which generally means, from a rising rate of inflation . . . A rising rate of inflation may reduce unemployment, a high one will not.

There would thus appear to be some scope for policy activism, but, on further inspection, it turns out to be very limited indeed. Unlike the original 'menu for policy choice' between inflation and unemployment, this is a trade off which no government worth its salt would dream of exploiting in all but the very short run. For as long as the marginal disutility of inflation remains positive, there will eventually come a point at which the government will be compelled to pursue policies which will push the unemployment rate back towards its natural value. Indeed, to the extent that inflationary expectations have built up a momentum of their own that it regards as excessive, the government may be forced to adopt demand management policies which aim to raise the unemployment rate above the natural rate so as to throw the process outlined above into reverse gear. In order to erode inflationary expectations, deflationary policies may be called for which temporarily raise the unemployment rate above U^*, thereby leading by degrees to downward revisions of the expected, and hence the actual, rate of inflation.

The non-accelerating inflation rate of unemployment

Many economists would subscribe to much of the above analysis. At the same time they would also wish to distance themselves from the connotations of full employment with which Friedman was to invest to the concept of the natural unemployment rate (see next section). This more eclectic group of economists accept that there probably does exist at any particular moment in time a single unemployment rate at which inflation neither accelerates nor decelerates: they describe this by the acronym NAIRU, the non-accelerating inflation rate of unemployment. Although they accept most of the reasoning behind the accelerationist hypothesis, these writers do not follow Friedman in identifying NAIRU with a condition of overall balance in the labour market. The fact that the economy is at NAIRU does not imply the absence of involuntary unemployment.

To illustrate this point let us postulate a hypothetical, though possibly unattainable, unemployment rate U_F which is the true *full-employment* unemployment rate: U_F is that unemployment rate where $L^d = L^s$ at w^*. It is the rate of frictional and structural unemployment. In Figure 6.8, the discrepancy between NAIRU and U_F measures the extent to which exogenous cost–push factors influence an inflationary process at levels of activity which are well below what may be reasonably considered to

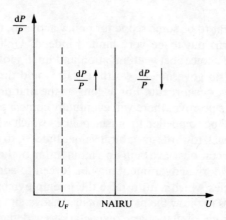

Figure 6.8   Inflation and NAIRU

correspond to full employment. The magnitude (NAIRU – U_F) may be taken as a measure of the inflationary bias which is imparted to the system by non-competitive forces, the most obvious of these forces being the influence of trades unions in the wage bargaining process.

An application of the concept of NAIRU to British circumstances is contained in Richard Layard's (1986) book *How to Beat Unemployment*. The theory that lies at the core of Layard's analysis is the 'real wage resistance' hypothesis: workers have a target real wage which they strive to achieve and defend through the wage bargaining process. The target real wage rate is not a specific number but will depend upon the unemployment rate: the higher the unemployment rate, the less ambitious are union negotiators and the more prepared are they to settle for a lower real wage. The inverse relation between the target real wage and the unemployment rate is illustrated by the curve TRW in Figure 6.9.

But there is, of course, another side to the wage bargaining coin. There will exist a real wage rate (Layard calls this the 'feasible real wage rate') which employers are prepared to grant to workers. The feasible real wage will be determined by, for example, unit labour costs and the mark up over unit labour costs. It may alter as a result of a variety of extraneous factors, in particular supply-side shocks, but Layard assumes that it is invariant with respect to the unemployment rate. The feasible real wage may thus be represented by the horizontal line FRW in Figure 6.9. The unemployment rate at which the TRW curve intersects with the FRW line defines NAIRU: it is the unique unemployment rate at which the real wage demands of workers can be reconciled with the real wage which employers are prepared to concede. If the pressure of demand were such

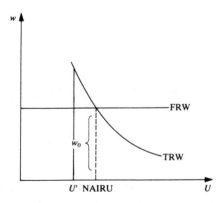

Figure 6.9   The determination of NAIRU

that the unemployment rate was U', the gap between TRW and FRW would provoke inflationary wage demands which would, if granted, push up prices. Price inflation would feed into inflationary expectations, as in the Friedman version of the accelerationist hypothesis, resulting in even higher money wage demands in the next round of bargaining. In this way the process of accelerating inflation gathers momentum. It can only be halted by cutting back on demand, thereby raising the unemployment rate to NAIRU.

Nevertheless, despite certain superficial similarities, the models proposed by Friedman and Layard contain numerous points of difference, the most important being that, for Layard, NAIRU is not determined by the operation of competitive forces in the labour market. The TRW curve cannot be derived mathematically from the L^s curve which has formed the basis of our analysis of both the classical and Keynesian models of the labour market. It is a relative – at several removes – of the L^s_{TU} function mentioned briefly in Chapter 5. The real wage rate w_0 which reconciles the target real wage with the feasible real wage at NAIRU should not be taken as a measure of Keynes's 'marginal disutility of employment'. The target real wage rate is something altogether (dare one say it?) 'sociologically' determined. This gives rise to the conventional neoclassical objection to all models of this sort, namely, that the concept of a target real wage rate is *ad hoc*, arbitrary and not grounded in the rational calculus of profit and utility maximization which should be the starting-point of all economic enquiry at both the micro and the macro levels. That the concept of a target real wage rate can be accounted for in terms of the behaviour of rational, maximizing agents is amply demonstrated in the works of Layard, of Carlin and Soskice (1990) and of the works of the new Keynesian school (see Chapter 8). It is early days yet, but, in my view, these models may form a more useful basis for analyzing actual inflationary processes in particular economies than the 'purer' neo-Walarasian models favoured by modern monetarists.

Money illusion and the natural unemployment rate hypothesis mark II

When we examined Friedman's demolition of the idea of a stable trade off between inflation and unemployment, we noted how there remained some scope for policy activism. Admittedly we also noted how hollow this observation rang in view of the fact that expansionary policies would entail accelerating inflation. If taken to extremes, such policies carried within them the potential to precipitate a catastrophic decline into hyperinflation. Nevertheless, setting these consequences to one side for the moment, Friedman's analysis did appear to countenance the possibility of pursuing expansionary, neutral or contractionary demand management policies. Monetary and fiscal policies could be combined in such a way as to achieve and maintain unemployment rates which differed from the natural rate.

But surely the proposition that the unemployment rate could be held below its natural value for fairly long periods of time runs counter to the neoclassical model of labour market behaviour? How could a discrepancy between the actual and the natural unemployment rates be made to persist simply as a result of the actions of the monetary and fiscal authorities? Was Friedman being unfaithful to the neoclassical *Weltanschauung* of which he was such a tireless defender? Some saw the irrational spectre of money illusion lurking menacingly in the wings.

In my view there was indeed an inconsistency here, though it was an inconsistency which Friedman only recognized implicitly when he started putting forward an alternative model, radically different from his accelerationist hypothesis, which denied any *direct* role for aggregate demand in influencing the level of employment. It will be recalled that, in the expectations-augmented Phillips curve, Friedman had assigned to aggregate demand a prominent, independent and direct role, summarized in the magnitude of $f(U)$, in determining the actual rate of inflation. In later versions of the natural rate hypothesis, Friedman was tacitly to abandon this view altogether. Aggregate demand shocks (alterations in the stance of monetary and fiscal policies were increasingly referred to as 'shocks') only affected real variables such as output and employment to the extent that they produced a state of confusion in the minds of agents regarding the behaviour of relative prices. The short-run inability to unscramble market signals was presumed to be the particular affliction of suppliers, i.e. the suppliers of commodities and the suppliers of factor services.

One way to appreciate the extent of Friedman's shift of position is to examine Figure 6.10. This diagram is, of course, the old and familiar friend which we first encountered in Chapter 2 when discussing Pigou's theory of employment. However it does have a rather novel twist: the actual and *expected* real wage rates, w and w^e respectively, are measured along the vertical axis. Suppose there is an increase in the money supply, M^s, or, in an economy already experiencing positive inflation, an increase in the rate of monetary expansion, dM^s/M^s. Prices and money wages will rise. (So firm is the grip held by the revived quantity theory of money nowadays that few of the monetarists or new classical macroeconomists who followed in Friedman's footsteps bothered to elucidate the mechanism by which changes in M^s (or in dM^s/M^s) affect W and P. They just do.)

If money is neutral, money wages and prices should rise in proportion to the rise in the quantity of money and the levels of output and employment should remain unchanged in Y^* and L^* respectively. Abstracting from inevitable stochastic disturbances, the neutrality of money requires that output and employment should *never* deviate from their full employment values. But many monetarist writers recognized that deviations from Y^* and L^* do in fact occur over and above those attributable to white noise disturbances. How do they account for this apparent non-neutrality of money?

Friedman's answer was disarmingly simple:

> Suppose something, say a monetary expansion, starts nominal aggregate demand growing, which in turn produces a rise in prices and wages of, say, 2 per cent per year. Workers will initially interpret this as a rise in their real wage – because they still anticipate constant prices – and so will be willing to offer more labour (move up their supply curve), i.e. employment grows and unemployment falls. Employers may have the same anticipations as workers about the general price level, but they are more directly concerned about the price of the products they are producing and are far better informed about that. They will initially interpret a rise in the demand for and price of their product as a rise in its relative price and as implying a fall in the real wage rate they must pay measured in terms of their product. They will therefore be willing to hire more labour (move down their demand curve). (Friedman, 1975, pp. 20–1)

In terms of Figure 6.10, workers would like to move up their labour supply function to a position such as point B since they mistakenly think that the real wage rate has risen to, say, w'. Employers, by contrast, mistakenly thinking that real wages have fallen to, say, w'', attempt to move down their labour demand function to a position such as point C. Assuming that actual trading in the labour market is determined on the short side, the level of employment rises to L''. Employers and workers make mistakes in unscrambling what is happening to real wages, but it is essential that these mistakes be made in *opposite* directions. By proposing this ingenious but patently artificial contrivance, Friedman was able to account for the non-neutrality of money in the short run. Obviously once market signals are correctly decoded by agents, output and employment revert to their natural values and money is once again neutral.

Finally there is a fundamental characteristic of Friedman's mark II version of the natural rate hypothesis which, in the light of Chapter 5, arouses considerable alarm among Keynesians. Figure 6.10 depicts a theory of labour market adjustment which is, to all intents and purposes, indistinguishable from that of A. C. Pigou and his classical contemporaries. Keynes's refutation of this theory as a description of labour

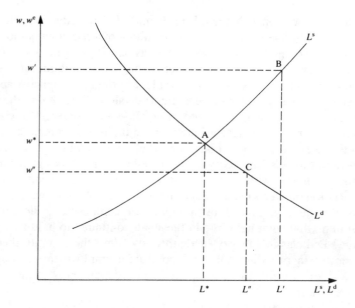

Figure 6.10   Friedman's account of disequilibrium in the labour market

market behaviour in a money using economy, and this formulation of a theory of labour market adjustment which was more appropriate to such an economy, have been glossed over by Friedman and his followers as if they were nothing more than minor, rather idiosyncratic footnotes in the history of economic ideas.

At the risk of repetition, it is important to be quite clear why Keynes would have found Figure 6.10, and the disequilibrium dynamics which are grafted on to it, so profoundly erroneous. In a money using economy, workers and employers are powerless to influence the real wage rate directly. The only variable that they can revise directly in either an upward and a downward direction is the money wage rate, but revisions of the money wage rate will have no direct effect on the real wage rate owing to the sympathetic variations in the general level of prices that they would provoke. Hence, no matter how competitive labour and commodity markets are (Keynes assumed perfect competition in the former and allowed for a high degree of competition in the latter), imbalances between the supply of and demand for labour would *not* be rectified through spontaneous variations in the real wage rate. In the case of general unemployment where $L^s > L^d$ the required fall in the real wage rate – the reader will recall that Keynes accepted the marginal productivity theory of the demand for labour – would not be forthcoming even if perfect competition were the rule in all markets. The reduction in the real wage rate which was a necessary concomitant of a rise in unemployment could only come about through an expansion of aggregate demand.[12]

Now Keynes may well have been wrong in his critique of classical labour market analysis. It is conceivable, as Friedman implicitly appears to suggest, that Pigou had been right all along.[13] If this is the case, however, several questions need to be answered in respect of classical theory before we can accept Pigou's rehabilitation as complete and can consign Keynes's theory of labour market adjustment to an unlamented oblivion: was classical theory guilty of confusing the workings of a money using economy with those of barter.[14] Was it muddled over the association between money wage changes and real wage changes? If so, was the muddle caused by a fallacy of composition, illegitimately assuming that what held true in the small continued to hold true in the large? Did classical theory surreptitiously admit the quantity theory of money – a theory which only holds good at full employment – through the back door in order to fix the price level independently of the level of money wages?

These are questions which were first posed over fifty years ago, but they have obviously made little lasting impact on a literature where the expenditure flows depicted in elaborations of the *IS–LM* model have been the principal focus of attention. The neglect of these important questions to which Keynes attempted to provide answers could, to some extent, account for the recent disenchantment with the Keynesian approach to macroeconomic theory and for the parallel reaction in the form of the rise of new classical macroeconomics.

---

[12]The reader who wishes to refresh his memory of the technical details of this proposition should run over the analysis underlying Figure 5.5.

[13]Despite Friedman's reference to Walras's model of general equilibrium in his definition of the natural unemployment rate (Friedman, 1968), K. D. Hoover (1988) has pointed to a far greater affinity between Friedman's model and that of A. C. Pigou. Why Friedman should have chosen to associate his ideas with those of Walras, who wrote virtually nothing on the theory of employment, instead of Pigou, could have something to do with intellectual one-upmanship: general equilibrium models, despite their limited practical applicability, are regarded as smarter than the more useful, though rather *déclassé* models of partial equilibrium. For an example of Friedman's Marshallian–Pigovian inclinations, see Figure 3 in Friedman (1975).

[14]Since the real wage could be directly adjusted in negotiations between workers and employers in a barter economy, Keynes often referred to such a system as a *real wage economy*.

Involuntary unemployment and the new classical macroeconomics

The Pigou–Friedman view that competitive market economies tend to gravitate towards a state of overall full employment is now such a firmly entrenched proposition in macroeconomics that it has almost gained the status of an axiom. Few adherents to the new classical macroeconomics trouble even to question it, let alone provide an analytical basis to justify it. Textbooks[15] on macroeconomics are written in which the assumption of full employment is taken as the starting-point. 'Markets clear' is the rallying cry of the new classical macroeconomics. Problems which had preoccupied macroeconomists (Friedman included) for decades are ruled out of court *by assumption*.

The quintessence of this approach can be found in Lucas (1978):

> Involuntary unemployment is not a fact or a phenomenon which it is the task of theorists to explain. It is, on the contrary, a theoretical construct which Keynes introduced in the hope that it would be helpful in discovering a correct explanation for a genuine phenomenon: large-scale fluctuations in measured, total unemployment. Is it the task of modern theoretical economics to 'explain' the theoretical constructs of our predecessors?

This is a sweeping statement which makes little obvious sense on first reading, so let us dissect it more carefully. The first sentence admits that involuntary unemployment may be a 'fact or phenomenon', that is, that it *may* exist; but that its possible existence does not require explanation from economic theorists. The second sentence is perfectly unexceptionable apart from the fact that it appears to be in flat contradiction of the first: involuntary unemployment is a 'theoretical construct' – surely theoretical constructs fall within the purview of economic theory! – which was developed to explain the very real and painful phenomenon of large-scale unemployment. Sound stuff. Unfortunately the third sentence sends us reeling back to square one in terms of methodological confusion: we are now told that just because Keynes had tried to provide a theoretical underpinning for the concept of involuntary unemployment does not, *ipso facto*, oblige subsequent theorists to '"explain" the theoretical constructs of our predecessors'. If the 'theorist' to whom Lucas was referring had, as his main area of interest, say, the axiomatic basis of social choice theory, his point would be well taken. To corral pure theorists specializing into other fields of economics into the enclosure of

---

[15]See, for example, R. J. Barro's *Macroeconomics* (1987) where he states in the preface: 'Here I present the market-clearing approach as a general method for analyzing real-world macroeconomic problems.'

macroeconomic theory simply on the grounds that Keynes had been there before would be perverse in the extreme. But when the 'theorist' in question is none other than Lucas himself, and when his views are being aired in an article called 'Unemployment policy', the befuddled reader is entitled to suspect that the confusion is not entirely one sided. Reading Lucas's article from this side of the Atlantic at a time when unemployment in Britain seems about to hit a post-war high, one is tempted to conclude that there may, after all, be a grain of truth in the mischievous quip attributed to Oscar Wilde: Britain and America are united by a common culture but separated by a common language.

Conclusion

Friedman was almost single handedly responsible for the emergence of the intellectual chasm between Keynesians and monetarists which grew increasing wide in the 1960s and 1970s. He had, of course, his followers, but they tended very much to follow in their master's footsteps. Friedman's Presidential Address to the American Economic Association, and the articles which followed it,[16] radically changed the agenda for macroeconomic research. Friedman had breathed new life into the Pigovian theory of labour market adjustment which, until the late 1960s, most economists had regarded as defunct and thoroughly discredited. This, coupled with the rise of a narrower version of monetarism, was to clear the ground for a far more extreme school of macroeconomics which would make adherents to old style monetarism look like liberal wimps. The new classical macroeconomists are committed believers in the power of market forces, being fired with an almost evangelistic enthusiasm. They sweep aside the qualifications and reservations which monetarists of the old school would occasionally express. In the new classical theory, Friedman's conviction that money is neutral in the medium term is held to apply to the short run also. Rational agents are not repeatedly and systematically duped by the actions of the monetary authorities. They learn from past experience how to read the actions of the monetary authorities and, as a result, nullify even the short-run scope for non-neutrality that Friedman had earlier been prepared to countenance. Apart from stochastic blips, markets always clear. And this observation carries over into the theory of employment: the labour market also clears,

---

[16]Many of these articles were published with amendments in R.J. Gordon, ed., 1974, *Milton Friedman's Monetary Framework*.

and any unemployment which remains is entirely the result of voluntary decisions by workers to withdraw from the labour market while still being officially classified as unemployed. We shall see in the next chapter how the combination of the new classical macroeconomics with the rational expectations hypothesis gave rise to the superneutrality of money: anticipated changes in the money supply have no effect whatsoever on the levels of output and employment.

7

Rational expectations and the new classical macroeconomics

Background

The arrival on the scene of the rational expectations hypothesis sent shock waves throughout the whole of macroeconomics. To those of a committed neoclassical persuasion it appeared to be a godsend. Monetarists had previously maintained that money was neutral only in the medium and long run, implying that there was some scope, albeit limited, for policy activism in the short run. By contrast, the rational expectations hypothesis, when applied to the theory of inflation, appeared to indicate that money would be neutral in the short run also, thereby denying any role to policy activism. This hypothesis is known under various names. We shall use only two: the 'invariance' proposition and the 'policy inefficacy' proposition. The constricted room for manœuvre that Friedman had been prepared to assign to monetary (but not fiscal) policy in affecting real variables was repudiated in the writings of the new classical school. In many new classical models – most conspicuously those associated with Robert Lucas – unemployment was almost never allowed to deviate from its natural, full employment value. Such fluctuations in the unemployment rate as were observed in practice came to be interpreted as fluctuations in the natural rate itself, not as deviations, temporary or otherwise, from the natural rate.

The rational expectations hypothesis, allied with the natural rate hypothesis had, so it was believed, driven the final nail into the coffin of policy activism and, by implication, of Keynesian macroeconomics. The role of government in macroeconomic management had to be pruned to a bare minimum. Monetary policy should steer a steady, clearly enunciated and generally comprehensible course. Targets for the rate of growth of the money supply should be announced and, once announced, should be strictly adhered to. No tricks should be pulled in an attempt to achieve transitory, and ultimately worthless, short-term gains. 'Monetary discipline' and 'public credibility', key phrases in this approach, would ensure the most favourable backdrop for the private sector to get on with its proper business of creating and allocating wealth. The provision of a placid monetary environment in which monetary policy was not itself a source of instability was the most that could be expected from the monetary authorities. What is now known as the rational expectations revolution, in conscious contradistinction to the Keynesian revolution four decades earlier, came to dominate macroeconomics, particularly in the United States where disillusionment with Keynesian ideas was particularly strong.[1] Once the post-revolutionary fervour had simmered down and the revolutionaries had become convinced of their victory over Keynesianism, questions started to be asked as to why, from 1936 onwards, so many of their august mentors, some of whom had won Nobel Prizes, had subscribed to a point of view which had been shown to be so palpably erroneous. It is hoped that this chapter will cast a little light on this question.

Needless to say the sense of elation with which the rational expectations hypothesis infected the new classical economists was not shared by Keynesians. The widespread acceptance of the invariance proposition with which the rational expectations hypothesis was so closely associated was met with a variety of reactions: glacial disdain; head scratching incredulity; stony, deafening silence; deep shock. The standing of Keynesianism seemed to ebb by visible degrees with the publication of each successive article which took as its starting-point the assumption of full employment. If one were to count heads, particularly among younger economists, Keynesian ideas were being eclipsed at quite an astonishing speed. The winter of Keynesian discontent probably occurred in the early 1980s, since when there have been signs of a marked rally.

The most widely held reason for the decline in Keynesianism was its supposed inability to explain the historically high rates of inflation which occurred in Europe and North America from the late 1960s onwards. The Keynesian model, by which was usually meant the *IS–LM* model, is a fix-price theory which, by definition, is incapable of explaining why

---

[1]The atmosphere of victorious self-assurance is graphically conveyed in Arjo Klamer (1984).

variations in the absolute price level occur.[2] This accusation had been set temporarily to one side after the discovery of the Phillips curve and its subsequent absorption into income–expenditure models. The missing equation had been found, the system had been closed and the Keynesian model at last formed a cohesive whole.

This cohesion came dramatically unstuck as a result of two developments, one theoretical and the other empirical. On the theoretical front Milton Friedman and, independently, Edmund Phelps, had powerfully rejected the idea of a Phillips curve as a trade off relation. If it was anything, the Phillips curve was a disequilibrium reaction mechanism, and even then it had been theoretically misspecified. Phillips and Lipsey had measured the rate of change of money wages along the ordinate instead of the expected rate of change of *real* wages. If one opts to play by neoclassical rules, as Lipsey in particular had, one should read the neoclassical rule book first.

At the time that Friedman was airing his dissatisfaction with the Phillips curve, the complex econometric models of inflation which its discovery had spawned were still predicting inflation reasonably well. But this happy state of affairs did not last for very long. After 1967, things started to go disturbingly awry on the empirical as well as on the theoretical front. The rate of inflation had increased to alarming levels. This, in itself, need not have posed much of a challenge to the conventional wisdom: if unemployment had been at unusually low levels at the time, the acceleration of inflation could have been explained in terms of the simple Phillips curve and contractionary demand management policies could have been implemented. But this was not the case: unemployment was already higher than its average post-war value and was itself rising. This pernicious combination of rising inflation and rising unemployment, usually referred to as 'stagflation', not only led economists to abandon the simple Phillips curve as a tool for modelling an inflationary process. (Many Keynesians who had never accepted the Phillips curve regarded its 'breakdown' as the long overdue come uppance of an uninvited and unwelcome intruder.) It also led to a fundamental questioning of the whole basis of the Keynesian model of which, since 1958, the Phillips curve had come to be regarded as an indispensable part.

By the early 1970s there was an almost tangible atmosphere of guilt by

---

[2]Even when applied to the *IS–LM* model this is misleading. The reader is referred to Figure 4.17 where the workings of the simple quantity theory of money are illustrated in terms of the Hicksian model. A perusal of the section in which this diagram appears – the section entitled 'Keynes's generalized quantity theory of money: price and output changes' – should provide an antidote to the fix-price canard.

association. The fact that the Phillips curve had appeared on the scene over thirty years after the publication of the *General Theory*, and that, in the interim, Keynesianism had managed to flourish without it, made little impression on those critics who were determined to strike at Keynesianism with any weapon which was to hand. The Phillips curve had been taken on board at the highwater mark of Keynesianism: by some mysterious logical twist its discredit was taken to imply that the ship itself would have to be scuttled.

So what is the rational expectations hypothesis and how does it interact with the new classical economics to produce the policy inefficacy proposition? Does the claim that agents form their expectations rationally have any substantive bearing on the quite fundamental issues which divide Keynesians from new classicals?

Rational expectations and unanticipated inflation

In what follows the exposition will focus not upon the general nature of rational expectations equilibria, but on the relation between the criteria for rationality on the one hand and the debate on the unemployment–inflation trade off on the other,[3] with the ultimate aim of arriving at the policy inefficacy proposition. This is, after all, the most spectacular and controversial example of the radical implications of rational expectations in macroeconomics.

We have already seen how the endogeneity of inflationary expectations played a central role in Friedman's critique of the Phillips curve. He claimed that, in a fully articulated theory of inflation, it was incorrect to assume that price expectations were static or, worse still, to ignore the role of price expectations altogether. The expected rate of inflation, $(dP/P)^e$, is an endogenous variable, being determined in Friedman's model by past mistakes in predicting inflation. If agents had underestimated the rate of inflation in one period, that is if $(dP/P)_t > (dP/P)_t^e$, they will take steps to revise upwards their expectation of the rate of inflation in the next period, that is, $(dP/P)_{t+1}^e > (dP/P)_t^e$. The adaptive expectations mechanism was widely used as a formal representation of this process of expectations revision.

In the early 1970s considerable disquiet started to be expressed with the

---

[3]There are many excellent introductory surveys of the application of the rational expectations hypothesis in macroeconomics. The reader who wishes to pursue matters further should read D. K. H. Begg (1982), S. M. Sheffrin (1983), M. Carter and R. Maddock (1984), C. L. F. Attfield, D. Demery and N. W. Duck (1985).

implications for economic rationality of mechanical, error learning processes in general and with the adaptive expectations mechanism in particular. It will be recalled from Chapter 6 that Friedman, while denying any lasting relationship between inflation and unemployment, nevertheless insisted that there did exist a relationship between *unanticipated* inflation and unemployment. That is,

$$(dP/P)_t - (dP/P)_t^e = \phi f(U_t) + e_t \tag{7.1}$$

where e_t is a randomly distributed error term.

In other words, errors in predicting the rate of inflation were made up of two component parts: a random stochastic component which is, of its very nature, unpredictable; and a systematic component, $f(U_t)$, which is related to the level of aggregate demand as reflected in the unemployment rate. The systematic component will persist for as long as the unemployment rate deviates from its natural value, U^*. For example in Figure 7.1, the systematic component is zero at U^* but is positive at U_1. The prediction error attributable to the systematic component has a magnitude v_t. Moreover, for as long as authorities pursued a monetary policy which held the unemployment rate at U_1, this prediction error will persist over time. Thus $v_t = v_{t-1} = v_{t-2} = \ldots = v_{t-n}$ if the unemployment rate is held at U_1 for n periods. Agents will be making persistent, systematic mistakes in predicting the rate of inflation. They are always one step behind.

The first and most fundamental requirement of a rational expectations equilibrium is that expectational errors should be distributed around a mean value of zero. In practice, of course, expectational errors are continually occurring: they are inherently unavoidable owing to the presence of the stochastic error term. Agents will always be making mistakes, and some agents will be making larger mistakes than others, but the rational expectations hypothesis stipulates that these mistakes should, on average over time, cancel each other out. In our inflation–unemployment example, this criterion of rationality requires that the mean value of v_t – the difference between the actual and the expected rates of inflation – should equal zero. That is

$$E(v_t) = E(e_t) = 0 \tag{7.2}$$

Obviously the accelerationist hypothesis embodied in equation (7.1) violates this criterion. The same mistake concerning the expected rate of inflation is made year in and year out. The actual rate of inflation stays ahead of the expected rate by a constant margin which, for as long as the unemployment rate is held at U_1, will never be closed. For this reason the accelerationist hypothesis stands accused of being based on irrational behaviour, for rational agents should not make persistent mistakes. We

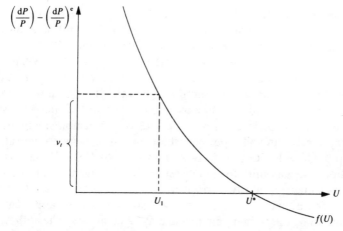

Figure 7.1 Inflation prediction error

referred above to the $f(U_t)$ term as the systematic component of an
accelerationist inflationary process: from an educated prediction of the
magnitude of $f(U_t)$ we should be able to make a reasonably good stab at
inferring the value of v_t. But rationality requires that there should be *no*
systematic element in the prediction error.

Let us assume that agents have been flirting for a while with the use of
the adaptive expectations mechanism but that, in the light of the
persistent, systematic errors which this mechanism entails, they quickly
abandon it. Reliance on a predictive procedure which is linked mechani-
cally to lagged values of the actual rate of inflation has been shown to be
wholly inadequate. How can agents improve their forecasts of inflation in
an uncertain world?

It is at this point that the rational expectations model becomes more
controversial. It postulates that agents will have an incentive to seek out
information on the underlying 'correct' model of the economy which, in
combination with adaptive expectations, had accounted for the systematic errors of the past. They will come to realize that the factor which had
given rise to their positive, constant prediction errors under adaptive
expectations was the excess demand component, $f(U_t)$. In order to
tighten up on their prediction of inflation, agents will take steps to predict
$f(U_t)$ on the basis of information which was available at the end of period
$t - 1$. In other words, they will form an estimate of the $f(U_t)$ term, $f(U_t)^e$.
The superscript 'e' denotes agents' subjective estimate of the $f(U_t)$ term in
contrast to the objective conditional estimate of $f(U_t)$, $E[f(U_t)]$. The
subjective estimate could be based on pure hunch and guesswork at the
end of period $t - 1$, but in order to introduce a degree of empirical

testability into the model it is normally assumed that $f(U_t)^e$ is arrived at by some policy rule which includes on the right-hand side only those variables whose magnitudes are known at the end of the period $t-1$. Since we have not, as yet, specified the instruments which will have to be used in achieving the target unemployment rate U_1 – should it be monetary or fiscal policy? Should it be both? If both, in what combination? etc. – we shall refer to a pseudo policy rule,[4] of which the simplest example is $_{t-1}U_t^e = U_{t-1} = U_1$; $_{t-1}U_t^e$ is the unemployment rate which is expected to prevail in period t, this expectation being formed at the end of period $t-1$ with the aid of a knowledge of U_{t-1}. What this pseudo policy rule amounts to is a presumption by agents that the demand management authorities consider an unemployment rate U_1 to be, in some sense, optimal and that they will adjust monetary and fiscal policies in such a way as to maintain this unemployment rate. The authorities are thought of as having committed themselves to the maintenance of a particular unemployment rate irrespective of the inflationary consequences and of being prepared to carry over this policy at least into period t.

Of course, there is nothing to guarantee that the authorities will stick by the same decision rules: they could become so agitated by public concern over the build up of inflationary pressure that they could jettison their employment objective and opt for contractionary demand management policies. Moreover, suspicion may grow in agents' minds during $t-1$ that the government may be on the verge of an about turn on employment policy. Nevertheless, since only variables which are observable at the end of period $t-1$ are admissible into the policy rule, these gut feelings are not allowed to have any direct impact on how $_{t-1}U_t^e$ is arrived at, although they may have an indirect influence through some other measurable variable which is admissible into the policy rule.

Generally in rational expectations models in macroeconomics the policy rule generating the prediction for a variable comprises an equation whose determining variables typically comprise both lagged endogenous variables (e.g. values of $(dP/P)_{t-s}, s > 0$) and lagged exogenous variables (e.g. $U_{t-r}, r > 0$). The common feature of these determining variables is that, being lagged, their values are known at the end of period $t-1$. As might be expected, policy rules of quite formidable complexity have been

---

[4]The reason for the qualifier 'pseudo' is that, in the vast majority of macroeconomic models, the unemployment rate is not an *instrument* of economic policy. In general the unemployment rate is regarded as one of the objectives of economic policy. Conventional usage applies the phrase 'policy rule' to the behaviour of the intermediate instruments of macroeconomic policy (e.g. the size of the government budget deficit, the rate of change of the money supply, etc.), not to the objectives themselves.

developed in the rational expectations literature, the best known of these being that proposed by Barro (1977) in which he attempts to model the process by which the growth in the money supply is determined and, on the basis of the prediction of what the money supply should have been given known values for its determining variables, to derive a time series for 'anticipated' changes in the money supply. We shall see in what follows that the distinction between anticipated and unanticipated changes in policy instruments plays an essential role in the application of the rational expectations hypothesis to the study of macroeconomic phenomena.

Two additional criteria need to be satisfied before we can definitely conclude that expectations are being formed rationally. Remaining with our inflation–unemployment example where $v_t = (dP/P)_t - (dP/P)^e_t + e_t$ we need to impose an additional restriction on the behaviour of the prediction error. Not only must the mean value of v_t be zero, as required in equation (7.2), but the prediction error must also not be systematically correlated with lagged values of itself. More formally this requires that restriction (7.3) be satisfied:

$$\text{cov}(v_t, v_{t-s}) = 0, s > 0 \tag{7.3}$$

The covariance of v_t with any lagged value of v_t should be zero. The reason for this once again centres on the role played by the information set available to agents at the end of period $t - 1$, which we shall refer to by the symbol I_{t-1}. The information included in I_{t-1} can be exploited by agents to tighten up their subjective prediction for $(dP/P)_t$. Suppose that v_t is not serially uncorrelated, as restriction (7.3) requires, but that it bears the following, hitherto unsuspected relationship to v_{t-1}:

$$v_t = a_0 + a_1 v_{t-1} + z_t, \text{ where } E(z_t) = 0 \tag{7.4}$$

Clearly once agents realize that v_t exhibits this pattern of serial correlation, they can include the information contained in equation (7.4) to augment the information set I_{t-1}, thereby eliminating any serial correlation which was previously present. This is another example of a procedure which is characteristic of the rational expectations approach to the use of information: the elements of I_{t-1} must be exploited in such a way that no better predictor of (dP/P) can be found without further, and by definition subsequent, enlargement of the information set. Such information as is available at the end of $t-1$ is put to its best use.

This essential characteristic of a rational expectations equilibrium – the efficient use of the relevant available information – suggests another criterion for rationality: the method that agents employ to predict (dP/P) should have a variance smaller than or equal to any other rival method of predicting (dP/P). We shall refer to this as the minimum variance criterion. Since the 'correct' model has the smallest variance of all, this criterion implies that agents employ a prediction method which is consistent with the model which 'correctly' determines (dP/P). Rational expectations theorists had realized early on that requiring agents to be in possession of 'the correct model' was straining the credibility of even the most sympathetic onlooker to breaking point. Instead they took refuge in the weaker claim that agents, on average over time, behaved *as if* they possessed the correct underlying model for the purposes of prediction. Agents may not know the correct model, but they behave as if they do. In this case their prediction model mimics the behaviour of the correct model so closely that there is no incentive for them to seek out further information to refine their predictions. (How agents perform this prodigious feat of mimicry without actually using *some* form of the correct model remains decidedly mysterious to this author.)

From the accelerationist hypothesis to the Lucas supply function

We have travelled a long way from the original accelerationist hypothesis as set out in Friedman's Presidential Address. The aggregate demand component of an inflationary process, $f(U_t)$, no longer exerts an independent influence on the rate of inflation which is, in principle, separable from that of the expectations component, $_{t-1}(dP/P)_t^e$, as it had been in the Friedman (1968) version. Expectations concerning the conduct of monetary and fiscal policies and their likely impact on the unemployment rate will enter into the rational formulation of inflationary expectations. Moreover, the absorption of the rational expectations hypothesis into the new classical economics led to a further, altogether more radical claim: the monetary and fiscal authorities would succeed in depressing the unemployment rate below U^* *only to the extent that* they could inveigle agents into formulating erroneous expectations. Thus the authorities' ability to raise the level of demand above Y^* is contingent on their success in deceiving the private sector into underanticipating inflation

This is not just a subtle shift of emphasis. It is one thing to assert that a consequence of sustained expansion of demand will be a direct increase in the expected rate of inflation by a process which efficiently circumvents the gradual error learning mechanism posited by adaptive expectations: individuals will have an incentive to search for the origins of their expectational errors and take the steps appropriate to keeping them to an absolute, unavoidable minimum. It is something altogether stronger to assert that the unemployment rate can *only* deviate from U^* as a result of the monetary (and fiscal?) authorities catching the private sector unawares. To take a specific example, the statement that a direct consequence of a publicly announced and widely believed monetary policy which aims at holding the unemployment rate at U_1 will be a higher expected rate of inflation does not imply the more extreme view that monetary policy can only reduce unemployment below U^* to the extent that the authorities increase the money supply at a rate in excess of what was generally anticipated. The conflation of these two completely distinct hypotheses has merely served to muddy the waters still further in the already turbulent and confused debate between Keynesians and new classicals.

In order to understand how this conflation has arisen it is instructive to trace through the steps which need to be taken to derive the Lucas supply function from the accelerationist hypothesis, the basic element of which is equation (7.1) above. This may also be written in the form

$$(dP/P)_t - {}_{t-1}(dP/P)_t^e = F(U_t - U^*) + e_t \text{ where } F(0) = 0 \quad (7.5)$$

Since $F(\ )$ is monotonic, we may take the inverse of (7.5):

$$U_t - U^* = F^{-1}((dP/P)_t - {}_{t-1}(dP/P)_t^e - e_t) \quad (7.6)$$

Now the Lucas supply function could be expressed in terms of equation (7.6). However, the more usual way to represent it is not in terms of deviations of the actual unemployment rate from its natural rate but in terms of deviations of the logarithm of output, y, from its natural value, y^*. One would normally expect there to exist an inverse relationship, derived, *inter alia*, from the short-run production function, between unemployment and the logarithm of output. Let the relationship take the form:

$$U = j(y) \quad (7.7)$$

It follows that

$$U - U^* = j(y) - j(y^*) = F^{-1}(\ldots) \quad (7.8)$$

In order to make the exposition more tractable let us assume that $j(\ )$ and $F^{-1}(\ )$ are linear so that, on rearrangement, an equation of the following general form is derived:

$$y_t - y^* = b((dP/P)_t - {}_{t-1}(dP/P)_t^e)) + w_t \quad (7.9)$$

Since the error term, w_t, is now a linear function of e_t, $E(w_t) = 0$.

Equation (7.9) is one version of the Lucas supply function, but it is not its usual representation. The term $(p_t - {}_{t-1}p_t^e)$ normally appears on the right-hand side in place of $((dP/P)_t - {}_{t-1}(dP/P)_t^e)$. In other words, the logarithm of the price level, p, appears on the right-hand side instead of the first derivative of its natural value. Of course taking logarithms and dropping down one time derivative does little to alter the spirit of the analysis and does much to expose the intuition behind this very influential relation. We shall therefore rewrite equation (7.9) in terms of the logarithm of the price level:

$$y_t - y^* = \theta(p_t - {}_{t-1}p_t^e) + u_t \tag{7.10}$$

where, once again, $E(u_t) = 0$.

The Lucas supply function is the more radical successor to the accelerationist hypothesis advanced by Friedman. It states that, apart from stochastic disturbances emanating from u_t, deviations of output from its full employment, natural value can only be the result of errors in predicting the price level. Hence a situation in which $y_t > y^*$ is the *outcome* of a situation in which $p_t > {}_{t-1}p_t^e$. This prediction failure is, in turn, the result of a series of unanticipated actions by the monetary authorities, that is, unanticipated departures from the policy rule which had governed the conduct of monetary policy down to period $t - 1$. Nevertheless, since a requirement of rationality is that the subjective expectation of the price level, ${}_{t-1}p_t^e$, should equal the objective conditional mathematical expectation for p_t, $E(p_t|I_{t-1})$, it follows that $E(p_t - {}_{t-1}p_t^e) = 0$. This is simply a more formal statement of the stipulation that, on average, expectations should be realized. Moreover, since $E(u_t) = 0$, it also follows that

$$E(y_t - y^*) = 0 \tag{7.11}$$

This is a most important result. Deviations from a state of overall full employment must be randomly distributed around a mean of zero. The origins of these short-lived discrepancies between y_t and y^* are to be found in similarly transient deviations of p_t from ${}_{t-1}p_t^e$. Since the condition for rationality contained in restriction (7.3) rules out any systematic relation between v_t, the prediction error, and lagged values of v_t, it rules out by the same token any persistent deviation of y_t from y^*. That is,

$$\text{cov}((y_t - y^*), (y_{t-s} - y^*)) = 0 \text{ for all } s > 0 \tag{7.12}$$

Applying these results to the unemployment rate implies that $(U_t - U^*)$ should be randomly distributed around a mean of zero and that $(U_t - U^*)$ should not exhibit any systematic relationship with $(U_{t-r} - U^*), r > 0$. In other words, the $f(U_t)$ term in equation (7.1) loses all meaning as a systematic relation linking v_t to U_t.

The requirement that $E(y_t - y^*) = 0$, or equivalently, that $E(U_t - U^*) = 0$, produced empirical difficulties which involved the problem of persistence. It appeared that output and employment in one period were correlated with lagged values of these variables over the phase of the business cycle. These perceptible correlations ran counter to the predictions of the invariance proposition. Lucas has advanced certain ingenious theoretical devices to explain the phenomenon of persistence which we shall examine later in this chapter. For the moment our principal concern will be to enquire into the forces which produce deviations of p_t from $_{t-1}p_t^e$.

The aggregate demand – aggregate supply framework

Two distinct justifications for the market clearing, full employment assumption of the new classical macroeconomics are to be found in the literature. The first has already been dealt with in Chapter 6 when we discussed Friedman's rehabilitation of Pigou's theory of labour market adjustment: in a competitive market economy, relative prices will respond in such a way as to eliminate any chance discrepancy between the demands for and supplies of goods and factors of production. In particular, the real wage will adjust spontaneously so as to prevent the emergence of excess supply in the labour market. Alterations in the level of aggregate demand have no significant impact on relative prices, although they may provoke temporary quantity responses owing to misperceptions concerning the behaviour of relative prices by the suppliers of goods (firms) and the suppliers of labour services (households).

But there is a second justification for the market clearing approach. If one were to peruse the extensive range of surveys of the applications of the rational expectations hypothesis to macroeconomics, one would come across a different framework of analysis, one which is so widely accepted that it is rarely explained in any detail, still less is its theoretical basis probed critically or its conclusions called into question. This is the aggregate demand–aggregate supply framework which, at its most elementary, postulates two functional relationships, one for the aggregate demand for output as a whole (AD) and the other for the aggregate supply for output as a whole (AS). The novel feature of this approach is the manner in which both AD and AS are posited as functions of the *absolute* price level, p, in such a way that, other things being equal, there will exist an absolute price level which will equate AD and AS at the full employment level of output, y^*. A sudden fall in aggregate demand resulting from, for example, fiscal contraction, will, in the short run, produce a fall in output, but eventually the induced fall in the absolute price level will have a countervailing influence which will restore demand to its original equality with y^*.

Consider Figure 7.2 in which the logarithm of the absolute price level, p, is measured on the vertical axis and the logarithms of the supply of and demand for output are measured on the horizontal axis. The aggregate demand function, AD, slopes downwards, indicating that, for constant values of our policy variable x, a lower absolute price level will entail a higher demand for output.[5] More formally, $AD = AD(p|x)$.

We shall have more to say about the properties of the AD function later in the chapter. At this stage suffice it to say that the naïve, unreconstructed quantity theory of money is normally introduced at this stage 'purely for the purposes of exposition'.[6] The policy variable, x, becomes identified with the money supply, m (note that $m = \log M$). In logarithmic form the Cambridge equation becomes:

$$m = k' + p + y \qquad (7.13)$$

The Marshallian k, and hence its log, k', is constant so that, for a given value of m, there is a one to one inverse linear relation between y and p, where y is interpreted in this context as the demand for output as a whole, i.e. $AD = m - k' - p$.

To depict the aggregate supply function we first need to draw a distinction between aggregate supply in the short run, where expectations *may* be sluggish in reacting to external events, and the long run where money is neutral and where the supply of output is invariant with respect to the nominal money supply and the absolute price level. The long-run aggregate supply function, AS^*, is therefore a vertical line in (p,y) space, touching the y axis at y^*. On that much – the shape of the long-run supply function – Keynesians and new classicals can agree: the willingness of firms to produce commodities does not depend upon the absolute price level.

Aggregate supply in the short run, AS_{sr}, is more problematical. Firms base their production plans for period t on the price they expect to prevail in t, this expectation being formed, as before, in the light of information available at the end of period $t - 1$. In other words, $AS_{sr} = AS(p_t|_{t-1}p_t^e)$. If the actual price level in t were equal to the expected price level, $AS_{sr} = AS^* = y^*$. However if the actual price level turned out to be

---

[5] In what follows we shall keep the use of time subscripts to a minimum, only reintroducing them where there is a danger of ambiguity.

[6] If a particular theory is invoked often enough 'purely for purposes of exposition' even the most sceptical reader gradually finds himself viewing this theory in a more favourable light. The almost universal exemplary use of the simple quantity theory of money sooner or later erodes any initial resistance that the reader may have had towards this approach.

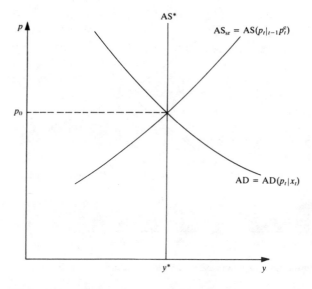

Figure 7.2 Aggregate demand/aggregate supply framework

higher in t than was expected at the end of $t-1$, firms would be more willing to produce extra output and y_t would exceed y^*. This is, of course, precisely the behaviour which is hypothesized in the Lucas supply function:

$$AS_{sr} - AS^* = AS(p_t|_{t-1}p_t^e) - y^* = y_t - y^* = \theta(p_t - {}_{t-1}p_t^e)$$

where u_t, the stochastic error term, has been omitted.

The upward slope of the AS_{sr} function reflects the response of firms to an actual value for p which turns out to be greater or less than they had expected at the end of $t-1$. But this still leaves unanswered the question: what factors will produce a discrepancy between p and p^e? Consider Figure 7.3. An increase in m from m_0 to m_1 catches the private sector by surprise. The AD schedule shifts upwards. In Keynesian economics, this increase in aggregate demand occurring at an initial state of full employment will simply raise prices: there will be no output response even in the short run. The economy moves from point A to point C and y never exceeds y^*. Not so in new classical economics. The increase in demand certainly raises prices but, since the increase in the money supply is unanticipated, so too is the increase in prices. (Note the almost instantaneous impact of a change in the supply of money on aggregate demand and the absolute price level – where are the 'long and variable' lags of yesteryear?) The Lucas supply function predicts that the economy

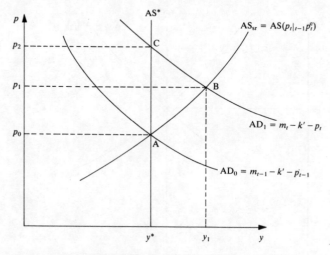

Figure 7.3 An increase in the money supply

will move along AS_{sr} to a point such as point B at which both prices and output are higher than at A: prices rise to p_1 and output rises to y_1. However, in the absence of a further aggregate demand shock, the realization in period $t+1$ that the money stock is now higher than previously will be incorporated into the information set I_t which is used to predict $_tp^e_{t+1}$. From equation (7.13) it is clear to agents that the price level appropriate to this money stock is p_2 so that $p_2 = {_t}p^e_{t+1}$. In $t+1$, the economy moves to point C, output reverts to y^* and prices bear the entire brunt of the increase in the money stock. Money is, once again, neutral.

The hardy perennial question of how an increase in the money stock is divided between a fall in velocity, an increase in output and an increase in prices gets short shrift in the new classical macroeconomics. Forget the string of elasticities with which Keynes embellished the simple quantity theory to arrive at his 'generalized quantity theory of money' (see Chapter 4). Keynes was concerned with producing a theory which was sufficiently general to embrace states of unemployment as well as full employment. Since it is axiomatic to the new classical macroeconomics that market economies are characterized by states of more or less continuous full employment, Keynes's elasticities analysis is ruled out as irrelevant *ex hypothesi*. In the new classical model the division of an increase in the money stock between price and output[7] increases depends

---

[7]In contrast to the conventional *IS–LM* representation in which the rise in the supply of money is partly absorbed in the form of a rise in the demand for money as a result of a fall in the rate of interest, it appears that k, k' and hence velocity remain constant in new classical models.

upon the extent to which the change in the money stock was anticipated or not. If the actual money stock in t is accurately predicted by agents at the end of period $t - 1$ (in symbols $m_t = {}_{t-1}m_t^e$), the actual price level in t will equal the price level which was expected at the end of $t - 1$ since expectations regarding the future behaviour of the money stock have been accurately generated by the efficient use of the information available in I_{t-1}. The economy will move directly from point A to point C without first stopping off at point B: no quantity response ensues from the monetary impulse. On the other hand if the increase in the money supply takes the private sector completely by surprise so that the whole of this increase is unanticipated, the short-run response of output will be much more pronounced.

But how do rational agents put themselves in a position of being able to anticipate changes in the money stock? Once again the new classical answer is simple, though by this stage common sense is being stretched to its limits. Having accepted the empirical validity of the crudest form of the quantity theory of money, agents search for a policy rule which determines changes in the money stock. Agents must try to burrow into the minds of central bankers to discover what motivates their actions governing the course of the money stock. Under what circumstances will the central bank increase the money supply?

The traditional Keynesian view of the conduct of monetary policy has been to assign to it the role of interest rate and/or exchange rate stabilization. The money supply should be adjusted in such a way as to fend off potentially damaging changes in the rate of interest and/or damaging changes in the exchange rate. The money supply is of no intrinsic significance: it only matters to the extent that it may be manipulated in such a way as to achieve other intermediate objectives of macroeconomic policy such as interest rate or exchange rate stability.

Naturally, monetarists and their new classical successors see things very differently. Control of the money supply should occupy centre stage in the conduct of macroeconomic policy. The central bank should abandon attempts to use the money supply to peg interest rates and exchange rates since, if left alone, these rates will 'naturally' settle down to their equilibrium values (see Friedman (1968) for a powerfully expressed plea for central banks to desist from trying to peg interest rates). The authorities should adopt a rule for the rate of growth of the money supply and should stick by it.

Suppose the central bank takes this line of argument seriously and opts for the following policy rule:

$$m_t - m_{t-1} = n \qquad (7.14)$$

where n is a constant. Since m is the logarithm of M, the left-hand side of equation (7.14) measures the proportional rate of change of the money supply. The private sector will have an incentive to form an estimate of this policy rule and use the resultant knowledge to arrive at their subjective estimate of what they expect the money supply will be in period t, $_{t-1}m_t^e$. In this example, the rational expectation of m_t is $_{t-1}m_t^e = (1+n)m_{t-1}$. Since both n and m_{t-1} are known at the end of $t-1$, they are available for inclusion in the information set I_{t-1} which forms the basis for $_{t-1}p_t^e$. Moreover, if the monetary authorities continue to adhere to the policy rule specified in equation (7.14), the discrepancy between the actual money supply and the anticipated money supply will be, on average, zero. That is, $m_t - _{t-1}m_t^e = z_t$ where $E(z_t) = 0$ since z_t is a randomly distributed, serially uncorrelated error term.

An implication of the preceding analysis is that the monetary authorities can only alter the level of output by engineering unanticipated variations in the money supply which, in turn, implies that they are continually altering their policy rule. But no matter how erratic the behaviour of the monetary authorities becomes, the private sector will sooner or later latch on to what is happening. Indeed, following Lucas (1973), it could be argued that the more volatile are demand management policies, the more adept does the private sector become at unscrambling the ever changing signals sent out by monetary policy and the less volatile output will be in the face of repeated changes in the direction of monetary policy. The general conclusion of the new classical macroeconomics is that the most that the monetary authorities can hope to achieve by shifting unexpectedly from one policy rule to another is to increase the variance of output around its given mean value of y^*, an objective which not even the most unrepentant policy activist would dream of advocating.

Reflections on the aggregate demand – aggregate supply framework

The policy inefficacy proposition derives its strength from the potent combination of the rational expectations hypothesis with the new classical macroeconomics. In fact, it will be argued below that the rational expectations hypothesis, the target of so many misdirected Keynesian barbs, may be combined with a model which does not assume market clearing in such a way as to allow considerable scope for discretionary demand management policies. The policy inefficacy proposition derives, not from the rational expectations hypothesis, but from the behavioural model which underpins the natural rate hypothesis of the new classical macroeconomics. The principal repercussion of introducing rational expectations into macroeconomic models is to shorten dramatically the lags in adjustment which have traditionally preoccupied macroeconomists from widely differing ideological positions.

Take the example of an increase in the money supply. In a new classical model, rational expectations will have the effect of eliminating many of the 'long and variable' lags of adjustment of the price level to an increase in the money supply so that the predictions of the simple quantity theory will be fulfilled with greater speed. On the other hand, in a Keynesian model where an increase in the supply of money can generally be expected to have real effects, i.e. where output will rise, the private sector will be able rationally to predict these quantity effects from the correct model (in this case Keynesian) which is included in the information set I_{t-1}. In other words the rational expectations hypothesis is ideologically neutral (see the final section of this chapter). There is nothing in the criteria which it stipulates for rational behaviour that confines its application to a market clearing framework.

The version of the natural rate hypothesis which we examined in the previous section contained just two behavioural relationships, the aggregate demand function and the aggregate supply function. We shall examine each of these relationships in greater detail in this section since they embody ideas and concepts which may not, at first sight, be either realistic or plausible.

In most accounts of the aggregate demand function, the reasons which are advanced for the inverse relationship between AD and p reduce, in essence, to the interaction between three complementary mechanisms. The first is the Keynes effect: as p falls, the real value of the money supply rises, the rate of interest falls and interest-rate-sensitive expenditures are stimulated. See Chapter 5, Figure 5.3 for a fuller account of this effect. The second is the real balance or Pigou effect: as p falls, the real value of private sector net worth rises which stimulates consumption expenditure. Once again, see Chapter 5, Figure 5.4 for greater detail on this effect. In the third, simple monetarist mechanism exemplified in the Cambridge equation for the demand for money (see equation (7.13) above) aggregate expenditure varies in proportion to changes in the real value of the money supply. This mechanism – what we called the cash balance transmission mechanism in Chapter 3 – is direct, in contrast with the Keynes effect where the stimulus to expenditure arises only indirectly from reductions in the interest rate. It is often erroneously confused with the real-balance effect since neither process requires the intermediation of the rate of interest. However, the real-balance effect is a pure wealth effect, operating only on the real value of the stock of outside money, whereas the 'money' referred to in the Cambridge or Fisher equations is almost entirely inside money which does not constitute part of the net worth of the private sector.

The Keynes effect and the real-balance effect – the first and second effects – formed an integral part of the neoclassical synthesis which played such a prominent part in mainstream economics until recently.

(The third effect should strictly speaking be regarded as a substitute for the first since it assumes a zero, or at least a very low, interest elasticity of the demand for money whereas the Keynes effect assumes that it is reasonably powerful.) The synthesis attributed demand deficient unemployment to downwardly rigid wages and prices. It went further in claiming that there existed a hypothetical price level at which the combined operation of the Keynes effect and the real-balance effect would stimulate aggregate demand by an amount sufficient to absorb the involuntarily unemployed into employment. On an operational level, however, the beneficial effects of price reductions on aggregate demand were never taken seriously in the neoclassical synthesis. Debate was confined to the purely theoretical properties of the income–expenditure model in which money wages and prices were allowed to go into free fall in the presence of general unemployment. In the original neoclassical synthesis the practical relevance of a process of price deflation for establishing full employment was regarded as minimal. The enormous extent by which prices might have to fall, together with the dynamic instabilities which might be encountered *en route*, were regarded as sufficient grounds for looking elsewhere for remedies for unemployment.

Inspection of Figure 7.2 should make it quite clear how the neoclassical synthesis has been modified by the new classical writers. The rather flat negative slope with which the aggregate demand curve is normally drawn insidiously suggests that quite a modest reduction in the absolute price level – 10% perhaps – will give a significant positive boost to aggregate demand. Orders of magnitude have changed. While Leontief, Pigou and Patinkin were speculating on the effects on demand of what might have to be, in principle, quite massive price reductions, the AD–AS framework gives the impression that relatively small price changes would make a powerful impact on aggregate demand. The neoclassical synthesis, which had started life as a series of 'in theory, what would happen if . . .?' questions, has been given operational teeth in the new classical economics. The synthesis has assumed a practical significance far beyond anything that its originators would ever have anticipated or – and here I conjecture – have approved of.

Nevertheless, one aspect of the AD–AS approach deserves brief mention. As far as its methodology is concerned this approach is firmly grounded in the income–expenditure approach of Keynesian macroeconomics. Thus the AD function is simply a collapsed form of the familiar *IS–LM* diagram where the price level is not taken as constant but is allowed to vary. The AD curve is a shorthand depiction in (p,y) space of what is happening to the *IS* and *LM* curves in Figure 5.4 as a result of falling money wages and prices.

The second behavioural relationship of this version of the natural rate hypothesis, the aggregate supply function, also needs some amplification, particularly in respect of short-run supply responses to policy shocks. The long-run aggregate supply function, AS*, poses no problem. It is in all respects identical to the description of the characteristics of a fully employed economy to be found in Keynes's *General Theory*. Full employment output, y^*, is invariant with respect to the absolute price level and the nominal money stock. Indeed Patinkin (1965) has suggested that one should regard Keynes's full employment aggregate supply function as one of an infinite set of vertical supply functions, each function corresponding to different values for the real wage rate as in Figure 7.4. The full employment aggregate supply function is that unique function corresponding to the market clearing real wage rate, w^*. At all other values for the real wage, output is constrained either by the unwillingness of firms to produce more output or by the unwillingness of households to provide more labour services *but not by both at the same time*. Only at w^* will firms and households be unwilling to alter their realized behaviour.

So AS* is the precise equivalent of the Keynesian $y(w^*)$ in Figure 7.4. Problems of interpretation arise with the non-vertical short-run aggregate supply function AS_{sr}. Why do suppliers, including the suppliers of factor services, increase output in the short run as a result of an increase in the absolute price level? Some new classical writers have sought to answer this question by referring to the 'island parable'. Suppose the economy is not one large, unified entity but is instead divided into a large number of islands. Each island is subject to economy-wide variations in

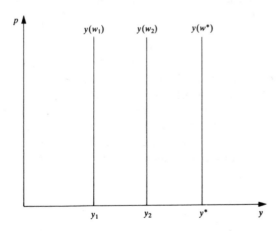

Figure 7.4 Aggregate supply functions at different real wage rates

demand as reflected in changes in the absolute price level for commodities, but news of what is happening on other islands and, by implication, of what is happening in the economy at large, takes time to filter through. An increase in aggregate demand and the consequent increase in the absolute price level affect all islands equally, though the mechanism of demand diffusion is unclear. On each island an increase in the demand for output is initially perceived as an increase in the demand for the island's output relative to that of other islands. In other words an increase in *aggregate* demand is mistaken on each island for an increase in the *relative* demand for the output of each island. The general increase in demand is misread by all of our hypothetical islanders: it is perceived on each island as an isolated (forgive the pun), specific phenomenon peculiar to that island. The aggregated reactions of all islands is illustrated in Figure 7.5. The initial rise in the general price level from p_0 to p_1 which results from the shift in the AD function from AD_0 to AD_1 is mistakenly interpreted on all of our hypothetical islands as an increase in the relative prices of their products. The output of all islands is raised as a result of what is believed (mistakenly) on each island to be a favourable shift in the pattern of demand in their direction. In terms of Figure 7.5, the rise in output from y^* to y_1 is the result of a series of individual decisions which were based on the assumption that, although the price of each island's output had clearly risen to p_1, the general price level in the rest of the economy would remain at p_0. On all islands the dug-outs embark in an attempt to sell the extra output to the other islands.

Eventually, of course, the dug-outs return[8] with the news that prices and demand had increased on other islands also and that what had erroneously been considered to be a series of relative price and demand shifts turned out to have affected all islands equally. When the realization of this news had permeated through to the remotest island, the initial market euphoria subsides, as does the level of output. The price level on other islands can no longer be taken as fixed at p_0 but will be seen to have risen. Once information concerning the shift in the AD schedule has been fully grasped throughout the economy, output reverts to y^*, the price level rises to p_2 and the relevant AS_{sr} function becomes $AS(_{t-1}p_t^e = p_2)$.

Unfortunately the island parable raises at least as many additional questions as it answers. First, by what mechanism are the demand and price signals so efficiently and rapidly diffused among all of the islands while information about events on other islands only becomes available

---

[8]Presumably the dug-outs return also bearing a cargo of unsold goods.

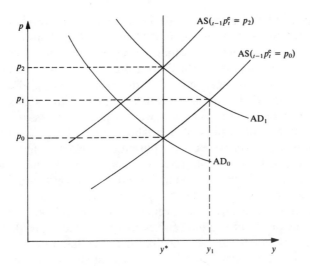

Figure 7.5 The 'island parable'

gradually? The process through which an increase in the supply of money[9] has an almost simultaneous and direct impact on prices and demand on all islands is glossed over as if it were a matter of trifling importance. This cavalier treatment of the transmission mechanism of monetary policy is one of the least attractive features of the new classical approach. It is also a feature which is likely to arouse the suspicions of the sceptical onlooker since it is part and parcel of a theory whose conclusions critically depend upon the combination of the sluggish dispersal of information on the one hand and the almost instantaneous diffusion of demand on the other. Such a theory will find it hard to repudiate the accusation of being little more than a clever but patently transparent artifice.

Secondly, what is supposed to be happening to the level of money wages following the increase in the money supply? Presumably they rise in line with prices. Workers could conceivably mistake a rise in money wages for a rise in real wage *à la* Friedman (1968), but the Friedman speculation only makes sense if employers think (perhaps mistakenly) that the real wage rate has fallen to a level such as w'' in Figure 6.10.

The island parable focuses not upon the reactions of workers and employers to what may turn out to be imaginary variations in the real wage rate but upon the reactions of producers to variations in the prices

---

[9]This must originate on an island called 'central bank'.

being paid for their products. This begs the question: do producers respond only to perceived changes in the prices paid for their products in comparison to those paid for other products *irrespective* of what is happening to their costs of production? Take the case of the inhabitants of an island who mistakenly think that the price which the rest of the economy is prepared to pay for its output has risen. In the absence of further information to the contrary, we are justified in assuming that money wages and the prices of non-labour inputs have also risen in proportion to the rise in price of final output. In deciding whether or not to increase the scale of their output, profit-maximizing producers will be favourably impressed by the rise in their product prices but, equally, they will be unfavourably impressed by the proportionate rise in input prices. In such circumstances there is every reason for believing that the representative producer will not raise output at all and hence that y will not deviate from y^*. Since the contributors to the literature on the new classical macroeconomics rarely take the trouble to furnish a fully articulated theory of the firm in which cost shocks are given equal prominence with demand shocks, one is entitled to take what they have to say on short-run supply responses with a large fistful of salt.

In the author's view the Lucas supply function comprises an arbitrarily concocted mishmash of conjectures and suppositions. Hypotheses seem to be effortlessly improvised out of thin air, the resulting theory giving the distinct impression of being a rather facile extemporization.

New classical macroeconomics and business cycles: unemployment as a leisure activity

Why does the measured unemployment rate vary so greatly over time? Is it for the usual Keynesian reasons, that is, because of periodic changes in aggregate demand and consequent changes in the demand for labour? Owing to their deep-rooted hostility towards the very concept of involuntary unemployment and their *a priori* conviction that the labour market clears 'more or less continuously', new classical macroeconomists are driven to look beyond this obvious explanation towards hypotheses which account for the acknowledged phenomenon of business cycles while at the same time preserving intact their beliefs in the robustness of all markets, including the labour market. Their objective is, in many respects, similar to that of Alfred Marshall some eighty years earlier, namely to graft a theory of the cycle on to a theory of value which asserts that, in a competitive economy, the interaction between the forces of supply and demand will ensure that all markets clear.

To this end Lucas (1977, 1978) devised a model which was quite a remarkable demonstration of his virtuosity in operating within the confines of the market clearing framework to which he is such a committed adherent. Lucas did not suggest that the observed fluctuations in unemployment were systematic deviations *from* the natural unemployment rate. Quite the contrary: they were fluctuations *of* the natural unemployment rate. His argument runs briefly as follows. Workers face a choice between work and leisure along the lines suggested in the classical theory of labour supply (see Chapter 2). Although, in principle, an increase in the real wage rate could raise the supply of labour significantly, in practice it appears that the 'underlying' supply of labour is fairly inelastic with respect to the real wage rate. When workers experience a rise in the real wage rate they face a decoding problem: they must decide whether this increase is a permanent rise, that is a rise which is likely to endure into the foreseeable future, or a temporary rise, that is a rise which is likely to be reversed in the near future. Generally speaking workers must decompose any given change in the real wage rate into a temporary component and a permanent component. If the rise in the real wage rate is perceived as mainly a permanent increase, the supply of labour is unlikely to be affected very much, because of the stylized empirical generalization mentioned above. On the other hand if it is perceived to be temporary, the effects on the supply of labour in the short run are likely to be substantial. *Carpe diem*: workers will take advantage of the short-term opportunity for financial gain afforded by abnormally high real wages by working longer hours, postponing holidays, working weekends, etc. The same behaviour operates in reverse: if the real wage rate is regarded as abnormally low, they will withdraw some of their labour services in the knowledge that they will be able to command a higher reward for their labour services when real wages return to normal. This partial withdrawal of labour supply is the mirror image of an increased preference by workers for more leisure: a rise in unemployment is seen as a sort of holiday or, at the very least, as a manifestation of an increased demand for leisure. Just as the measured unemployment is not 'involuntary', neither is the increased consumption of leisure 'enforced'. Involuntary unemployment and enforced leisure are Keynesian concepts which are precluded by assumption. Workers are responding rationally and entirely voluntarily to external events. Hence, even though unemployment may be fluctuating markedly over time, workers are never 'off' their notional labour supply curve. They are riding happily along on the roller-coaster of the business cycle.

The preceding account assumes that workers are in a position to distinguish with a reasonable degree of accuracy between changes in their real wages which are temporary and those which are permanent. The larger the temporary component of a real wage change, the more significant will be the response from the suppliers of labour. Lucas maintains that, in an economy in which all nominal prices are rising, workers face a twofold 'signal extraction' problem (see Sheffrin, 1983): (a) ascertaining whether the real supply price of labour is changing when all other prices are in a state of flux; (b) evaluating the temporary and permanent components of a change in real wages which, in the light of (a), may accompany across the board changes in prices. Problem (b) has already been dealt with, but problem (a) reflects the difficulty of determining what is happening to relative prices when prices in general are rising. In the labour market it reduces to the need by workers and employers to calculate what changes, if any, are taking place to the real wage rate when money wages and the absolute price level are rising. In economies where there is a history of high and variable rates of inflation, workers and other suppliers will have become adept at the semiotics involved in decomposing price changes into relative price changes on the one hand and absolute price changes on the other. They will be skilful at separating 'noise' from 'signal'. As a result they will be less susceptible to being 'fooled' or 'surprised' by the actions of the monetary authorities. On the other hand, in economies where rates of inflation have historically been relatively modest, the scope for confusion in decoding the messages imparted by price changes is greater. In times of rising money wages, therefore, workers must first decide whether or not the real wage is rising (problem (a)), and secondly decompose any increase in the real wage which may be suspected to have occurred into a permanent component, eliciting minimal labour supply response, and a temporary component, which could elicit a significant rise in the supply of labour services (problem (b)).

The solution to problem (a) should be relatively straightforward in economies where information on changes in the cost of living is given prominent news coverage when up to date figures become available and where labour is organized under the umbrella of trades unions with sizable economic research departments. In Britain, for example, there is no excuse for not knowing recent trends in the cost of living. The most up to date figures are flashed on to television screens in news bulletins as soon as they are available, and when abnormal rises occur they make banner headlines in the press. And one must add to this information on the very recent history of the price level the plethora of informed predictions by economic pundits of the likely future course of the price level. There has long been a lucrative private market in econometric models and the predictions that arise from them: nowadays these predictions come free of charge in the daily media prognostications of the specialist forecasters. In these circumstances is it realistic to assume that workers, particularly workers covered by union agreements, make significant blunders in dividing W by P? The idea that the temporary real effects produced by demand stimuli are due to a lack of information which is readily available at zero cost is surely far fetched when it comes to calculations of the real wage rate.

Problem (b), the task of apportioning a given perceived increase in the real wage rate between a temporary increase and a permanent increase, may prove to be altogether more formidable. Presumably workers will have to derive a trend path for the growth in real wages and calculate temporary changes in real wages as deviations from this trend line. Or perhaps more sophisticated methods are applied along the lines suggested by Friedman's permanent income hypothesis. No matter: Lucas assumes that workers follow *some* procedure for arriving at an estimate of their normal or permanent real wage rate.

So let us take stock of where we have reached so far in our analysis of the Lucas business cycle model. When prices are fluctuating, general confusion prevails regarding the behaviour of relative prices. In particular workers may come to the conclusion that their real wage rate is fluctuating procyclically (this surmise may, in fact, turn out to have been erroneous, but that is another story): when prices are rising more rapidly than previously, workers suspect that the real wage rate has also risen. A significant part of the suspected increase in the real wage rate will be conceived of as a temporary increase, eliciting a substantial supply response from workers. This supply response takes a variety of forms depending on the institutional arrangements within particular labour markets, but the Lucas model postulates that there will be a diminished demand for holidays and other leisure activities and an increased demand for overtime or weekend working. The temporary increase in the supply of labour will lead to an increase in employment and output, but since the rise in employment is entirely voluntary, the rise in output is a rise in the natural rate of output, y^*.

By this stage the reader may be becoming a little uneasy. Granted that fluctuations in employment may result from fluctuations in the real wage rate around its permanent, normal value which may, in turn, give scope for intertemporal speculative behaviour in the supply of labour; granted that these fluctuations may be caused by the confusion surrounding fluctuations in the general price level or in the rate of inflation. But by this stage the patient reader will be asking: what causes fluctuations in absolute prices? Enter the quantity theory of money in its simplest guise. Governments and their agents, the monetary authorities, are continually changing course in the conduct of their monetary policies. These course changes give rise to significant fluctuations in the money supply and in the rate of monetary expansion which, in turn, set the Lucas business cycle in motion. By corollary monetary policies which are geared to stabilizing the rate of growth of the money supply (or, more generally, reducing the unanticipated component of a given change in the money supply) will eliminate the cyclical fluctuation in unemployment.

Lucas's account of the business cycle lays almost exclusive emphasis on supply-side phenomena such as the high degree of intertemporal substitutability between employment and leisure. Workers are intertemporal speculators and abnormally high unemployment rates reflect the subjective speculation by workers that the real wage rate will rise to its normal value in the near future. But once again microeconomic problems arise since there are two parties to the contract of employment. How do employers react to the supposed increased willingness of workers to offer more labour services resulting from a monetary stimulus? Since the new classical macroeconomics is grounded in old classical macroeconomics in its emphasis on the role of real wage adjustments in accounting for variations in employment, presumably they have also taken on board that essential element of the classical theory of employment, the marginal productivity theory of the demand for labour (see Chapter 2). Even if, for the sake of argument, one were to take at face value the Lucas hypothesis that an unanticipated increase in the money supply raises the notional supply of labour, what incentive do employers have to take on any extra labour? If the real wage rate has temporarily risen, as workers are supposed to believe, employers will have the incentive to take on *fewer* workers. Even if individual employers were fairly bullish about the prospects for their own firm and intend expanding output and employment, they would postpone doing so until the real wage rate had reverted to its permanent value.

In other words, speculative behaviour works both ways: workers may engage in it, but so too may employers. Only when some convincing reason can be adduced for believing that both employers and workers not only misread market signals, but also misread them in the *opposite* direction from each other, will it be plausible to infer that both the supply of and demand for labour will rise with the general rise in prices and money wages. Friedman (1968) had earlier wriggled out of this tight corner by assuming that only workers, not employers, were subject to short-run money illusion: workers were supposed to think that the real-wage rate had risen while, as it turns out, it had fallen *ex post*. For Friedman the realized decline in the measured real wage rate – a decline which only becomes apparent to workers with the passage of time – was sufficient incentive for employers to take on more labour. Later Friedman (1975) shifted position somewhat in that he allowed for employers' mistakes concerning the behaviour of the real wage rate: the *ex post* real wage need never deviate from its market clearing value for fluctuations in the level of employment around its natural value to occur. Only when employers perceive real wages to be abnormally low will they be prepared to take the workers up on their offer of extra labour.

Lucas's account of the effects of monetary expansion on the level of employment could not be more different from that of Keynes's *General Theory*, in which an increase in the money supply, by reducing the rate of interest, raises the level of demand. The consequent rise in the level of output raises the price level relative to the level of money wages, i.e. it reduces the real wage rate. The level of employment rises as a result of the complementary stimulus to the demand for labour afforded by the rise in the demand for commodities and the fall in the real wage rate. Action by the monetary and fiscal authorities may succeed in relaxing the constraints imposed on the behaviour of the private sector by a deficiency of aggregate demand. In Lucas's model a deficiency of aggregate demand can never occur since markets always clear. Any fluctuations in measured unemployment which may, from time to time, be observed is the result of workers' fluctuating preferences between work and leisure. Unemployed workers are like unemployed actors: they are 'just resting between engagements'.

Side by side with the increasing popularity of monetary theories of the cycle, the late 1970s witnessed the emergence of alternative theories of the business cycle which, though firmly rooted in new classical macroeconomics, attributed the causes of the business cycle to real as opposed to monetary phenomena.[10] Real theories of the cycle bear many of the family characteristics of the earlier monetary theories, in particular the retention of the intertemporal substitutability theorem within a market clearing framework. These theories are 'real' in the sense that they trace the origins of business cycles to supply-side shocks such as exogenous shifts in technology. To take a specific example, let us assume that the production function all of a sudden shifts 'upwards'. The marginal physical product of labour curve shifts to the right. Real wages and output rise in consequence. Workers face the signal extraction problem of deciding whether the increase in real wages is transitory or lasting. To the extent that a significant proportion of the increase is regarded as transitory, the supply of labour will rise. From now on the chain of events is very similar to that of monetary theories of the cycle. Whereas the critical statistic in monetary models is the unanticipated increase in the money supply, the all important statistic in real models is

---

[10] A very lucid account of the variants on the new classical theme is to be found in K. D. Hoover (1988).

the variance of capital productivity. Changes in output which *cannot* be accounted for by changes in the input of capital and labour are *assumed* to be accounted for by autonomous shocks in technology. The bewildering ingenuity of the new classical macroeconomists is matched only by the tenacity with which they cling to the market clearing paradigm.

It is small wonder that Keynesians stood in perplexed amazement when they tried to relate the new classical theory of unemployment to the unemployment rates which were being experienced in the late 1970s. For example, this theory is incapable of accounting for the phenomenon of redundancies: workers surely do not *want* to be made redundant in order to indulge their desire for longer holidays. Is it not far fetched and fanciful to regard lay-offs and redundancies as cleverly disguised methods of electing to consume more leisure? To a Keynesian this explanation for general unemployment sounds perversely counterintuitive. Britain in the early 1990s appears to be on the precipice of the worst recession since the 1930s. How do the new classical macroeconomists explain *that* predicament? Given that they have ruled out of court the concept of demand deficient unemployment, the new classical writers have left themselves with no alternative explanation: if markets are clearing, they must be clearing at different measured unemployment rates. Governments should learn to treat published unemployment statistics with much greater circumspection than was the case in the past. For the new classicals, high unemployment rates should not be the object of discretionary government intervention since they are mere epiphenomena. For Keynesians, persistently high unemployment rates are an indication that the labour market is not clearing, that there is chronic excess supply in the labour market, and that some action by the monetary and fiscal authorities may eventually be warranted.

Rational expectations in a Keynesian context: a naïve example

In the preceding analysis the rational expectations criteria were introduced piecemeal within a context which assumed market clearing, at least in the fairly short run. This seemingly symbiotic link has been damaging to the more general applicability of these criteria in other contexts. Indeed, one of the reasons for the rapid absorption of the rational expectations hypothesis into new classical circles was that the underlying model of neoclassical economics in general and new classical macroeconomics in particular was the belief that this hypothesis conformed with the distinguishing feature of neoclassical theory, that of profit and utility maximization. Agents maximize, and part of the maximization procedure is the efficient use of all information available at reasonable cost. Keynesian economics, by contrast, was supposed to be built upon non-maximizing, *ad hoc* assumptions and constructs such as fixed prices and money wages, money illusion, curious 'psychological laws of consumption', etc. As usual, these critics of Keynesian theory were referring to the *IS–LM* model in which tangency solutions and the like make no appearance whatsoever. The fact that the Keynesian consumption function is based on maximizing behaviour by households which are already quantity constrained in the labour market was splendidly demonstrated by Barro and Grossman (1976) (yes, the same Barro). Moreover the Keynesian analysis of the labour market as set out in Chapter 5 should have made it fairly clear that Keynes was not denying any of the neoclassical assumptions motivating self-interested households and firms to engage in trade in *attempts* to achieve Pareto-efficiency. What he was denying was their *ability* to achieve the outcomes to which the opportunities for mutually advantageous trade clearly pointed. Workers and employers, motivated by the self-interest of neoclassical theory, endeavour to arrive at trades which would, if they became effective, clear the labour market. Nevertheless the only means at their disposal – cutting money wages – will fail to produce the required outcome for all of the reasons outlined above.

Moreover the commonly held view that the rational expectations hypothesis is the natural offspring of neoclassical and new classical economics has considerably limited the wider application of the concept of rational expectations in macroeconomic models which do not take the assumption of market clearing as their point of departure. The same sort of guilt by association which had tainted Keynesian economics in the wake of the Phillips curve *débâcle* has tainted the rational expectations hypothesis owing to its close connection, through Keynesian eyes, with the policy inefficacy proposition of the new classical macroeconomics. The fact that the rational expectations hypothesis is a free-standing set of criteria which can be applied to a wide variety of macroeconomic models was rarely grasped by early Keynesian critics. A corrective is clearly called for in the form of an illustrative counterexample.

Consider the chain of reaction which follows from an increase in the money supply in the *IS–LM* system.[11] 'Shocks' of this type form the

---

[11] In the light of the criticisms of the *IS–LM* model which are liberally peppered throughout this book, the reader may find it strange to see it reappear as a representation of the Keynesian approach. Two points should be borne in mind. First the example given here is solely for purposes of illustration and, since the *IS–LM* system is so well known, it serves that purpose reasonably well. Second, most of the criticism of the *IS–LM* model revolves around the indiscriminate application of a model which was only intended to highlight certain prominent features of Keynes's *General Theory*. If the *IS–LM* model has been found to be wanting, it is mainly because far too much was expected of it.

bedrock of the new classical literature which, combined with the rational expectations hypothesis, yield the superneutrality result outlined above. In the standard account of expansionary monetary policy illustrated in Figure 7.6, the economy is seen to move from point A to point B very quickly owing to the immediate impact that the increase in the supply of money has upon the rate of interest. After a while, however, entrepreneurs, realizing that interest rates are now lower, start to invest more, thereby raising income and the rate of interest. The economy embarks on a rather sluggish crawl up the new *LM* curve until it eventually comes to rest at point C where there is a new, higher equilibrium level of income, Y_2.

How does the introduction of the concept of rational expectations alter the above account? First, there is the question of the correct model on which agents base their expectations of the outcomes of particular policy actions. We shall assume not only that the *IS–LM* model *is* the correct model but also that agents *know* that it is the correct model. Suppose that the increase in the money supply is announced in time to be included in I_{t-1}, that agents fully believe the central bank, and that the central bank behaves in period t in the way that it announced it would behave at the end of $t-1$. In other words, the realized change in the money supply is fully anticipated and hence $M_t - {}_{t-1}M_t^e = 0$. In the new classical model such exact anticipation will generate – random errors apart – a perfect forecast of the price level in period t. By contrast, in this example, the fact that the unanticipated change in the money supply is zero, coupled with

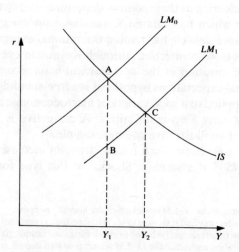

Figure 7.6 Fully anticipated increase in money supply with Keynesian 'correct' model

the inclusion of the 'correct' model depicted in Figure 7.6 in the information set I_{t-1}, will generate a similarly perfect forecast of the new equilibrium level of output in period t, that is, Y_2. In symbols, $Y_t = {}_{t-1}Y_t^e = Y_2$ on account of the fact that $M_t - {}_{t-1}M_t^e = 0$. If this is the case the economy will move with great speed from point A to point C, completely bypassing point B. At no stage in the rapid transition from A to C has any criterion of the rational expectations hypothesis been violated. What has happened is that all of the tiresome lags in adjustment of activity to changes in monetary policy which used to worry macroeconomists have been dramatically foreshortened by the introduction of the rational expectations hypothesis.

The moral of this simple tale should be clear. The rational expectations hypothesis does not pose a threat to Keynesian theory in the way that was thought to be the case when it first entered into macroeconomics. The rational expectations hypothesis challenges macroeconomists of widely differing outlook to re-examine the short-run dynamics of their respective models so as to check that no assumption of irrational behaviour has been implicitly or inadvertently embedded within the structure of the model.

Unfortunately, even when this fairly uncontroversial observation is accepted, the debate occasionally assumes an additional layer of confusion when the underlying structure of the Keynesian model is called into question on account of the supposedly irrational behaviour of the suppliers of labour in that model. Should the rational expectations hypothesis be grafted on to a 'correct' model which is basically the Keynesian theory of economic activity? It is sometimes darkly hinted that there is little point of applying the rational expectations hypothesis to a model which is so irredeemably based on the non-optimizing (i.e. irrational) assumptions of sticky money wages and money illusion. The reader who wishes to recap on why the Keynesian treatment of the theory of labour supply is *not* based on irrational behaviour is referred to Chapter 5, the section entitled 'Wage stickiness and money illusion'.

Concluding remarks

The strong links between the rational expectations hypothesis and the new classical macroeconomics initially sent out confusing signals. Partly this was a matter of timing: both approaches penetrated the mainstream of macroeconomics at more or less the same time. Partly this was because many of the enthusiastic supporters of the rational expectations hypothesis also tended to subscribe to the market clearing paradigm. But by far the most powerful link connecting the two approaches was the common assumption of economic rationality. By implication, other approaches were based on irrational behaviour.

Although most of this chapter has been given over to an exposition of the policy inefficacy proposition which was grounded in the aggregate demand–aggregate supply framework where variations in the absolute price level figure prominently, the reader should note that many new classical writers simply take it for granted that, in a competitive economy, markets clear on average over time. Unlike Lucas, these writers rarely attempt to justify this conviction formally, preferring instead to allude vaguely to the Walrasian model of general equilibrium and to the behavioural assumptions which underpin that model. As usual the assumptions centre on the motives that spur *Homo œconomicus* to action: firms maximize profits and households maximize utility. It beggars belief how the fairly uncontroversial assumption of traditional price theory that agents optimize subject to constraints should be taken by these writers as *sufficient* grounds for supporting the inference that all markets clear. Although this area of research is beyond my technical competence, I am assured by experts in neo-Walrasian economics that very strong *a priori* restrictions need to be imposed before even a glimmer of a general market clearing solution can be discerned. The likes of Arrow, Hahn and Malinvaud would certainly not rule out the possibility of Keynesian demand deficient unemployment. The hypothesis that firms aim to maximize profits and that households aim to maximize utility does not, *ipso facto*, imply that markets will always tend to clear. The path breaking work by Barro and Grossman (1976) elegantly shows how the existence of Keynesian unemployment alters the nature of the budget constraint subject to which agents optimize. For example, if all of a sudden households discover that they can no longer sell as much of their labour services as they would ideally like, their realized incomes will be reduced. Their utility functions may remain unchanged, but the income constraints which now confront them have altered. This is the second round of Clower's 'dual decision hypothesis': agents must now optimize subject to constraints which are themselves partly determined by realized outcomes. If household income falls short of full employment income ($Y < Y^*$) for Keynesian reasons, no one would suggest that household decisions will continue to be based on the palpably false premise that households will be able to sell as much of their labour services as they would ideally like. The constrained maximization problem becomes one where the level of income for the representative household ceases to be a choice variable, as it is in new classical theory, but becomes a datum, determined at the aggregate level by effective demand. In other words, the conventional assumption that agents attempt to optimize does not guarantee that the eventual outcome of such attempts will be a market clearing equilibrium. Referring back to Figure 5.9 in Chapter 5, it is evident that households would prefer to be at point A rather than at points B or C, but that they have no means at their disposal to effect the move to this optimal position. Workers can optimize until they are blue in the face and still remain powerless to reach their notional labour supply function L^s.

The reader will by now have become thoroughly jaded with the constant repetition of this fundamental tenet of Keynesian economics, but how do the new classical writers respond to it? The simple answer is, they do not. Perhaps Lucas gave one too many hostages to fortune when he jocularly confessed in an interview, 'In economics, you can get a book out written in English like Harberler's *Prosperity and Depression* without being able to read it. Or Keynes's *General Theory*. I still can't read Keynes [laughter]' (R. E. Lucas in A. Klamer (1984), p. 30). Not even the most unreconstructed Keynesian would ever claim that the *General Theory* was an easy read. Quite the contrary – at times it is infuriatingly obscure. Nevertheless, the peremptory dismissal of the book which established the modern discipline of macroeconomics is disconcerting. Disconcerting but, on further reflection, hardly surprising when one bears in mind that, for more than two generations, Keynesian economics has been taught almost exclusively through the medium of the *IS–LM* model. The *General Theory* appears to have assumed the dubious status of a 'classic': a work to which everyone refers but which no one reads.

8

Recent developments in Keynesian macroeconomics

Despite the sustained onslaught from the monetarists and, more virulently, from the new classical macroeconomics, the Keynesian research programme has continued to make significant progress on a variety of fronts. We shall briefly discuss three[1] interconnected lines of enquiry and, although the success of these approaches is hard to evaluate at this stage, they have certainly raised many issues which either expose the incompleteness of the simple Keynesian model or point to fundamental inadequacies within it.

The first development of the Keynesian system which we shall consider revolves around the important distinction between classical and Keynesian unemployment and highlights the policy implications which flow from this distinction. The second area of current research in macroeconomics centres on a phenomenon known as *hysteresis*. Economists working in this field are attempting to find answers to the question of why the various estimates of NAIRU exhibit a persistent tendency to rise over time. The third major development in Keynesian macroeconomics is the growing literature on 'prices versus quantities': when there is a nominal demand shock, why do quantities (output and employment) bear more of the onus of adjustment than prices (money wages and the absolute price level)?

We shall examine these three lines of enquiry below. But there is a fourth major avenue of current research which, for reasons of its technical complexity, cannot be covered in this book. This concerns the

---

[1]The choice of these three topics reflects my own interests. Other writers would provide a different and probably more extensive list.

analytical deficiencies in the treatment of the relationship between stocks and flows in Keynesian macroeconomics. For example, the Keynesian saving function in which the rate of acquisition of new financial and real assets is a function of the level of income has long been a source of dissatisfaction. Many prominent Keynesians have sought to replace the simple $S = S(Y, r)$ formulation and substitute in its place a set of equilibrium relationships between stocks (e.g. the desired stock of financial assets) and flows (e.g. the flow of national income). This is in marked contrast with the *IS–LM* system where the only stock–flow equilibrium relationship which is explicitly modelled is between the stock of money and the flow of income, this being summarized in the *LM* curve. No other stock–flow relationship enters the analysis.

This neglect of stock–flow equilibrium relationships is equally conspicuous in the treatment of the process of capital formation: in common with all short-run macroeconomic models, the *IS–LM* system posits a constant stock of physical capital while at the same time permitting the rate of net investment to vary. But how is it possible to reconcile a variable rate of capital formation with a fixed stock of capital? The answer which is usually proffered is a variant of the 'snapshot' argument: the stock of capital is so large in comparison with variations in the relevant flows that it would take a timespan considerably longer than the Keynesian short run for variations in the rate of net investment to have a significant impact on the size of the stock of capital. Fortunately much recent research in the Keynesian tradition has sought answers to many of these stock–flow problems, though once again a consensus view has yet to emerge.

Classical and Keynesian unemployment: models of temporary equilibrium

A general dissatisfaction with the lever-pulling macroeconomic models that the *IS–LM* model had spawned gathered momentum in the early 1970s. The feeling that Keynesian economics, at least in its textbook distillation, lacked robust microfoundations had become widespread. One reaction to this rather clichéd allegation took the extreme form of the new classical macroeconomics which jettisoned Keynesian ideas lock, stock and barrel, and which reinstated a modified, rather more mathematical version of the old classical system. The new classical school was distinctly more categorical in both analysis and prescription than its predecessor of over six decades earlier. For example, the extensive list of qualifications and caveats which Marshall appended to his exposition of the quantity theory of money had threatened to cast such a long shadow over its validity that Marshall appeared to take freight and retarait behind the *ceteris paribus* stipulation which so typified his approach to economics. By contrast with the old classical school, qualification, self-doubt or simple pragmatic open-mindedness are not conspicuous attributes of the adherents to the new classical macroeconomics.

Since the publication of the *General Theory* there had always been a nagging sense of unease at the treatment of prices in Keynesian macroeconomics. The mid-1960s saw the development of models of temporary equilibrium, which took as their starting-point the assumption that the initial values of relative and absolute prices were arbitrarily given in the short run. Models of temporary equilibrium, exemplified in the work of Barro and Grossman (1976) and of Edmond Malinvaud and the French Keynesian school, were inspired by the exceptionally penetrating insights of Robert Clower (1965 and 1967). Although a satisfactory account of these models requires a level of technical exposition well beyond the scope of this book, the basic question which they attempted to answer is quite simple to grasp. In what circumstances will an initial state of general unemployment require the real wage to *fall* for employment to increase, and in what circumstances will the real wage rate have to *rise* for employment to increase? This is the point at which the by now famous distinction between classical and Keynesian unemployment enters the picture. To reduce the extent of classical unemployment the real wage rate must fall, while to reduce the extent of Keynesian unemployment the real wage may have to rise, or at least remain unchanged. Not surprisingly, expansionary demand management policies will be successful in reducing Keynesian unemployment. On the other hand, if they are undertaken in isolation, these same policies could actually exacerbate the problem of unemployment if the unemployment is classical in origin. It is clearly imperative to arrive at a correct diagnosis of the origins of involuntary unemployment.

The sources of classical unemployment have already been touched upon in Chapter 2. General unemployment occurs when the initial real wage rate, w_1, exceeds the market clearing real wage rate, w^*. Workers are off their notional labour supply function, L^s, but employers are on their notional labour demand function, L^d. The marginal productivity condition of perfect competition is continuously operative so that, given the conventional shape of the short-run production function and of its derivative, the marginal physical product of labour function, an increase in the demand for labour will have to be accompanied by a reduction in the real wage rate.

The reader will recall how Keynes would not have disagreed with a single syllable of the above diagnosis. Where Keynes and Pigou parted company was in the mechanism through which the requisite decrease in real wages would occur. Pigou argued that, in a competitive economy, unemployed workers would vie with employed workers in an attempt to gain employment, possibly at the expense of those already in work. The only means at the disposal of the unemployed would be to offer their labour services at money wages which were lower than those being commanded by the employed. The general decline in the level of money wages would lead to reductions in real wages, which in turn would encourage employers to hire more workers.[2] It follows that the persistence of unemployment was the result of forces which prevented this mechanism from operating freely. The most obvious culprits were the monopolistic practices of the trades unions which impeded the downward adjustment of money (and hence real) wages. The policy implications of the old classical approach were far reaching, particularly insofar as they suggested that measures should be taken to curb the exercise of monopoly power by trades unions. Despite the failure of the old classical writers to form a coherent set of policy prescriptions, their view remained that any attempt to reduce general unemployment must have as its cornerstone policies which would reduce real wages.

Although the partial equilibrium diagram in Figure 2.6 conveys the gist of the classical position, an alternative diagrammatic representation of the same approach in terms of simple general equilibrium theory turns out to be more illuminating when we contrast states of classical unemployment with states of Keynesian unemployment. The first step in the construction of this diagram is to consider separately the conditions for equilibrium for the representative firm on the one hand, and for the representative household on the other. To illustrate different positions of equilibrium for the firm, consider Figure 8.1. Two points of neoclassical equilibrium for the firm, points A and B, lie along the short-run production function, $Y = f(L)$. Consider point A. The slope of the production function, $f'(L)$, measures the marginal physical product of labour at this point. It is clear that the slope of the tangent to the production function at this point is also equal to the marginal product of labour. Hence the angle of the arrowhead measures the marginal product of labour. Applying the marginal productivity theory of the demand for labour in perfect competition permits us to interpret the same angle as a measure of the real wage rate. We therefore observe that, with a real wage rate w_1, the tangency solution of conventional price theory yields values for both the profit maximizing level of output, Y_1^s, and the demand for labour, L_1^d, for the representative firm. A fall in the real wage rate from w_1 to w_2 results in both a rise in the notional demand for labour to L_2^d

---

[2]Much of Chapter 5 above is given over to Keynes's rebuttal of this proposition.

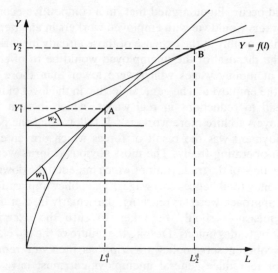

Figure 8.1   Equilibrium for the firm

and a rise in the notional supply of output to Y_2^s. Clower referred to magnitudes such as Y_1^s and L_1^d as 'notional' quantities in the sense that firms, if they are constrained only by the parameters of their production function and a given real wage rate, w_1, would ideally like to supply Y_1^s output and demand L_1^d labour services. These magnitudes are the outcomes of hypothetical thought experiments on the part of firms. The L^d curve in Figure 2.6 is a partial equilibrium depiction of one of the outcomes of this more general optimization procedure.

A very similar analysis may be applied to depict states of equilibrium for the representative household. Consider an indifference curve AA' in (Y, L) space. Households exchange their labour services for goods. It is normally posited that the marginal disutility of employment is an increasing function of the actual level of employment. This hypothesis generates an infinite set of indifference curves which are convex to the L axis. One such indifference curve is AA'. For a real wage rate w_1, utility maximizing households would be willing to exchange L_1^s of their labour services in exchange for Y_1^d goods. This optimization procedure thus yields the equilibrium values for two important magnitudes: the notional supply of labour, L^s, and its mirror image, the notional demand for goods, Y^d.

A state of general equilibrium can be depicted by combining Figures 8.1 and 8.2 in Figure 8.3. Point Z is a position of Walrasian equilibrium in the sense that both the goods market and the labour market are cleared at

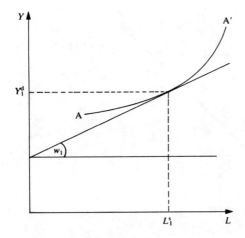

Figure 8.2 Equilibrium for the household

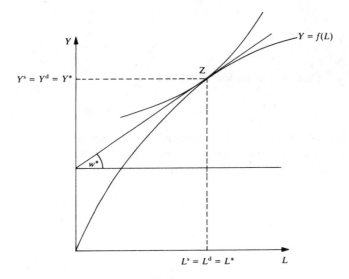

Figure 8.3 Walrasian equilibrium

a real wage rate w^*. Both firms and households are in equilibrium. Neither group has any incentive to alter its mode of behaviour.

But what would happen if the real wage rate were wrong? What would happen if the real wage rate were w_1, a value in excess of the market clearing real wage, w^*? Figure 8.4 illustrates such a state of disequilibrium. The optimal position for households is represented by point B,

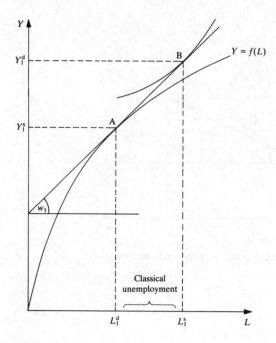

Figure 8.4   Classical unemployment

while point A represents the optimal position for firms. Hence there is notional excess supply in the labour market ($L^s > L^d$), which is necessarily mirrored in notional excess demand in the goods market ($Y^d > Y^s$). This is the upshot of a more general principle of general equilibrium theory known as Walras's Law. When households initially decide the flow of their labour services that they are willing to supply at different values for the real wage rate they are simultaneously deciding the quantities of goods which they demand in exchange for those services. The decision that determines Y^d is simply the flip side of the decision that determines L^s. The magnitude Y^d is the demand for goods which would materialize if households actually managed to sell all of the labour services which they notionally offer.

At this stage the 'short-side' rule is normally introduced. Actual trading in the labour market will be determined by whichever quantity is the smaller, the supply of labour or the demand for labour. More formally $L = \min(L^d, L^s)$, where L denotes the actual amount traded in the labour market and where 'min' refers to the minimum – or, in this case, minor – quantity inside the parentheses. Inspection of Figure 8.4 reveals that, since $L^d < L^s$, $L = L^d$: the actual employment of labour will be demand determined. The application of the short-side rule to the goods market reveals that $Y = Y^s$: the actual volume of output, Y, will be determined on the supply side. The economy will settle down at point A, a position of neoclassical equilibrium from the point of view of firms, though obviously not from the point of view of households, which would prefer to be at point B. Households must therefore revise downwards ‧ their planned expenditure on goods in the light of their failure to sell all of their labour services. The magnitude Y^d thus ceases to have any practical relevance since it is an entirely hypothetical quantity: *if* L_1^s labour services were sold, the demand for goods *would* be Y_1^d. But this representation of the aggregate demand for goods is patently misleading since realized trading in labour services and goods only amount to L_1^d and Y_1^s respectively. In other words, *effective* demand is conditioned by actual trading in the labour market. The level of effective excess demand, $Y - Y^s$, is zero, despite the fact that notional excess demand, $Y^d - Y^s$, is positive. The level of notional excess demand is the magnitude which is relevant to Walras's Law, but it is of no operational significance either for firms or for households. As Clower pointed out, it takes a strange contortion of language to characterize the 1930s as a period in which the basic problem was that of an excess demand for goods!

The concept of quantity rationing is obviously relevant here. Since households cannot sell their notional supply of labour services, i.e. $L < L_1^s$, they are said to be rationed in the labour market. Households are similarly rationed in the goods market, i.e. $Y < Y_1^d$, on account of (a) their failure to sell L_1^s labour services and (b) the unwillingness of firms to produce any more than Y. By way of contrast, firms are in continuous neoclassical equilibrium and are not subject to quantity rationing in either the goods market or the labour market. They are hiring just the right number of workers, L_1^d, that the calculus of profit maximization dictates. By the same token they are producing just the right level of output, Y_1^s. No external quantity constraints impinge upon the behaviour of firms.

General unemployment is the most conspicuous outcome of this failure to reach a Walrasian equilibrium. Such unemployment is labelled *classical* in the sense that its sole root cause is an excessively high real wage ($w_1 > w^*$). Quantity constraints on firms do not figure at all. A necessary and sufficient condition for the eradication of classical unemployment is hence a direct downward adjustment of the real wage rate to a level where $w = w^*$. Once this adjustment has been achieved, a state of Walrasian general equilibrium will prevail (see Figure 8.3). Precisely *how* this requisite adjustment is effected is rarely discussed satisfactorily in this literature, particularly when one bears in mind the close connection between changes in money wages and changes in prices which is such a prominent feature of the pricing decision in most advanced market economies. To take a concrete example, an established characteristic of the pricing decision across many Western economies over several decades has been the tendency for firms, particularly firms in the manufacturing sector, to set prices as a mark up over variable costs, the most prominent among which is the money wage. If the phenomenon of mark up pricing (alternatively known as 'administered' pricing) is as widespread as is generally believed, what instruments of macroeconomic policy can governments bring to bear to alter – in this context, to reduce – the real wage rate? Malinvaud assigns a special role to prices and incomes policies to effect a differential adjustment of W in relation to P, but how such a policy would operate in the absence of quite massive and probably unacceptable levels of state interference both in wage bargaining and in the pricing decisions of firms remains a disconcertingly moot point. Prices and incomes policies have been justified historically on the grounds that, if successful, they serve directly to scale down the rates of increase of money wages and absolute prices while minimizing the rise in unemployment which a policy of demand restriction would entail. In other words, prices and incomes policies were devised with the objective of short-circuiting the painful process of adjustment to a lower rate of inflation. On the other hand apologists for such policies rarely if ever sought to justify them on the grounds that they would reduce the real wage rate *à la* Malinvaud. Of course, in open economy models of temporary equilibrium, alterations in the nominal exchange rate might do the trick of reducing real wages through their impact on the terms of trade; but, in the case of a devaluation, this would succeed only to the extent that the phenomenon of real wage resistance were not encountered.

In brief, the mechanisms through which policy makers might bring about a reduction in classical unemployment have not been systematically worked through in most models of temporary equilibrium. Both the origins of classical unemployment and the nature of the remedy for it remain stubbornly obscure.

The second broad category of general unemployment is labelled *Keynesian*. The origins of Keynesian unemployment must be traced, not to wrong relative prices – specifically to a wrong real wage – but to a deficiency of aggregate demand. As we saw in Figure 5.9 in Chapter 5, it is perfectly conceivable that Keynesian (demand deficient) unemployment is consistent with a real wage which is at its market clearing value, w^*.

Point Z locates a position of Walrasian equilibrium; but this point is unattainable despite the fact that the real wage rate is at its market clearing value. The economy finds itself in a suboptimal state of temporary equilibrium at point C owing to a sales constraint on output:

firms would ideally like to produce Y^* output and employ L^* workers but, being unable to sell all of this output and employ this number of workers, they are obliged to produce a level of output Y_1 compatible with constraint on sales and hence employ only L_1 workers. The fact that Y_1 falls short of Y^* is attributable to a deficiency of aggregate demand. Both firms and households would prefer to be at point Z but they are prevented from realizing their optimal mode of behaviour by a general lack of demand in the economy. In terms of the simpler partial equilibrium framework illustrated in Figure 8.6, both firms and households are off their notional labour demand and supply functions.

Points Z and C in Figure 8.5 correspond to points Z' and C' in Figure 8.6. At C and C', two marginal conditions fail to be satisfied: the real wage rate is neither a measure of the marginal disutility of employment nor a measure of the marginal physical product of labour. The traditional marginal conditions of simple price theory cease to be operative in the presence of Keynesian unemployment. (Recall Keynes's retention of the 'real wage equals marginal product' principle, so that only the first marginal condition failed to hold in the *General Theory* model.) It follows that no adjustment of the real wage rate may be required to reduce unemployment. In our example the real wage rate remains at its market clearing value, w^*, despite the presence of involuntary unemployment. In contrast with the case of classical unemployment, the short-side rule no longer applies: $L \neq \min(L^s, L^d)$. In fact L^s and L^d, interpreted as notional quantities, are equal, but both

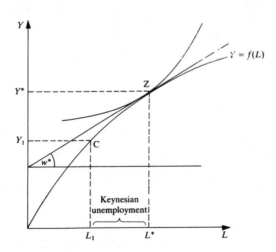

Figure 8.5 Keynesian unemployment

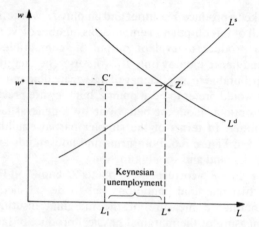

Figure 8.6 Partial equilibrium depiction

magnitudes exceed the amount of realized trading in the labour market, L.

Models of temporary equilibrium attribute the persistence of both classical and Keynesian unemployment to the short-run stickiness of money wages and prices. In the long run the economy will tend to gravitate towards a position of Walrasian equilibrium. In this vein Malinvaud (1983) writes: '[T]he Walrasian equilibrium . . . is appropriate for long-run economic analysis, because in the long run prices are actually flexible and play the role that was traditionally given to them.' In order to come to grips with the reasoning behind this rather sanguine conclusion we must consider three important magnitudes: the money wage rate, W, the absolute price level, P, and the nominal stock of *outside* money, OM. In most of the models of temporary equilibrium the only financial asset which is explicitly modelled is the stock of fiat money – effectively notes and coin in circulation. Other financial assets – bonds, equities, *inside* money – scarcely feature at all. The relationship between these three important variables is supposed to determine the characteristics of a state of temporary equilibrium. In essence classical unemployment stems from an inappropriate relationship between W and P, i.e. $W/P > w^*$, while Keynesian unemployment stems from an inappropriate relationship between OM and P.

This latter relationship needs some amplification. The expenditure decisions of the private sector depend upon an extensive array of variables – the rate of interest, the real wage rate, the realized level of income, etc. Within this array of determining variables, great prominence is accorded to the ratio *OM/P*, the stock of real balances. Consumption expenditure depends, *inter alia*, on the stock of real balances. The higher is *OM/P*, the higher is consumption expenditure and the higher is the level of aggregate demand. The ratio *OM/P* can rise either as a result of an increase in *OM* or through a fall in *P*. The only route through which *OM* can rise is a temporary budget deficit financed by the issue of fiat money. This is the case where the graphic monetarist image of governments printing or minting new money is quite literally accurate since no alternative source or finance is available to them as a result of the restrictive assumptions of the model. Once *OM* has been 'topped up' by a sufficient infusion of new money, the budget can again be balanced.

A similar chain of reasoning applies to the real-balance effect. With a constant nominal stock of fiat money, a falling price level raises *OM/P*, which raises consumption expenditure, which in turn raises the level of aggregate demand. To appreciate how a falling price level serves to stimulate employment, consider Figure 8.7. Point *B* represents a state of labour market clearance: the $L^d(OM_0/P^*)$ curve which passes through point B is the usual notional demand for labour function which would apply if employers were not subject to a sales constraint in the goods market. The only factor which determines the position and slope of this function is the short-run production function.

The $L^d(OM_0/P_0)$ curve is, however, something altogether different since it is the effective, as opposed to the notional, demand for labour function: its position is determined by the effective demand for goods

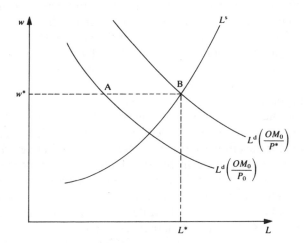

Figure 8.7 Falling prices and the demand for labour

which will, in turn, depend upon the magnitude of OM/P. The initial stock of real balances fixes the $L^d(OM_0/P_0)$ function to the left of the notional demand for labour function. The horizontal distance AB measures the extent of Keynesian unemployment.

What this diagram clearly exposes is the temporary nature of Keynesian unemployment in these models. With the passage of time, money wages and prices will be revised downwards in the presence of excess supply in both the labour market and the goods market. Real balances will rise, and so too will aggregate demand. The sales constraint on firms will progressively diminish and the $L^d(OM_0/P)$ function will shift to the right. This process will continue until a price level is reached which is so low as to make OM_0/P so high as to ensure that the effective labour demand function eventually coincides with the notional labour demand function. For a given initial stock of nominal money balances, OM_0, there will exist a unique absolute price level, P^*, which will establish full employment.

This is a similar conclusion to that of the neoclassical synthesis except that there is no scope for the Keynes effect to operate. This is hardly surprising since temporary equilibrium models lack a coherently articulated theory of interest which would allow the Keynes effect to be activated. The phenomenon of liquidity preference can find no place in a model that admits of only one asset, fiat money. The full burden of long-run equilibration is thrown on to the slender base of the real balance effect. Now while it is plausible to argue that consumption expenditure will partly depend upon the real value of private sector net worth, to concentrate all attention on a tiny fraction of this magnitude is to lose all sense of proportion. Sheer orders of magnitude matter, and the orders of magnitude do not come down on the side of the real-balance effect. To take the British example, I would hazard that the ratio of real balances to total private sector net worth is less than 1% (see Dow and Saville (1988) for a breakdown of the constituent parts of private sector wealth). The undoubted benefits of the greater mathematical rigour which these models incorporate may have been bought at the cost of a loss of perspective on the world 'out there'. One would have thought that the Great Depression years in the United States had provided a suitable testing ground for the efficacy of the real-balance effect, but, as Patinkin pointed out at an early stage in the development of the neoclassical synthesis, a large *increase* in real balances appeared to be accompanied by a large *fall* in output. The experience of this catastrophic episode in American economic history can do little to inspire confidence in the recuperative powers of advanced market economies.

The broad distinction between classical and Keynesian unemployment has far-reaching implications for the conduct of macroeconomic policy. If unemployment is classical, steps must be taken to reduce the real wage rate. Policies of demand expansion are worse than useless since they could intensify the rationing of households in the goods market. On the other hand, if unemployment is Keynesian, steps must be taken to boost aggregate demand. Policies to reduce the real wage rate in the face of Keynesian unemployment could make matters far worse since a common feature of temporary equilibrium models is the positive functional dependence of consumption expenditure on the real wage rate. Real wage cuts, by reducing aggregate demand, raise the level of Keynesian unemployment.

In most of the early work on quantity constrained models it was assumed that any observed general unemployment had to be either classical or Keynesian but not both at the same time. This monocausal approach had the advantage of clarity of distinction but it could be highly misleading as a guide to macroeconomic policy since it is perfectly conceivable that classical and Keynesian unemployment may coexist at one and the same time. For example, it is possible that $W/P > w^*$ and that $OM/P < OM/P^*$. In other words, a given level of unemployment may comprise a classical component attributable to excessive real wages and a Keynesian component attributable to deficient aggregate demand. We must therefore confront the empirical problem of separating out classical from Keynesian influences in order to answer a very simple question: is the unemployment which is observed in a particular economy over a given period of time predominantly classical or predominantly Keynesian in origin?

R. M. Coen and B. G. Hickman (1987) have attempted to provide a tentative answer to this important question. Figure 8.8 represents a simplified version of their model.

The real wage is measured along the vertical axis and labour services are measured along the horizontal axis. The L^d curve is the notional demand curve for labour, i.e. along L^d firms are not subject to quantity constraints in either the goods market or the labour market. The $L^d(Y_0)$ curve, by contrast, is the effective demand curve for labour: firms, considered in the aggregate, cannot sell more than Y_0 units of output on account of a sales constraint in the goods market, which in turn is the result of a deficiency of aggregate demand. The downward slope of the effective labour demand function reflects the hypothesis that, even if they face quantity constraints in the goods market, firms would be willing to employ more workers if the real wage rate were lower.[3]

---

[3] In the short run the slope of $L^d(Y_0)$ is likely to be much steeper than that of L^d.

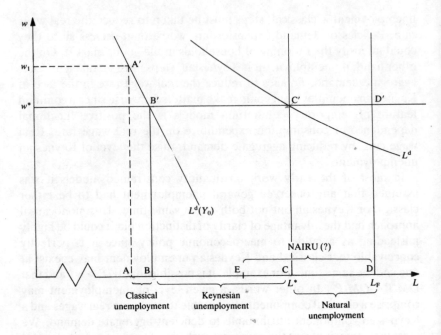

Figure 8.8 Coen–Hickman model

The total volume of the available labour force is L_F. Since there will always be some unemployment which can be attributed to microeconomic factors, the maximum feasible level of employment will fall short of L_F. The natural level of employment, that is that level of employment consistent with overall labour market clearance at a real wage rate w^*, is L^*. The discrepancy between L_F and L^* is thus a measure of the natural unemployment rate U^*.

But the natural unemployment rate is only part of the total unemployment rate which is measured by the horizontal distance DA. Total unemployment can be decomposed into three constituent parts: Keynesian unemployment, measured by CB; classical unemployment, measured by BA; and natural unemployment, measured by DC. Coen and Hickman's empirical methodology proceeds as follows. First arrive at an estimate of the natural unemployment rate. Secondly, estimate the magnitude of the wage gap, that is the magnitude of $(w_1 - w^*)$. Thirdly, estimate the elasticity of the constrained labour demand function with respect to the real wage rate. The second and third results will jointly yield an estimate for the classical component of observed unemployment. This estimate of classical unemployment, when added to the first estimate of natural unemployment, will determine the magnitude of the Keynesian component of observed unemployment. The Keynesian component is clearly a residual which is arrived at by subtracting the natural and classical components from overall unemployment. Coen and Hickman conclude that, by and large, observed unemployment rates in the United States, the United Kingdom, Germany and Austria from the early 1970s have their origins in deficient aggregate demand. While classical factors were often present, and for brief periods predominated, Keynesian factors were the proximate forces accounting for the rise in unemployment over this period. This is the result of the combined effects of a low estimated real-wage elasticity of demand for labour and of controversially low estimates of the natural unemployment rates for these four countries.

Coen and Hickman rightly mistrust the use of NAIRUs to form estimates of natural unemployment rates. Not only are estimates of NAIRU notorious for their lack of robustness, they also have a disconcerting tendency to shadow the actual unemployment rate suspiciously closely. The case of the United Kingdom is particularly graphic. In the first column in the following table they compute the average unemployment rates over four sample periods. In the second column they insert the corresponding estimates for NAIRU which they had extracted from a variety of empirical studies.

	Actual unemployment rates	NAIRU estimates
1967–70	2.2	2.4
1971–75	3.0	4.0
1976–80	5.4	4.7
1981–83	10.6	9.2

Is it mere coincidence that, over a period in which the observed unemployment rate rose almost fivefold, the estimate for NAIRU rose almost fourfold?[4] The suspicions of the disinterested onlooker are likely to be aroused against the whole notion of NAIRU as an operationally useful construct. Moreover even if these sceptical grumblings are set to one side, are we to interpret the proposition that there has been a secular rise in NAIRU as pointing to a rise in the *natural* unemployment rate? Coen and Hickman dispense with the common practice of linking changes in NAIRU with changes in the natural unemployment rate, preferring

---

[4]The most recent estimate for the natural unemployment rate for Britain is given by Nickell (1990) at 8.7%.

instead to rely on demographic and other data to arrive at direct estimates of the natural rate, estimates which do not take as their reference point the behaviour of the rate of inflation. They thereby avoid a circularity of reasoning which has plagued the natural rate–NAIRU literature from its earliest days: if a sustained rise in the unemployment rate is *not* accompanied by an abatement of inflationary pressure, then this literature can admit of only one explanation – that NAIRU, a concept which has often been conflated with that of the natural unemployment rate, must itself have risen. Many ingenious hypotheses have been advanced to account for this supposed rise in NAIRU, the most promising of which is the notion of hysteresis discussed in the next section.

As James Tobin pointed out in his comments on the Coen and Hickman paper, a feature of their approach which exposes it to criticism from those macroeconomists who accept some variant of the NAIRU hypothesis is that it lacks a coherent explanation of the relationship between unemployment, be it Keynesian, classical or some mixture of the two, and inflation. Tobin colourfully dubs these critics as 'Euro-pessimists' or 'Euro-hypochondriacs'. Even if it is accepted that a substantial proportion of any given unemployment rate is Keynesian in origin, Euro-pessimists fear that any expansion of demand to reduce such unemployment will hit up against supply-side constraints. These supply constraints are not the usual physical barriers to increased output imposed by the productive potential of the economy. Rather they take the form of the greater danger of an intensification of the wage–price–expectations spiral which would result from an expansion of demand. The more extreme Euro-pessimists would view *any* attempt at expanding demand to reduce unemployment as being necessarily inflationary. They are likely to be distinctly unimpressed by the policy implications of the taxonomic exercise undertaken by Coen and Hickman. A thorough examination of the inflationary repercussions of policies to reduce both classical and Keynesian unemployment needs to be undertaken before such policies can be advocated safely. The decomposition of observed unemployment rates into their classical and Keynesian parts can only serve as a first step in the formulation of macroeconomic policy since such an exercise must take place within a broader framework which encompasses concepts such as short- and long-run Phillips curves, the natural unemployment rate, and NAIRU. For example, how should policy makers react if, having been persuaded that the larger part of observed unemployment is Keynesian, they are also persuaded that NAIRU lies well within the range BC in Figure 8.8? The larger is the interval CE, the greater are the inflationary dangers inherent in removing Keynesian unemployment by a traditional demand expansion. So we must go further in our exploration of the ever more complex relationship between inflation and unemployment.

Hysteresis and the non-accelerating inflation rate of unemployment

The concept of the non-accelerating inflation rate of unemployment, NAIRU, was introduced into macroeconomics in the 1970s as a more acceptable version of the Friedman–Phelps notion of the natural unemployment rate, denoted above by the symbol U^*. One of the problems which arose from Friedman's definition of the natural unemployment rate was that, apart from a list of qualifications mostly of a microeconomic nature, it appeared to possess characteristics which were usually associated with an economy in overall full employment. If the actual unemployment rate coincides with the natural rate, we must infer, following Friedman, that the overall supply of labour equals the overall demand for labour at the market clearing real wage rate. As we saw above, Friedman went further: the natural unemployment rate was also a stable equilibrium unemployment rate in the sense that deviations from the natural rate, produced, typically, by misguided monetary policies, would only be transitory. As if this further proposition were not strong enough, Friedman went on to claim yet another property for the natural rate: the natural unemployment rate was that unique rate at which inflationary expectations were exactly fulfilled and hence was that unique rate at which agents had no incentive to revise their expectations of inflation either upwards or downwards. Thus in the original formulation by Friedman, the natural unemployment rate possesses two analytically separable characteristics: (a) it corresponds to a state of overall full employment; (b) it is that single rate at which the expected rate of inflation, and hence the actual rate of inflation, is neither rising nor falling.

Many non-monetarist economists were prepared to absorb characteristic (b) into their macroeconomic models, but were reluctant to take on board its more strictly classical partner, characteristic (a). These economists[5] were ready to accept that there probably did exist a particular unemployment rate at which inflation was neither rising nor falling but they were unwilling to associate this rate with a state of overall full employment. The concept of NAIRU referred only to the behaviour of the actual and the expected rate of inflation. It bore no connotation of overall equilibrium in the labour market. Any particular estimate of NAIRU could include a large proportion of workers who were involuntarily unemployed.

Nevertheless, even though the concept of NAIRU was considerably

---

[5] These would include many economists who would broadly describe themselves as Keynesians.

more palatable to mainstream macroeconomists than the Friedman natural unemployment rate, it hit up against formidable practical problems. Consider what were generally believed to be the policy implications of the NAIRU hypothesis. If a government wishes to take action to reduce the rate of inflation, it must deflate aggregate demand along traditional Keynesian lines, thereby raising the actual unemployment rate, U, above NAIRU. The more severe is the deflation of demand, the larger will be the induced discrepancy between U and NAIRU and the more rapidly will the rate of inflation fall. Moreover once inflation has levelled out at an acceptable rate, aggregate demand can be expanded once again with the result that the actual unemployment rate will fall back towards NAIRU. To the extent that policies are widely publicized and are regarded as credible by agents, the grafting on of the rational expectations hypothesis simply speeds up the process of adjustment to a lower rate of inflation.

Many governments, most prominent among which was the former Conservative government of Mrs Margaret Thatcher, accepted the logic of the above argument and were thereby persuaded to swallow the bitter pill of demand deflation and abnormally high unemployment rates in exchange for the boon of a sustained fall in the rate of inflation. Unfortunately the application of the anti-inflation policies which were associated with this particular interpretation of the NAIRU hypothesis was to expose many unforeseen drawbacks. From the 1970s onwards governments restricted aggregate demand by a variety of means. Although politicians tended to steer clear of acknowledging this aspect of policy too publicly, in their more candid moments they admitted that this cure for inflation went hand in glove with a rise in unemployment above NAIRU. For as long as U remains above NAIRU, inflation should be falling. The catchphrase 'If it isn't hurting, it isn't working' came to epitomize this approach to anti-inflation policy.

Unfortunately the predictions of this very simple hypothesis were not borne out by the facts of subsequent experience.[6] The deflation of aggregate demand and the rise in unemployment did appear to reduce the rate of inflation, but once unemployment had settled down at a higher level, the rate of inflation ceased to fall. An unemployment rate well in excess of what had hitherto been considered to be a stable NAIRU was failing to produce sustained reductions in the rate of inflation beyond the initial impact effect of the fall in aggregate demand. Some critics of the

---

[6]It should be obvious that criticisms of the NAIRU hypothesis apply *a fortiori* to the more extreme natural rate hypothesis.

NAIRU concept hazarded that, if there was any connection at all between unemployment and inflation, it was likely to run from *changes* in the unemployment rate to *changes* in the rate of inflation.[7] Hence rising unemployment should be correlated with falling inflation, but once unemployment has steadied at a new, higher level, so the rate of inflation will also steady at a new, slightly lower, but probably still unsatisfactory level. At the very least the NAIRU hypothesis stands in need of radical modification if it is to serve as a useful guide to the conduct of anti-inflation policy.

There are two alternative ways of reacting to the stylized facts outlined above. The first is to jettison the whole notion of NAIRU. This would certainly accord with a powerful strand of Keynesian opinion in Britain which, from the outset, had regarded the unearthing of the Phillips curve with great circumspection and which, despite the subsequent deluge of econometric studies of the relationship between unemployment, inflation, and inflationary expectations, remained unconvinced that there existed any precise relationship between the rate of increase in money wages and the pressure of aggregate demand. These cost–push Keynesians could look at the bleak unfolding of events from the late 1970s onwards with a justifiable sense of *Schadenfreude*. To a considerable extent I share many of the views of these writers.

However there was a problem which the cost–push explanation of inflation found impossible to surmount, namely, that it does not readily lend itself to rigorous empirical verification. Consider just one instance, one in which there has been, according to a version of the cost–push hypothesis, an intensification of trades union militancy. How on earth does one set about devising a convincing measure of something as impalpable, though nevertheless real, as the degree of trades union militancy? All attempts at providing such a measure have proved to be abortive. Moreover, cost–push writers tend to subscribe to several versions of the same basic hypothesis at one and the same time. It is perfectly possible, for example, to attribute upward pressure on wages to real wage resistance in certain circumstances and to competitive inter-union leapfrogging in other circumstances. Indeed, it is likely that both phenomena will be at work simultaneously within an industrial relations structure such as prevails in Britain where trade unions are anxious not only to protect the real wages of their members from erosion by exogenous price increases but also to preserve their position in the pecking order of wage differentials.

---

[7] The hypothesis that the change in the unemployment rate rather than its absolute level is more important in explaining the dynamics of an inflationary process goes back to the earliest days of the Phillips curve literature.

We saw earlier how such explanations of inflation were greeted with pontifical disdain by monetarists. At one stage writers who subscribed to a cost–push position were in danger of having their economists' union cards taken away from them. The basis for the mainstream dismissal of the cost–push hypothesis concerned, as we indicated, its untestability. The techniques of applied econometrics could not be deployed upon a hypothesis in which most of the relevant variables could not be directly measured and in which the focus of attention was continually shifting – sometimes leapfrogging was the problem, sometimes real wage resistance, sometimes a Marxian class struggle for shares in the national income, but at most times some miscellany of all three problems was present contemporaneously. The grunts of exasperation among applied econometricians were almost audible.

The reaction of the mainstream in macroeconomics was to pursue a second, less extreme line of inquiry. Instead of switching allegiance to the 'unscientific' or, worse still, the 'sociological' cost–push hypothesis,[8] most economists have kept faith with the concept of a determinate NAIRU and have attempted to recast it in a way which would help to explain why NAIRU tends to track the path of the actual unemployment rate so closely. One particular attempt at explaining the troubled experience of the 1980s retained the notion of NAIRU but claimed that NAIRU was not a constant number but depended on the past history of the unemployment rate. The behaviour of NAIRU, which we shall also call the equilibrium unemployment rate, is itself path dependent. Powerful ratchet effects produce a situation in which a sustained rise in unemployment above NAIRU results in a rise in NAIRU itself. Following upon a sustained reduction in aggregate demand, a succession of doors slam shut. Changing metaphor, the equilibrium unemployment rate is seen to be shackled to the actual rate. Only during the transitional period when unemployment is rising will the chain be lengthened somewhat. However once the unemployment rate has stabilized at a new, higher level, so too will the equilibrium rate of unemployment.

This rather skeletal account of the phenomenon of hysteresis, suggesting a connection between the time paths of the actual and the equilibrium

---

[8]Lest he should fall into the trap of thinking that only Keynesians of a certain vintage offend against the canons of scientism, the reader should note the hostility which has long been expressed at the application of naïve scientism in economics by Friedrich Hayek. Hypotheses in economics may be true but intrinsically untestable statistically. Hayek persisted in believing that the neoclassical explanation of the interwar unemployment was correct but untestable. It is ironic to recall that his adversaries in this debate were the Keynesians, though Keynes himself had scant regard for the new discipline of econometrics.

unemployment rates, needs to be substantially fleshed out.[9] Through what mechanisms will a rise in the unemployment rate have only an evanescent impact on the rate of inflation? Three distinct mechanisms feature in the literature on hysteresis:

1. The insider–outsider mechanism.
2. The effect of the growth in numbers of the long-term unemployed on the money wage bargain.
3. The dependence of the size of the capital stock on the degree of capacity utilization and hence on the level of aggregate demand.

Insider–Outsider Effects

Insider–outsider models are a more rigorous articulation of ideas which have been current in one form or another for many years, particularly in British Keynesian circles. Formal insider–outsider models are exemplified in the recent work by Lindbeck and Snower (1986) and Blanchard and Summers (1986).

Insiders are those workers who are currently employed and who are in a position to exercise considerable muscle in the wage bargaining process owing to the major discontinuity between the skills possessed by insiders and the skills possessed by outsiders. Most of the insiders' skills are assumed to be firm specific, acquired over the years and difficult to replicate in the short to medium run. Because of this skill differential between insiders and outsiders, and hence the strong preference of firms to continue to employ insiders, the power of outsiders, who are unemployed, to affect the outcome of the wage bargain struck between firms and insiders is minimal over a significant range of wage changes. The model presented below is a simplified version of that contained in Carlin and Soskice (1990).

Three characteristics describe the behaviour of insiders:

1. Because of the significant skill differential between insiders and outsiders, insiders can be treated at a first approximation as monopolists.

---

[9]We cannot, for want of space, do full justice to the variety of models of hysteresis which have been developed in recent years. Fortunately an excellent collection of seminal papers is contained in R. Cross (1988). Alternatively Carlin and Soskice (1990) provide a clear résumé of the dominant themes in this growing literature.

2. Insiders attempt to maximize the utility only of the representative *employed* worker (that is, the representative insider); they attach no utility to the welfare of unemployed workers (outsiders).
3. Insiders are hermetically sealed from the intrusion of outsiders by the assumption of zero labour turnover.

The demand for labour for all firms, L^D, is a function (a) of the real wage rate, w, and (b) of the level of effective demand for output as a whole, Y^D. A decline in the level of aggregate demand will reduce Y^D, thereby shifting the L^D curve to the left in (w, L) space.[10] Firms set prices as a mark up over average cost. In its simplest form this reduces to equation (8.1):

$$P = (1 + \mu)(W/LP) \tag{8.1}$$

where μ is the fractional mark up and LP is output per worker. If we define the fraction m as

$$m = \mu/(1 + \mu)$$

we obtain

$$W/P = LP - mLP \tag{8.2}$$

In other words, the real wage rate equals output per worker minus real profits per worker. Numerous empirical studies have suggested that both m and LP are invariant with respect to alterations in normal levels of output and employment. Hence equation (8.2) defines a *price determined real wage* (*PRW*) which employers seek to defend from erosion in the face of money-wage demands by insiders in order to protect their real profitability. This price determined real wage is represented in Figure 8.9 by the horizontal line PRW.[11] The initial level of employment for insiders is L_1, determined by the intersection of the PRW line with the initial demand for labour curve, $L(Y_1^D)$. The contraction in aggregate demand brought about through restrictive macroeconomic policies serves to shift the demand for labour curve to a position $L(Y_2^D)$.

What are the wage–price dynamics which ensue from this contraction in aggregate demand? The representative insider now fears that his job, which he had previously assumed to be safe, might now be in jeopardy. He is therefore prepared to countenance a reduction in his real wage so as to stave off the threat of dismissal. Let us assume that insiders are now

---

[10]Note that L^D is the *effective* demand for labour in the sense of Clower, not the notional demand denoted by the symbol L^d above.

[11]There is a close connection between the Carlin and Soskice price determined real wage line and Layard's (1986) feasible real wage line depicted in Figure 6.9.

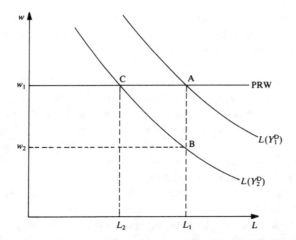

Figure 8.9   Hysteresis as insider–outsider phenomenon

willing to accept a real wage reduction so as to protect their jobs. Figure 8.9 represents this as a fall in the real wage acceptable to the L_1 insiders from w_1 to w_2.[12] If initially money wages and prices were rising at 10% per annum, insiders attempt to reach point B by restricting their money wage claims to, say, 5% per annum, that is, they are willing to accept a 5% cut in real wages. But can they achieve this real wage cut? Can they reach point B, thereby preserving their privileged position as insiders? The answer is negative. The reduction in the rate of increase of money wages will, through the mark up pricing hypothesis, lead to a similar decrease in the rate of price inflation, leaving the real wage rate unchanged at w_1. In other words, instead of preserving a level of insider employment L_1 at a lower real wage rate w_2, the level of employment among insiders falls to L_2 owing to the inability of insiders directly to influence the real wage rate. The number of insiders who are displaced into the pool of outsiders is $(L_1 - L_2)$. Outsiders, even those who were until recently insiders, cannot penetrate the ranks of the insiders and, as a result, can no longer influence the course of wage bargaining. Once the level of insider employment has levelled out at L_2, there is no longer an incentive to moderate the pace of money wage demands which will continue at 5%. The volume of equilibrium unemployment has therefore been swollen by the influx of $(L_1 - L_2)$ former insiders: NAIRU has risen. The key

---

[12]Specific assumptions are being made here regarding the properties of insiders' utility functions. See Carlin and Soskice (1990) for further amplification.

feature of all models of hysteresis is obviously present in the insider–outsider model: it is only during the process of adjustment from a higher to a lower level of employment that there will be significant downward pressure on the rate of increase of money wages and prices.

As was intimated earlier, less formal approaches to the inflationary biases which may be endemic within certain systems of industrial relations have been in circulation among Keynesians for many decades. For many Keynesians, and certainly Keynes himself, the celebrated 'problem of money wages' was essentially one which could only be tackled on a political as opposed to an economic front. Generally speaking the 'political' cure for inflation comprised some form of prices and incomes policy, and was regarded as the only alternative to the less palatable 'economic' cure of demand deflation. In the heady days immediately following the Keynesian revolution, many of Keynes's followers[13] began to express concern at the consequences which might flow from a commitment to full employment. Whereas the massive unemployment which had plagued the interwar period has at least served to keep the lid on money wages, the switch to Keynesian policies, with their emphasis on the objective of maintaining full employment, might open a Pandora's box of inflationary money wage claims. The transformation of the industrial relations climate which would be brought about by adherence to Keynesian principles could produce a potentially catastrophic spiral of money wage increases leading to price increases leading to a build-up of inflationary expectations.

Many Keynesians went further. They argued that, even if governments were prepared to use demand restriction and high unemployment to reduce, or at least to contain, upward pressure on money wages, there was no longer any guarantee that such policies would work. In the British case the problem lay in the structure of collective bargaining. Trades unions, which regarded their principal objective as being to protect the interests of their employed members (insiders), were not particularly moved – public rhetoric apart – by the plight of outsiders. Providing that there was no threat to their members' jobs, trades unions felt that they had a free hand in wage negotiations, often seeming to pluck numbers out of thin air and try it on with employers. A long list of criteria was trundled out to justify the eminent reasonableness of their wage claims: their members had fallen behind in the league table of wage differentials; the cost of living had increased; productivity had risen; firms' profits were

---

[13]This is a group of economists, mainly British, who tended to dominate thinking in the higher reaches of the Civil Service, in Oxbridge, in most of the quality newspapers, and in other organs of opinion, down to the late 1960s.

high and their members were entitled to their 'fair' share. And lurking behind the smokescreen of public utterances justifying their case, there remained that most potent of sanctions, the strike threat, and with it the knowledge that employers would not defy the union by taking on and training outsiders to fill the boots of striking insiders. The problem, neatly summarized by Blackaby (1980), was that Britain's collective bargaining structure lay betwixt and between two polar extremes: at one extreme was the highly centralized system which was prevalent in some countries of continental Europe; at the other extreme was the model of atomistic competition in labour markets which appeared to feature only in textbooks. Britain's union structure was one of a series of 'fragmented monopolies', each monopoly looking over its shoulder at other monopolies and exploiting the comparison whenever it was to its advantage. The behaviour of these fragmented monopolies is unlikely to be affected by abnormally high levels of unemployment. Admittedly the zeal with which trades unions seek to achieve increases in the money wages of their members is likely to be tempered in times of rising unemployment, an outcome which is also predicted in the more formal models of hysteresis. The difference between the old Keynesian and the new Keynesian approaches[14] arises from the latter's retention, albeit in radically modified form, of the notion of an equilibrium unemployment rate, and the former's wholesale rejection of the usefulness of the NAIRU concept.

Hysteresis and the long-term unemployed

A second line of inquiry focuses on the role played by the long-term unemployed in the wage bargaining process. Statistically there appears to exist a stable relationship between the proportion of the long-term unemployed in the total unemployment rate, denoted by the symbol LT, and the actual unemployment rate. This relationship is represented in Figure 8.10. A rise in the unemployment rate from U_1 to U_2 tends to raise the proportion of that rate consisting of the long-term unemployed from LT_1 to LT_2. Enter the distinguishing behavioural hypothesis of this version of the hysteresis model: the higher the proportion of long-term unemployment in overall unemployment, the smaller will be the impact of any given unemployment rate upon the bargaining power of trades unions.

---

[14]The new Keynesian school should not be confused with the 'neo-Keynesian' or 'post-Keynesian' schools.

Perhaps the simplest way of showing how the statistical regularity depicted in Figure 8.10 interacts with this behavioural hypothesis is to consider a modified version of Figure 6.9 derived from Layard (1986). The feasible real wage line, FRW, is, to all intents and purposes, identical to the price determined real wage line of Carlin and Soskice. For a given value for LT, there will be a unique inverse relationship between the target real wage, TRW, and the unemployment rate. The intersection of the TRW curve with the FRW line determines the value of NAIRU. Hence, if the proportion of long-term unemployment is 20%, the value of NAIRU will be $NAIRU_1$. Let us now suppose that the government, unhappy with what it considers to be an unacceptably high rate of inflation, embarks on a policy of demand contraction, which produces as its inevitable side effect a rise in unemployment. From the statistical regularity between U and LT depicted in Figure 8.10, we infer that the proportion of long-term unemployment rises to, say, 40% of the total unemployment rate. This has the effect of shifting the TRW curve to the right and of raising the value of NAIRU to $NAIRU_2$.

The reasoning behind this prediction runs as follows. The most active participants on the supply side of the labour market comprise those workers who are already in employment and those workers who, though not currently in employment, have only been unemployed for relatively short periods of time and are anxious to regain employment at the earliest opportunity. By contrast, the long-term unemployed have effectively dropped out of active participation in the labour market. The passage of time has led to a deskilling of the long-term unemployed, a relentless depreciation of human capital in the face of changing technological requirements; it leads to increased demoralization among the long-term unemployed as, week after week, their attempts to find jobs prove to be fruitless; the work ethic becomes more remote, being progressively supplanted by an alternative culture of dependency which eventually ceases to attract social stigma.

These negative effects on the supply side of the labour market will be reinforced on the demand side by a reluctance among employers to recruit new workers from among the ranks of the long-term unemployed. A worker's unemployment record becomes a form of screening device for employers who consider workers with a record of only short-term unemployment to be safer bets than the long-term unemployed. Many employers regard the long-term unemployed with suspicion: is there anything *wrong* with a worker who has been so consistently turned down by other employers? In all events the combined influence of negative effects on both the supply side and on the demand side of the labour market render the long-term unemployed increasingly irrelevant when it comes to determining the outcome of collective bargaining. They have become outsiders with a vengeance.

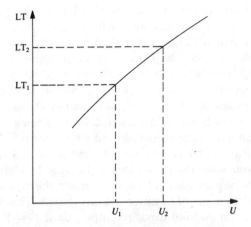

Figure 8.10 Relationship between U and LT

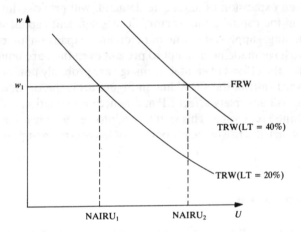

Figure 8.11 NAIRU and the long-term unemployed

Capital scrapping and the rise in NAIRU

In most macroeconomic models it is normally assumed that the size of the capital stock is exogenously given by investment decisions which stretch back over decades. However there is one model of hysteresis which critically turns on the relaxation of this assumption, treating the capital stock as an endogenous variable, its size being determined mainly by the degree of capacity utilization. The argument is fairly straightforward, though it can be refined and elaborated in a variety of directions.[15] Following Malinvaud (1980) we shall compare three numbers: Y, Y_c and Y_F which correspond to actual output, normal full capacity output, and full employment output respectively. The conventional Keynesian model assumes that $Y_F = Y_c$: if the labour force is fully employed, so too will be the capital stock, though not *vice versa*. For Malinvaud, general unemployment is Keynesian when $Y < Y_F \leq Y_c$ and is classical when $Y = Y_c < Y_F$. In other words unemployment is classical when a capacity constraint impedes an expansion of output and employment.[16] Malinvaud points out that an economy may initially find itself in a state of Keynesian unemployment but that, in the face of prolonged underutilization of capacity which the persistence of this state entails, the capital stock will shrink through the impact of negative net investment. This has the effect of lowering Y_c, normal full capacity output, until $Y = Y_c < Y_F$. What started off as Keynesian unemployment has ended up as classical unemployment. A sustained restriction of demand, pushing Y below Y_c and Y_F, has once again slammed doors shut. A reversal of policy, taking the form of an expansion of aggregate demand, will provoke inflation, particularly in the capital goods sector, since a deficient capital stock is now the binding supply-side constraint on the expansion of output. Although we have made no attempt to present even the bare bones of a formal model, the effects of capital shrinkage are probably best depicted by a downward shift in the FRW line in Figure 8.11: the decline in the capital stock will adversely affect LP and hence, via equation (8.2), the price determined real wage. This shift will reinforce the upward pressure on NAIRU which the rise in the proportion of long-term unemployed will exert.

Prices and quantities

One of the more positive contributions to the debate on macroeconomic policy which the monetarist counter-revolution produced was to highlight an already glaring deficiency in the *IS–LM* model: the fix-price restriction which is normally imposed on this model necessarily implies that alterations in the level of nominal demand will manifest themselves exclusively in the form of changes in the level of real income. In terms of Keynes's 'generalized quantity theory of money', e_Y, the elasticity of real

---

[15]See Carlin and Soskice (1990) for their own version of the capital scrapping model.

[16]The reader should note that the classical unemployment referred to in this context differs from that in the previous section where an excessive real wage, rather than a deficient capital stock, is responsible for classical unemployment.

income with respect to nominal demand, is equal to unity. At the other extreme, the naïve quantity theory of money imposed the restriction that $e_Y = 0$ and hence that e_P, the elasticity of the absolute price level with respect to nominal demand, is equal to unity. Typically the initial state of an economy will lie somewhere between these two extremes, neither languishing in a deep Keynesian recession nor hitting up against a state of classical full employment.

So the question remains: how will a given increase in nominal demand be divided between an increase in real income and an increase in the price level? At the end of Chapter 4 we hazarded that e_Y would be much larger than e_P when there is widespread unemployment; that e_P would rise as aggregate demand rose; that there would exist a critical level of aggregate demand where $e_Y = e_P = 1/2$; and that e_P would tend to unity, and e_Y to zero, as full employment was approached.

This conjecture sounds intuitively plausible but it really does not cast much light on why these elasticities should assume certain values at different levels of activity. What we require is a series of hypotheses which would explain the stylized fact summarized by Nordhaus (1983): '[T]he evidence for the United States is that the short-run division of nominal demand shocks between quantities and prices is closer to 90-10 than the 10-90 or 0-100 envisaged by other paradigms.' To state the question rather differently, why is it that prices, and in particular the level of money wages, are so insensitive to changes in nominal demand? In Britain in the early 1990s, this seemingly esoteric question is being addressed as a matter of urgency by politicians who usually fight shy of venturing into the rarefied arena of macroeconomic debate. Professional economists who had been closely associated with the monetarist experiment a decade earlier can be seen scratching their heads in bafflement at the lack of success of a prolonged period of monetary restraint in substantially reducing the pace of money wage increase. Nowadays one reads more and more about the old-fashioned 'problem of money wages' from the most unlikely sources. The hysteresis literature discussed in the previous section obviously dovetails into a more wide-ranging inquiry into the sources of money wage–price rigidity in the face of significant alterations in nominal demand.

Implicit contracts as a source of wage rigidity

According to the continuous market clearing postulate of the new classical macroeconomics, random fluctuations in the demand for labour should manifest themselves principally in variations in the real wage rate and not in the level of employment. (Recall the assumption that the long-run supply of labour is inelastic with respect to the real wage rate.) In practice, however, we observe wide fluctuations in the level of employment and comparatively small variations in real wages. Why should this be? More specifically, is it possible to explain the relative stability of the real wage within the conventional neoclassical paradigm of optimizing agents?

It is to this latter question that implicit contract models are addressed. Starting with the pioneering work of Baily (1974) and Azariadis (1975), these models are at once simple and far fetched. The analysis starts at the level of the individual firm and its employees, building up to the level of the economy as a whole by assuming that firms and workers in the aggregate behave in much the same way as individual firms and individual groups of workers. The firm and its workers consult with each other to arrive at an implicit understanding or contract concerning the set of permissible reactions of the firm to changed market circumstances. What are grandiloquently referred to as 'alterations in the state of nature' turn out, on closer inspection, to be variations in the demand for the firm's product. Both the firm and the union know from past experience that these fluctuations in demand occur from time to time. Workers are risk averse and seek to dampen the instability of income which fluctuations in product demand could bring in their wake. The absence of complete insurance markets denies workers of access to the capital market, thereby forcing them to look elsewhere for insurance cover. What more obvious source of insurance is there than the firm that gives them employment? They therefore agree with their employers, who are assumed to be less risk averse than workers, to draw up a wage–employment package which would provide a form of insurance cover for a set of different 'states of nature'. Firms and workers enter into unwritten – implicit – contracts to guarantee a greater stability of income for workers. The employer willingly enters into such contracts since the negotiated wage will be less than the marginal product of labour. Hence the employer is able, during normal times, to cream off this discrepancy which is, in essence, the insurance premium paid by workers. Typically implicit contracts will entail much greater stability of real wages and corresponding instability of employment than the standard auction model would predict. Workers voluntarily enter into contracts in which they recognize *ex ante* the firm's right to lay some of them off during hard times.

An enormous and technically complex literature has grown up around implicit contract theory to which it would be impossible to do justice in a book of this nature. We shall make only two observations regarding the original model. First, the type of unemployment which the model attempts to explain is not involuntary unemployment in the sense of Keynes. Workers enter into implicit contracts with their eyes wide open.

The fact that, as a result of entering into these contracts, they are accepting the distinct possibility of being laid off in hard times points to the voluntary nature of such unemployment. Of course, every *ex ante* decision has its *ex post* corollary, so that workers who find themselves laid off *ex post* could be ruing the day that they entered into the implicit contract; but it is only in this very limited sense that they can be regarded as involuntarily unemployed.

The second observation is far more fundamental and once again calls into question the 'involuntariness' of the unemployment which implicit contract theory attempts to explain. It is an essential tenet of Keynesian theory that, on a macroeconomic level, neither workers nor employers are in a position to exercise *any* discretion in setting the real-wage rate. Implicit contract theorists appear to have fallen into exactly the same macro/micro confusion which, decades earlier, had bedevilled Pigou's theory of labour market adjustment. A large part of Keynes's *General Theory* was devoted to exposing the various fallacies of composition in classical economics which had illegitimately inferred that what held true in the small also held true in the large. Adam Smith's analysis of the effects of an increase in the propensity to save ('What is prudence in the conduct of every private family can scarce be folly in that of a great Kingdom') and Pigou's analysis of labour market adjustment are two of the best known examples of fallacies of composition in classical macroeconomics. By starting their analysis at the level of the individual firm, and then by assuming that the behaviour of firms in the aggregate was similar to the behaviour of individual firms writ large, implicit contract theory falls victim to confusing money-wage adjustment with real wage adjustment. Implicit contract theory has virtually nothing to say on this vital distinction which lies at the heart of the successful transition from micro to macro analysis. On a microeconomic level, an adjustment in money wages *is* an adjustment in real wages on account of the enabling stipulation of *ceteris paribus*. On a macroeconomic level, however, *cetera* certainly do not remain *pares*: for Keynes, the only 'wage' which can be directly influenced in the wage bargain is the money wage. Voluntary, cooperative actions on the part of workers and employers can have no direct effect on the real wage. At best, implicit contract models provide a possible rationale for money wage stickiness in the face of substantial fluctuations in employment.

However, to those with even a nodding acquaintance of how wage bargains are struck between employers and workers, these models fly in the face of observation and experience. If the search is on for the sources of money wage inflexibility, the redoubtable energies of researchers in this field could profitably be redirected towards Keynes's embryonic treatment of this question in the *General Theory*. The high degree of interdependence between Blackaby's 'fragmented monopolies' in the labour market, coupled with prisoners' dilemma choices facing each monopoly, impart a substantial degree of downward inflexibility to *money* wages, but, as Keynes repeatedly emphasized, such inflexibility had nothing whatever to do with *real* wage inflexibility nor with the cognate origins of *general* unemployment.

Inflexible product prices

One of the most enduring propositions in macroeconomics, surviving even the turbulent experience of the 1980s, is the hypothesis that firms, particularly those in the manufacturing sector, do not fix the price of their output 'competitively', but resort instead to conventional or habitual rules of thumb. The most widely investigated rule of thumb is the mark up pricing mechanism: prices are fixed as a mark up over average costs, this latter variable often being 'normalized' by reference to a benchmark level of economic activity (the 'normal cost pricing' hypothesis). The simplest version of mark up pricing has already been touched upon in the form of equation (8.1).

$$P = (1 + \mu)(W/LP) \tag{8.1}$$

An important characteristic of equation (8.1) is the absence of any term summarizing the pressure of demand for commodities. Thus, when the demand for their products rises, firms do not respond by raising μ, thereby taking advantage of a short-run opportunity for extra profit. They run down inventories and, beyond a certain point, raise output. If the combination of inventory decumulation and an increased scale of output still fails to satisfy the higher demand for output, firms ration supply according to a variety of criteria: perhaps they favour long-standing customers or perhaps they introduce a first come first served method of allocation. In all events the rise in demand elicits quantity responses and not price responses.[17]

Mark up pricing has both fascinated and baffled macroeconomists for many decades. In the 1950s Gardner Ackley had referred to mark up pricing as 'a phenomenon in search of a hypothesis' – it obviously existed in a wide range of markets, but its origins were hard to explain within the framework of traditional price theory. One of the leading American

---

[17] Of course, to the extent that higher product demand may be accompanied by increased tightness in the labour market, there may be some upward pressure on prices arising from the correlative upward pressure on money wages.

Keynesian economists of his generation, the late Arthur Okun (1981), pointed to the origins of Ackley's 'phenomenon' of administered pricing in what he called 'customer markets'. Unlike auction markets, where alterations in the balance between demand and supply produce corresponding alterations in prices, customer markets are characterized by the elusive concept of 'fairness' in the relationship between sellers (firms) and buyers (customers). A sudden increase in the demand for commodities clearly presents sellers with the opportunity for extra profit, but sellers in customer markets forgo this opportunity since to do otherwise would constitute an unacceptable breach of the implicit contract binding sellers to buyers. To increase prices in such circumstances would be generally regarded as exploitative, as 'unfair'. By contrast an increase in costs, most notably caused by an increase in money wages, is generally regarded as sufficient justification for increased prices. The application of a conventional rule of thumb in setting the prices of commodities in the face of changing cost conditions is generally accepted as 'fair'. In such circumstances the most widely applied convention will therefore be mark up pricing.

Much of the research into why money wages and product prices appear to be insensitive to variations in nominal demand has been conducted by economists who would generally accept the tag of new Keynesian. The feature which distinguishes new Keynesians from their predecessors of three decades earlier is the former's keen perception of the need to furnish adequate microeconomic foundations for the Keynesian principle of effective demand. New Keynesians abandon the standard Walrasian auction model in favour of other models characterized by the market structures of imperfect competition and monopoly. Earlier Keynesians were often loftily dismissive of the microfoundations of macroeconomics, quoting with obvious approval Gerald Shove's famous put-down remark 'Maynard never spent the twenty minutes necessary to understand the theory of value'. Whatever the truth of this remark in respect of Keynes, the new Keynesians are clearly not guilty of such an oversight.

The initial impetus for the development of new Keynesian models came from the failure of the new classical, market clearing models to explain movements in output, employment and inflation in the United States and Europe during the 1970s, the 1980s and, *a fortiori*, the early 1990s. Old Keynesian macroeconomics, with its arbitrary stipulation of given money wages, was clearly ill equipped to fill the vacuum. The search was on for the sources of wage–price rigidities which could be reconciled with the assumption of rational, maximizing agents. Models of imperfect competition were obviously much better suited to the task than the neo-Walrasian models favoured by the new classical macroeconomics.

, Nevertheless, although this research programme could prove to be highly productive in casting further light on the dynamics of inflationary processes, I must express a lingering reservation: why do new Keynesians feel the need to rationalize the prevalence of nominal price rigidities? It appears that, in new Keynesian models, nominal demand disturbances manifest themselves in the form òf changes in real variables *only because* nominal prices are inflexible. It follows that, if only nominal prices *were* sufficiently flexible, demand induced fluctuations in output and employment would be very small indeed. But the reader will recall from Chapter 5 how, in a closed economy, this conclusion rests principally upon the combined strength of the Keynes effect and the real-balance effect. Until recently it had been assumed that these two effects, though of considerable theoretical interest, were very weak in practice. No compelling theoretical or empirical reasons have been adduced hitherto which might require a revision of this view.

Conclusion

The analytical distinction between classical and Keynesian unemployment is a clear advance on the simple Keynesian approach which had assumed that all unemployment of a macroeconomic nature could only be attributed to a deficiency of aggregate demand. In certain circumstances, general unemployment can be classical in origin, being the result of excessively high real wages. Indeed, as Coen and Hickman have pointed out, the two forms of unemployment are not mutually exclusive and could exist side by side. As economies become more open and as the world economy takes further steps to a return to a system of fixed but adjustable exchange rates, the probability of classical unemployment becoming more widespread in countries with abnormally high rates of wage inflation rises considerably. Britain in the early 1990s is a classic case in point. One way of looking at a devaluation of a currency is to view it as a back door method of keeping an economy's real wages in line with those prevailing among its competitors. The abandonment of floating exchange rates effectively closes this back door.[18]

---

[18]At the time of writing – summer, 1991 – this question is one of great political acrimony and recrimination in Britain. Entry into the Exchange Rate Mechanism of the European Monetary System had been forced upon Margaret Thatcher by her Chancellor of the Exchequer and her Foreign Secretary. According to Nicholas Ridley, one of her most ardent supporters, Mrs Thatcher had set her face against entry into a system in which British sovereignty over the conduct of its macroeconomic policies would have to be seriously curbed. Once one has cut through all of the political flimflammery with which Mr Ridley's recently published memoirs are liberally peppered – pistols to the head, treachery, back stabbing and similar manner of macabre metaphor – it appears that the aspect of 'sovereignty' which Mrs Thatcher and her allies were so eager to protect from foreign interference was the ability to devalue sterling when the occasion demanded it.

Nevertheless our discussion of the distinction between classical and Keynesian unemployment was defective in one critical respect: it assumed away the problem of inflation. At a time when policy makers put the conquest of inflation at the top of their macroeconomic agenda, economists must come clean about the inflationary consequences of the different courses of action which they recommend to reduce unemployment.

In the section on hysteresis we examined the attempts which have been made to explain what, at first sight, was the breakdown of the relationship between inflation and unemployment which the original NAIRU hypothesis suggested. The idea that the time path of NAIRU was itself path dependent on the actual unemployment rate opens up an alarming prospect in which demand management policies alone will have only a transitory impact on the rate of inflation. Perhaps other policies will have to be tried – or retried – such as prices and incomes policies, though the British experience is not one to inspire confidence in the efficacy of such policies.

In the final section we continued our discussion of some of the sources of rigidities in money wages and prices. Many writers in this field are deeply pessimistic over the prospects of reducing inflation through policies of unaided demand restriction. The late Arthur Okun had long been an advocate of some form of incomes policy, though the short-lived and ultimately pyrrhic triumph of monetarism had appeared to cast him in an increasingly isolated light. Although the advocates of incomes policies readily acknowledge their less than glorious track record, particularly in Britain,[19] they persist in the view that some method for directly moderating inflationary money wage claims must be found. In response to the TINA acronym prompted by Mrs Margaret Thatcher's 'There is no alternative' remark, they aver that there has to be an alternative to mass unemployment in taming the inflationary tiger. That this alternative may be riddled with certain bureaucratic inefficiencies does not, *ipso facto*, rule it out of court. There could be no greater contrast than between the optimism of the monetarists in the early 1970s, who estimated the output and employment of loss of a successful anti-inflation

---

[19]Britain has long been regarded as the testing ground for rival economic theories. J. K. Galbraith, in an amusing and thoroughly mischievous newspaper interview, considered that the choice of Britain as a guinea-pig to be injected with the monetarist virus verged on the divinely inspired on account of its robust social structure and its concomitant distaste for violent revolutionary upheaval.

programme to be relatively modest,[20] and the pragmatic approach of modern Keynesians who take the world as they find it, warts and all, and strive to find solutions to messy problems bequeathed by an indifferent, capricious past.

---

[20]As late as 1980 both Milton Friedman and David Laidler, in their evidence to the British House of Commons Treasury and Civil Service Committee, were sceptical of suggestions that there would be large output and employment losses resulting from a monetary contraction. By one of those quirky ironies of history the collected evidence of this Select Committee was published just at the time when the monetary restriction that they had been advocating was about to plunge the British economy into the worst recession in its post-war history. At the time of writing Britain seems to be poised on the brink of an even deeper recession.

9

Concluding observations

Although I have attempted in the preceding eight chapters to keep the use of the first person singular to a bare minimum, I feel that, in this concluding chapter, I may be allowed a certain latitude to give a personal gloss on some of the matters arising from the body of the book.

Keynes versus the classics once again

Hicks's celebrated 1937 essay in *Econometrica* in which he introduced his version of the *IS–LM* system had the twin objectives, first of reducing the disparate and often confusing elements of Keynes's *General Theory* to a manageable form; and secondly, of providing a framework within which one may contrast the Keynesian and the classical approach to macroeconomics. It is this later objective which I should like to subject to further scrutiny here.

From the earliest days, many Keynesians, most vociferously the Cambridge branch of the family, had complained that the *IS–LM* model was a travesty of Keynes's ideas. They poured scorn on Hicks's model, accusing its author of omitting certain vital aspects of the *General Theory* and, worse still, of playing straight into the hands of Keynes's classical opponents. Much ink has been spilled in heaping opprobrium on what Joan Robinson called 'bastard Keynesianism'.

So, for what it is worth, here is my twopennyworth. The Keynesian purists are misguided in their criticism of Hicks's model since the *IS–LM* system *does* contain many of the quintessential innovations of the *General Theory*. Indeed I have a nagging suspicion that Keynes himself was a bit of a bastard Keynesian.

The aspect of the *IS–LM* system which has been a persistent source of unease for me lies, not in its misrepresentation of Keynes's ideas – an impressive amount of the *General Theory* has been successfully captured in this simple, two-dimensional diagram – but in the inadequate treatment of the classical position. We saw in Chapter 4 how it was virtually impossible to portray most of the central classical insights within the confines of a model which was devised, first and foremost, as a didactic construct to expose Keynes's ideas to a wider audience. The classical case is particularly badly served in textbooks which impose certain elasticity conditions on the *IS* and *LM* curves to highlight the difference between Keynes and the classics.

Figures 9.1(a) and (b) purport to expose the essential distinction between classical and Keynesian approaches to macroeconomics. Keynesians are supposed to believe that the *LM* curve is non-vertical (9.1(a)), reflecting the hypothesis that the demand for money is elastic with respect to the rate of interest, whereas classical writers are supposed to believe that the *LM* curve is a vertical line (9.1(b)), reflecting the rival hypothesis that the interest elasticity of the demand for money is zero. Moreover, although the *IS* curve is downward sloping in both (a) and (b), in the Keynesian case the slope of the *IS* curve is usually much steeper than in the classical case: Keynesians are normally thought of as 'elasticity pessimists', that is, they play down the influence of prices (the interest rate in this case) on quantities (the rate of investment).

The impropriety of portraying the workings of the classical model by reference to the *IS–LM* system can best be appreciated by considering the chain of reasoning behind the construction of the *IS* curve. We start by asking the following hypothetical question: what would be the repercussions of a fall in the rate of interest from r_1 to r_2? The Keynesian answer is simple: investment expenditure rises, leading to a multiplier effect on income, which, in turn, raises saving by an amount just sufficient to fund the rise in investment. The slope of the *IS* curve thus reflects (a) the interest elasticity of the investment decision and (b) the magnitude of the investment multiplier. It is hard to conceive of a construct which is *more* Keynesian than the *IS* curve.

Classical writers would have approached the question from a very different angle. For a start they would have inquired into the reasons behind the fall in the rate of interest from r_1 to r_2. In the classical system such a fall in the rate of interest could only come about either through a decline in the desire to invest or through an increase in the desire to save. Let us assume that there has been an increase in the desire to save. The saving schedule in (r, S) space has been bodily displaced from S_1 to S_2. The resulting excess supply of investible funds rapidly depresses the rate of interest until a new natural interest rate, r_2, is established. Investment

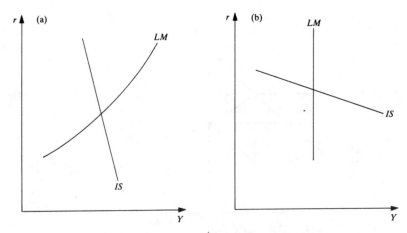

Figure 9.1   (a) The 'Keynesian' case; (b) the 'classical' case

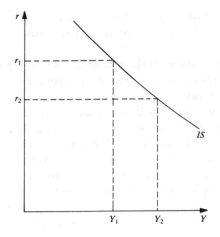

Figure 9.2   Logic behind the *IS* curve

expenditure will rise ($\Delta I > 0$) but this will be matched by an equal fall in consumption (i.e. $\Delta C < 0$ and $\Delta I = -\Delta C$). In other words, despite the fall in the rate of interest from r_1 to r_2, the overall levels of real expenditure and real income remain unchanged ($\Delta Y = 0$). We cannot perceive anything of a downward sloping *IS* curve emerging from this particular exercise. In fact the classical *IS* curve will be vertical. The increase in the desire to save reduces the natural interest rate from r_1 to r_2

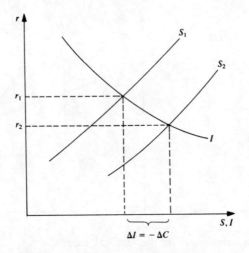

Figure 9.3   Classical theory of interest once again

at an unchanged level of income, Y_1. Once again we see the rate of interest playing its role as one of the two most important shock absorbers in the classical system.

The second critical shock absorber is the real wage rate. In Figure 9.4 the level of income Y_1 – and hence the position of the vertical *IS* curve – is determined by the real wage rate.

It is clear from the top panel in Figure 9.5 that, since the real wage rate w_1 is in excess of the market clearing real wage rate w^*, the resultant levels of employment and output are below their full employment values i.e. $L_1 < L^*$ and $Y_1 < Y^*$. In such circumstances classical theory predicts that, in a competitive labour market, there will be a tendency for the real wage to fall towards w^* and for employment and output to rise towards L^* and Y^* respectively. Moreover, as national income rises towards Y^*, the vertical *IS* line will shift to the right until it comes to rest in a position $IS(w^*)$ in Figure 9.6.

The above analysis enables us to draw an even sharper distinction between the weak and the strong versions of Say's Law: for a level of income $Y_1 < Y^*$, alterations in the desires to save or invest produce movements up or down the vertical *IS* curve $IS(w_1)$ at an unchanged level of income (the weak version of Say's Law); alterations in the real wage rate, leading to the eventual elimination of the gap between w and w^*, will shift the *IS* curve to a position $IS(w^*)$ (the strong version of Say's Law).

Clearly the only variable which is capable of altering the position of the *IS* curve in the classical system is the value of the real wage rate. Any attempt to reduce unemployment through a fiscal expansion (e.g.

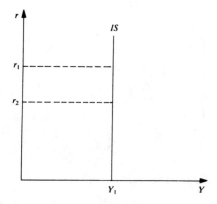

Figure 9.4 'Classical' *IS* curve

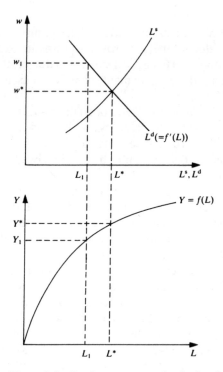

Figure 9.5 Real-wage rate as shock absorber

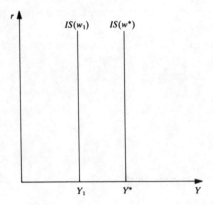

Figure 9.6 The real wage rate and the 'classical' *IS* curve

through a rise in G) is doubly damned since (a) such an expansion simply raises the natural interest rate and thereby crowds out private expenditure (this is the Treasury view); and (b) a fiscal expansion does nothing to attack the root cause of general unemployment, namely, an excessively high real wage rate.

I hope that this example exposes how ill equipped the *IS–LM* model is in highlighting the differences between Keynes and his classical adversaries. From 1937 onwards the cards had been stacked heavily against the classical system. I still consider that system to be fatally flawed, but my grounds for reaching this conclusion do not rest on any putative difference of *a priori* restriction regarding the elasticities of the *IS* and *LM* curves. Indeed, it is curious how Milton Friedman, that champion of a return to classical methods of analysis, should have chosen to do battle with the Keynesians on ground which so favoured his opponents. We saw earlier how Friedman (1974a) proposed a 'common model', the elements of which would, he thought, be acceptable to Keynesians and monetarists alike. The common model turned out to be the various equations which defined the *IS* and *LM* curves. As we pointed out in Chapter 4, the *IS–LM* system is one equation short. Friedman claimed that it is in the provision of this missing equation where the essential differences between Keynesians and monetarists are supposed to reside: Keynesians assume that the price level is fixed ($P = P_0$) and that real income is the variable to be determined, while monetarists assume that the level of real income is fixed ($Y = Y^*$) and that the price level is the variable to be determined. By following this procedure, Friedman was simply arbitrarily swapping one model-closing stipulation for another within the basically Keynesian framework of the *IS–LM* system.

An adequate exposition of the logic behind classical macroeconomics should be conducted using classical, not Keynesian, methods of analysis. By strapping the classical system to the procrustean bed of the *IS–LM* model, Hicks concealed so much that was interesting and distinctive in classical macroeconomics that he unwittingly erected barriers to a proper appreciation of modes of thought which had dominated economics for well over two centuries.

Keynes and money

Two contradictory claims are often made in relation to the treatment of money in Keynesian economics. The first is the monetarist assertion that Keynesians downgraded the role of monetary policy to such an extent that its influence was regarded as, at best, subordinate and ancillary to fiscal policy and, at worst, was discounted altogether. Depressing vistas of liquidity traps and interest-inelastic expenditure propensities are opened up to justify this claim. We saw in Chapter 4 how, despite the back of an envelope doodlings of a few of his followers, Keynes himself was not an elasticity pessimist. Nevertheless he insisted that an expansionary monetary policy would only be successful (a) to the extent that the increase in the supply of money was accompanied by a significant fall in the rate of interest; and (b) to the extent that the fall in the rate of interest succeeded in stimulating private expenditures, most notably investment expenditure. In all events Keynes, despite his earlier total immersion in and adherence to the traditional quantity theory of money, came to regard changes in the supply of money as being of little intrinsic importance. Given his background in Cambridge monetary theory, he would have *understood* the primacy of place accorded to the supply of money in monetarist models, but the mature Keynes would have – and did – reject it.

The second claim is almost the polar opposite to the first. Many Keynesians assert that the market failures pinpointed in Keynesian economics arise from the fact that modern economies are money using. Thus demand deficient unemployment is a 'monetary phenomenon'. This is a theme which suffuses much of the more esoteric literature on Keynesian economics, which I have had, and occasionally still have, some difficulty in grasping. Certainly Keynes himself conceived of a money using economy as operating in a very different manner from that of a barter economy. Early drafts of the *General Theory* were entitled *A Monetary Theory of Production*. But how can aggregate demand failures only occur in a money using economy? Which are the characteristics distinguishing money using economies from barter economies that give rise to the possibility of unemployment equilibrium? We shall consider two cases, both of which figure prominently in the *General Theory*, in which the existence of money both as a means of exchange and as a store of value may account for aggregate demand failures.

Real and money wages

In a barter economy, workers are, by definition, paid in kind. If there is a pool of unemployed workers who wish to work for real wages marginally below the current rate, competition between the employed and the unemployed will depress the real wage, thereby ensuring that the eventual outcome will be one of full employment. The essential feature of the above mechanism which produces this happy state of affairs is that the real wage rate is directly under the control of workers and employers. Providing there are no barriers to entry in the labour market, an initial state of unemployment will be eliminated as a result of workers revising the real wage rate downwards. The distinction between real and money wages is obviously meaningless in barter. Since, in a barter system, competitive forces would tend to eliminate divergences between the supply of and the demand for labour through variations in the real wage rate, Keynes tended to refer to a barter economy as a *real wage economy*: in such an economy, the real wage is directly negotiable between employers and workers.

This is not true of a money using economy where the distinction between money wages and real wages is of paramount importance. The means of exchange function of money severs the link between changes in money wages and changes in real wages. It is hard to exaggerate the contextual significance of this severance for Keynes's critique of Pigou's theory of labour market adjustment. Even if the labour market is competitive, Keynes maintained that excess supply in the labour market would depress the general level of money wages, but would do nothing to nudge the real wage downwards towards its market clearing level on account of the ensuing 'balanced deflation' of money wages and prices. A large part of Chapter 5 is given over to Keynes's analysis of this matter, so little more need be said here, apart from repeating that it is the inability of workers and employers to influence the level of real wages directly which makes Keynesian unemployment *in*voluntary.

Keynes's monetary theory of interest

Compared with the turmoil which surrounded the 'liquidity preference versus loanable funds' debate in the two decades following the publication of the *General Theory*, one hears very little nowadays of the theory of interest. Not so in Keynes's day. It may seem strange to the modern reader, but the validity or otherwise of Keynes's theory of interest was seen to be a matter of vital importance in forming one's attitude towards the Keynesian revolution. So what made the liquidity preference theory of interest such an integral part of Keynesian economics? To answer this question we need to consider its rival, the classical theory of interest, the essentials of which were outlined in Chapter 2. If the classical theory of interest is correct, all shocks which, for Keynesians, threaten to lead to changes in the levels of output and employment, will spend themselves entirely in the form of alterations in the natural rate of interest. The rate of interest is, as we have seen, one of the principal shock absorbers in the classical system: alterations in the rate of interest ensure continuous equality between *ex ante* investment and saving at unchanged levels of real income.

But what would happen if the rate of interest failed to perform this delicate balancing act, not because of any *ad hoc* assumption of price sluggishness, but because the rate of interest is determined by factors extrinsic to the market for investible funds? If the rate of interest is first and foremost determined by considerations of liquidity preference, a sudden increase in the desire to save will not put downward pressure on the natural rate of interest. A discrepancy opens up between the desire to save and the desire to invest which leads to a decline in real income, this decline continuing until equality between *ex ante* investment and saving is restored at a lower level of real income. The 'failure' of the rate of interest to maintain continuous equilibrium between investment and saving at unchanged levels of income is not the result of any inefficiencies or frictions in the market for investible funds which prevent the interest rate from falling sufficiently rapidly. Rather it is the result of the fundamental Keynesian proposition that the rate of interest is determined in a separate market, the market for *stocks* of financial assets of differing degrees of maturity. The 'stock' principle dominates the 'flow' principle. The implications of the dominance of the stock principle over the flow principle are illustrated in Figure 4.5 of Chapter 4. The monetary theory of interest is an indispensable part of the principle of effective demand: without it the quantity adjustments arising from exogenous shocks could not occur.

Sundry reflections on monetarism, inflation and unemployment

Money and inflation

Though monetarism has often been viewed as a monolithic approach to monetary theory and policy, it has, in fact, developed in a variety of directions, not all of them compatible with each other. Two distinct strands in the development of monetarism will concern us in this subsection. The first, which we may call the traditional version of monetarism, postulates a link between changes in the money supply and changes in absolute prices which has at its core the intervening influence of the pressure of aggregate demand. The claim that inflation is 'always and everywhere a monetary phenomenon' can thus be decomposed into two more elementary propositions: (a) that changes in the money supply or in the rate of monetary expansion are the most important determinants of changes in the level of aggregate demand; (b) that increases in the rate of inflation are the consequence of the authorities' attempts to run the economy at 'excessive' levels of aggregate demand, that is, at unemployment rates which are below the natural rate of unemployment, U^*. In other words recklessly expansionary monetary policies produce a state of excess demand in commodity and factor markets, the rise in aggregate demand being mirrored in the fall in the unemployment rate below U^*. Moreover the fact that U has been pushed below U^* leads to an increase in the rate of price inflation on account of the $f(U)$ component of the expectations augmented Phillips curve $dP/P = f(U) + (dP/P)^e$. Proposition (b) is, in essence, a more elaborate and sophisticated version of Keynes's theory of the inflationary gap where U^* corresponds to a state of overall full employment and the magnitude $(U^* - U)$ is an indicator of the extent of the inflationary gap.

Keynesians could – and did – dispute both propositions (a) and (b). For Keynesians other variables, most notably the size of the budget deficit and the levels of interest rates, exerted a more powerful influence on aggregate demand than changes in the money supply or the rate of monetary expansion. Furthermore, although inflation could be the result of excess demand in certain circumstances, more typically it was the result of cost–push influences on the level and the rate of change of money wages at levels of economic activity well below what could reasonably be thought of as corresponding to full employment levels of activity. In other words, there existed no precise relationship between the pressure of aggregate demand and the rate of inflation. Attempts to estimate Phillips curves, augmented or otherwise, were doomed to failure.

Neverthelesss, fundamental though these differences of approach appeared to be at the time, the fact remains that traditional monetarists and Keynesians were speaking more or less the same language. They were using similar methodological approaches – normally the *IS–LM* representation of the Keynesian income–expenditure model – so that the potential for the emergence of a consensus clearly existed. What blew the process of finding common ground irreparably off course was the revival of the classical theory of labour market adjustment which became incorporated into what we may call the *new classical* version of monetarism. The first signs of this revival were perceptibly present in Friedman (1968) and unmistakably pervasive in Friedman (1975). In the latter pamphlet, the classical approach to disequilibrium in the labour market is depicted in Friedman's Figure 3 and the classical theory of labour market adjustment, in which the rate of change of *real* wages is a function of the level of excess demand in the labour market, is presented in the amended version of his Figure 2: it is pure Pigou! This is a much more extreme position than had been embraced in traditional monetarism. In the more virulent new classical brand of monetarism changes in the stance of monetary policy only produce real effects to the extent that they dupe the private sector into believing that relative prices (especially real wages) are behaving in a manner in which they are patently not behaving. It follows that a process of monetary contraction to combat inflation will have minimal side effects on real magnitudes provided that the implementation of these contractionary policies is fully anticipated by the private sector: no mistakes will be made concerning either the conduct of monetary policy or the behaviour of relative prices so that there can be no policy induced deviations from the natural rates of output and employment.

Although some fragments of the traditional version of monetarism can just about be rescued from the debris of the current, ever deepening recession in Britain, it is hard to see how *any* version of the new classical monetarism can be vindicated by events as they unfold daily. At the time of writing, the OECD predicts that the British unemployment rate will rise to well over three million, possibly to a post-war high, and record numbers of bankruptcies are being recorded. The only comfort which can be derived from this sorry state of affairs is that the *rate of increase* in unemployment might be falling. It would take a very cloistered monetarist to suggest that the seemingly inexorable rise in unemployment in Britain is the result of recurrent failures by both employers and workers to unscramble the correct signals concerning the behaviour of the real wage rate. Not even the most hard-nosed believer in the merits of market capitalism would claim that the current rise in unemployment is voluntary, the outcome of an increased preference for leisure over work. The plummeting levels of employment and, to a lesser extent, of output are, quite simply, the result of the decline in both consumption and investment expenditure which, in turn, were brought about, not through adherence to strict money supply targets (they were discarded long ago), but through the punishing impact of high interest rates over a long period of time. It is hard to imagine a recession which is more *Keynesian* in origin!

Aggregate demand, the natural unemployment rate and incomes policies

European experience in the 1980s and the early 1990s does not inspire confidence in the 'stability of the private sector' hypothesis which plays such a prominent part in both versions of monetarism. Inflationary pressure remains stubbornly ingrained despite levels of unemployment which are unprecedentedly high by post-war standards. Those who have continued to keep faith with either the natural unemployment rate hypothesis or the milder NAIRU hypothesis have been forced to take refuge in one version or another of the concept of hysteresis, while the less convinced have started to ask, is there anything out there? Keynesians of the cost–push school have seen their dogged mistrust of Phillips curves, natural rates of unemployment and the like amply vindicated by the course of events. The costs of an anti-inflation policy which relies on demand restriction alone are proving to be much greater than had been suspected in the 1960s and 1970s, and it is still not certain that the inflationary tiger has been tamed.

The time is long overdue for the reappraisal of alternative anti-inflation policies. In particular, incomes policies, which have been the victim of a bad professional press over the last two decades, should be re-evaluated. Supporters of incomes policies tend also to be Keynesians, though there is nothing in the structure of the Keynesian system which necessarily implies such support apart, perhaps, from a rejection of the quantity theory of money. Few of these Keynesians would argue that incomes policies are anything more than second-best solutions to inflation. Even fewer would welcome increased state intervention in the processes of wage and price setting which, in a first-best world, should be the sole province of the private sector. Nevertheless, if an incomes policy succeeds in bringing inflation down to acceptable levels while at the same time avoiding the deleterious side effects that a policy of unaided demand restriction will otherwise bring in its wake, then it is certainly worth giving such a policy further consideration.

The question regarding the form which incomes policies should take does not lend itself to easy generalization. It all depends on the circumstances which confront particular countries at particular stages of their economic development. Obviously the industrial relations structure is of paramount importance, as is the degree of social cohesion in the relations among the different classes of society. For example, in Austria there appears to exist an extensive social consensus which enables the successful implementation of incomes policies. On the other hand in Britain such a consensus has, in the past, been difficult to discern.

The predicament confronting the British economy in the early 1990s graphically illustrates the need for a widening of the economic agenda for tackling inflation. Britain is experiencing historically high and rising unemployment rates, but inflationary pressure is abating only slowly. Money supply targets, and the much trumpeted Medium Term Financial Strategy which was introduced in 1980 to attain these targets, were long ago abandoned in favour of what was thought to be the only alternative, short-term fine-tuning through interest rates. The impact of high interest rates has bitten deep into aggregate demand, resulting in rising unemployment, falling output and a record number of bankruptcies. In these circumstances it is hardly surprising that many British and American economists have resumed the search for a generally acceptable incomes policy, the most favoured candidate being some form of tax-based incomes policy (see, for example, Layard (1986)).

Stable 'demand' for money functions?

The empirical breakdown of 'demand' for money functions, briefly touched upon in Chapter 4, was the principal reason for the abandonment of money supply targets in favour of interest rate fine-tuning in Britain in the 1980s. The monetarist cure for inflation critically revolves around the idea that the money supply can be treated as an exogenous variable. Monetarists accept that the money supply *can* be an endogenous variable in certain circumstances, the classic examples occurring when the monetary authorities pursue interest rate or nominal exchange rate targets. Nevertheless they insist that, if only governments had the political will to abandon alternative targets for monetary policy, they would be in a position to target the money supply. The first step in the implementation of the monetarist cure for inflation would then have been taken.

We suggested in Chapter 4 that the breakdown of the relationship between changes in the money supply, M^s, and changes in money income, PY, might be attributable to the abandonment of monetary policies whose primary objective had been to control interest rates. Kaldor (1970) suggested that the relationship that was being estimated statistically using data generated *before* such a shift in policy was, in fact, a stable *supply* of money function. Figure 4.18 illustrates the highly stylized case where the pursuit of a particular interest rate target implies that changes in the supply of money will be called forth by exogenous changes in money income. Many factors could account for these changes in PY, but Keynesians, particularly in Britain, have traditionally laid strong emphasis on autonomous cost–push pressures on money wages which feed into prices on account of mark up pricing, which, in turn, feed into inflationary expectations. In these circumstances it should come as no surprise that a close correlation between changes in money income and changes in the money supply had been observed, though the direction of causation is the opposite to that of the monetarists, running from PY to M^s and not *vice versa*. By the same token it should come as no surprise to discover that this correlation weakens to the point of collapse when interest rate targets are abandoned.

The unearthing of a statistical regularity between two macroeconomic aggregates as important as the money supply and money income naturally gave rise to the temptation among policy makers to exploit it with a view to achieving some measure of control over the behaviour of one of the aggregates. The statistical association between changes in the money supply and changes in money national income which appeared to have existed down to the early 1980s could not bear the strain of the change in policy regime, the new regime placing almost exclusive reliance on curbing the rate of growth of the money supply in order to contain the rate of growth of nominal income, and particularly the P component of PY. In other words, the precondition for the existence of a significant association between M^s and PY before, say, 1980, had been that policy makers would not 'lean on' this association for control purposes. Once this association is 'leaned upon' by being made the centrepiece of an anti-inflation policy, its erstwhile stability disintegrates, thereby depriving targets for monetary aggregates of their putative efficacy.

Of course, in practice, few governments can be entirely indifferent to what happens to interest rates so that, even with a firmly committed monetarist government such as Mrs Thatcher's former administration, changes in the money supply will generally have some endogenous component. Indeed, it has been persuasively argued by Dow and Saville (1988) that, in Britain, changes in the money supply are almost always endogenous, irrespective of whether or not the government is avowedly monetarist. Increases in bank deposits form far and away the largest component of increases in the money supply, these increases being, in turn, the result of increases in bank advances to the non-bank private sector. The overriding criterion which a bank applies when granting an advance to one of its customers is the customer's creditworthiness, i.e. his ability to repay the advance. The customer's money income will obviously loom large in the bank's estimate of its customer's credit-worthiness. Aggregating over all customers, it follows that increases in the volume of bank advances to the non-bank private sector will be mainly determined by increases in money income. Dow and Saville leave the question of what determines increases in money income as a moot point, though I suspect that they may subscribe to a cost–push explanation of inflation.

One of the major stumbling blocks in the monetarist analysis of inflation lies in its treatment of the M variable in 'demand' for money functions. In most econometric studies which investigate the relation between changes in M on the one hand and, on the other, changes in PY and in other variables, it is simply *assumed* that what is being estimated is a demand for money function. In other words, it is being assumed that the money supply is an exogenous variable. The separation of the forces which determine the demand for money from those which determine the supply of money lies at the heart of monetarism. The supply of money must be exogenous and the demand for money must be a stable function of a small number of variables. The analytical basis of monetarism is shaken to its very foundations if either of these requirements fails to hold good.

Is credit money similar to gold?

Finally I must confess to a recurrent sense of unease at the occasional monetarist conflation of the analysis of a modern economy, in which credit money is the overwhelmingly dominant means of exchange, with that of an economy in which the typical means of exchange is commodity money, normally gold. I must emphasize that such conflation is only occasional, but it is symptomatic of more general cast of mind among some monetarists.

One example of this conflation is the vogue which was enjoyed by the works of David Hume during the rise of monetarism in the 1970s. The monetary theory of the balance of payments proudly traced its ancestry back to Hume's price–specie–flow mechanism of balance of payments adjustment. For Hume, the origins of balance of payments deficits could often – though not always – be found in excessive increases in the issue of paper money by private banks which had the effect of 'banishing bullion', i.e. they produced a drain from the stock of gold which was circulating domestically. Although they substantially modified the price–specie–flow mechanism, these 'global monetarists' retained the broad analytical structure of Hume's approach and were impressed by his exposition of the mechanism through which the drain from the domestic supply of gold would operate.

Another example of the pervasive influence of early writers in the tradition of the quantity theory of money on their intellectual heirs, the monetarists, surfaces in the works of Milton Friedman (see Chapter 3 above). We have already noted how irksome Friedman found the 'black box' allegations which were persistently levelled against the monetarist model. By what mechanism, inquired the sceptics, do changes in the money supply affect the price level? Go back to David Hume, retorted an exasperated Friedman (1974b). So what *did* Hume have to say on the transmission mechanism? Apart from Hume's rather skeletal account discussed in Chapter 3, the answer is – not all that much. The reader will recall that the embryonic model proposed in Hume's *Essays* takes as its starting-point a sudden increase in the supply of gold brought about as a result of an equally sudden balance of trade surplus. The resultant importation of gold accrues initially in the form of higher incomes for exporters and a subsequent multiplier-style increase in total national income. Hume percipiently acknowledged that, in the short run, output and employment would be stimulated by the inflow of gold. Nevertheless he took it for granted that, since the initial state of the economy was one of overall full employment, the ripple effect of the increase in the supply of money would eventually spend itself entirely in the form of higher levels of absolute prices and money wages.

So how valid is it to transfer modes of analysis appropriate to economies in which the predominant means of exchange is commodity money to modern credit-money economies where the exchange of *inside* money is far and away the most important means of effecting transactions within the private sector? Exposition by use of analogy can be fraught with perils. It is particularly misleading when it is implied that the effects of changes in the supply of money in late twentieth-century economies, in which what Keynes called 'bank money' is the almost universal means of exchange, are analogous to those which result in an early eighteenth-century economy on the gold standard.[1]

Nor is my sense of unease at the occasional conflation of the operation of credit-money economies with that of commodity-money economies dispelled by the more frequent reference in monetarist circles to 'printing money' as the usual channel through which the money supply increases. The image of the printing presses of the central bank functioning at full tilt is certainly a graphic one which is likely to appeal to the layman; but it is particularly wide of the mark when describing the workings of a modern banking system. The money supply is normally defined as comprising two

---

[1] 'I shall, as in my *Treatise on Money*, assume that money is co-extensive with bank deposits' (*GT*, p. 167n).

components: (a) notes and coin in circulation; (b) the volume of bank deposits. Quantitatively bank deposits form by far the larger component of the money supply. Indeed an increase in the money supply resulting from an increase in the volume of bank deposits need not be accompanied by *any* increase in the supply of notes and coin: an increase in the money supply need not involve 'printing money' at all! I suspect that part of the appeal of the image of newly printed money being 'injected' into the economy can be explained by the fascination that the operation of the gold standard continues to exercise over monetarists since notes and coin, though quantitatively insignificant components of the money supply, are the closest approximations to Hume's 'bullion' which modern economies possess.

Keynesianism and classical economics, old and new

The study of the history of economic ideas used to be considered an essential component of a well-rounded curriculum for undergraduate courses in economics. Over the past twenty-five years, however, the study of the history of thought has ebbed to such an extent that it is rare to come across a young economist who is thoroughly versed in the works of the pioneers of their subject – Smith, Ricardo, Marx, Marshall, Walras, Fisher, Keynes, to name but a few. The ascendancy of quantitative methods in economics in recent years, and the parallel concentration on formal techniques of analysis, have displaced the study of the works of the classic writers in economics, most of whom tended to eschew mathematical modes of presentation in favour of almost exclusively verbal analysis.[2]

This neglect of the intellectual history of one's subject would astonish those trained in other branches of the humanities. Even nowadays it is barely conceivable that a graduate in, for example, philosophy would *not* have read the works of Plato, Aristotle, Descartes and Kant. Unfortunately the same cannot be said of economics. Many modern economists may be inclined to dismiss my expression of regret at the decline in the study of the history of ideas as merely the grumblings of a dyed in the wool traditionalist, a *laudator temporis acti se puero*. Certainly I believe that

---

[2]Both Alfred Marshall and John Maynard Keynes gained first class degrees in the Mathematical Tripos at Cambridge, Marshall being placed second in the list of wranglers. Nevertheless both Marshall and Keynes shared a life-long distrust of the use of mathematical methods in economics. Keynes refused to include any mathematics in the *General Theory*, and the only diagram which he eventually agreed to include was the result of Harrod's prompting.

the study of the intellectual evolution of the discipline of economics forms a fascinating subject for scholarly inquiry in its own right. I have more than a little sympathy for J. K. Galbraith's (1977) observation 'Perhaps it is a sense of history that divides good economics from bad.' But I would justify the study of the history of thought not only on the grounds of 'art for art's sake'. Nowhere is the need for a sense of the history of economic ideas more pressing than in the current debate on the state of macroeconomics.

The reader will recall how the starting-point of Keynes's *General Theory* was a critique of the constituent parts of the classical theory of the macroeconomy which he had first to assemble from a variety of sources. Although there were some exceptions,[3] examination of the original sources reveals that Keynes's version of classical theory was not all that wide of the mark. He did not succumb to the obvious temptation of erecting rows of easily demolished straw men.

Keynes's wide-ranging critique of classical theory was just the point of departure for the formulation of his own alternative vision of the workings of a money using economy in the large. His most fundamental insight, the principle of effective demand, can be expressed on a variety of levels of abstraction, but its basic prediction, that the level of output will adapt itself to the aggregate expenditure plans of different sectors of the economy, captures the essence of his analysis: 'For the proposition that supply creates its own demand, I shall substitute the proposition that expenditure creates its own income, i.e. an income just sufficient to meet the expenditure' (*CW*, XIX, pp. 80–81). In order to arrive at this conclusion Keynes had to develop a fully articulated model of the macroeconomy, the essential features of which were analyzed in Chapters 4 and 5 above. The task which Keynes had set himself was formidable: not only had his theory to be internally consistent, it had also to be more generally applicable than its classical rival.[4]

The success of the Keynesian revolution went largely unchallenged for over thirty years after the publication of the *General Theory*. It became widely accepted that classical macroeconomics was irredeemably flawed. Even the redoubtable A. C. Pigou, in two lectures delivered in 1949, generously conceded that much of his own analysis had been faulty, that his earlier criticisms of Keynes had been misplaced, and that, by and large, Keynes had got it right (see Pigou, *Keynes's General Theory: A*

---

[3]For example, I share many of D. H. Robertson's misgivings about Keynes's peremptory treatment of the *neo*-classical (loanable funds) theory of interest.

[4]Keynes regarded the classical model as a special case of his own more general model, the classical model only applying in a state of full employment.

Retrospect, 1950). A couple of decades later Lionel Robbins, the dominant figure in the economics department at the London School of Economics in the interwar period,[5] handsomely admitted that his diagnosis of the origins of general unemployment had been erroneous. Ironically his warm endorsement of the power of Keynes's vision took place at a time when many around him were abandoning Keynesian economics altogether, opting instead for the new classical macroeconomics.

So how are we to account for the rise of the new classical economics in the light of the conversion of such stalwarts of the old classical economics to Keynesianism? I can only hazard three related hypotheses to explain the mysterious revival of classical economics: that the new classical writers have only a nodding acquaintance of the works of their intellectual antecedents, the old classical economists; that they are unaware of Keynes's devastating critique of old classical economics; and that they are therefore unable to appreciate the *differentiae* which separated old classical modes of analysis from Keynesian modes of analysis and the manner in which the latter logically superseded the former. New classical models appear to have been conceived in a thought historical vacuum, showing scant awareness of the half-century of intellectual speculation and controversy which ultimately led to the acceptance of the Keynesian model and to the recognition of macroeconomics as an independent field of economic inquiry.

---

[5]Lionel (later Lord) Robbins continued to be the towering influence at the LSE both during and for many years after the war.

References

Attfield, C. L. F., D. Demery and N. W. Duck (1985), *Rational Expectations in Macroeconomics: An Introduction to Theories and Evidence*, Oxford: Blackwell.

Azariadis, C. (1975), 'Implicit contracts and underemployment equilibrium', *Journal of Political Economy*, **83**, 1183.

Baily, N. (1974), 'Wages and employment under uncertain demand', *Review of Economic Studies*, **41**, 37.

Barro, R. J. (1974), 'Are government bonds net wealth?', *Journal of Political Economy*, **82**, 1095.

Barro, R. J. (1977), 'Unanticipated money growth and unemployment in the United States', *American Economic Review*, **67**, 101.

Barro, R. J. (1987), *Macroeconomics*, Chichester: John Wiley.

Barro, R. J. and H. I. Grossman (1976), *Money, Employment and Inflation*, Cambridge: Cambridge University Press.

Baumol, W. J. (1977), 'Say's (at least) eight laws, or what Say and James Mill may really have meant', *Economica*, **44**, 145.

Begg, D. K. H. (1982), *The Rational Expectations Revolution in Macroeconomics*, Hemel Hempstead: Philip Allan.

Blanchard, O. J. and L. Summers (1986), 'Hysteresis and the European unemployment problem', *NBER Macroeconomics Annual* p. 15.

Blackaby, F., ed. (1980), *The Future of Pay Bargaining*, London: Heinemann.

Blaug, M. (1962), *Economic Theory in Retrospect*, Cambridge: Cambridge University Press.

Blinder, A. and R. M. Solow (1973), *The economics of public finance*, Washington, DC: Brookings Institution.

Cagan, P. (1956), 'The monetary dynamics of hyperinflation', in M. Friedman, ed., *Studies in the Quantity Theory of Money*, Chicago: University of Chicago Press.

Carlin, W. and D. Soskice (1990), *Macroeconomics of the Wage Bargain*, Oxford: Oxford University Press.

Carter, M. and R. Maddock (1984), *Rational Expectations: Macroeconomics for the 1980s?*, London: Macmillan.

Chick, V. (1983), *Macroeconomics after Keynes*, Hemel Hempstead: Philip Allan.

Clarke, Peter (1988), *The Keynesian Revolution in the Making, 1924–1936*, Oxford: Oxford University Press.

Clower, R. W. (1965), 'The Keynesian counter-revolution: a theoretical appraisal', in F. H. Hahn and F. Brechling, eds, *The Theory of Interest Rates*, London: Macmillan.

Clower, R. W. (1967), 'A reconsideration of the microfoundations of monetary theory', *Western Economic Journal*, **6**, 1.

Coddington, R. A. (1983), *Keynesian Economics: the search for first principles*, London: Allen and Unwin.

Coen, R. M. and B. J. Hickman (1987), 'Keynesian and classical unemployment in four countries', *Brookings Papers on Economic Activity*, **1**, 123.

Cross, R., ed. (1988), *Unemployment, Hysteresis and the Natural Rate Hypothesis*, Oxford: Blackwell.

Dornbusch, R. and S. Fischer (1978), *Macroeconomics*, New York: McGraw-Hill.

Dow, J. C. R. and I. D. Saville (1988), *A Critique of Monetary Policy: Theory and British experience*, Oxford: Oxford University Press.

Dunlop, J. G. (1938), 'The movement of real and money wages', *Economic Journal*, **48**, 413.

Flemming, J. S. (1976), *Inflation*, Oxford: Oxford University Press.

Friedman, M. (1953), 'The methodology of positive economics', in M. Friedman, *Essays in Positive Economics*, Chicago: University of Chicago Press.

Friedman, M. (1956), 'The quantity theory of money: a restatement', in M. Friedman, ed., *Studies in the Quantity Theory of Money*, Chicago: University of Chicago Press.

Friedman, M. (1968), 'The role of monetary policy', *American Economic Review*, **58**, 1.

Friedman, M. (1969), 'The optimum quantity of money', in *The Optimum Quantity of Money and Other Essays*, Chicago: Aldine.

Friedman, M. (1974a), 'A theoretical framework for monetary analysis', in R. J. Gordon, ed., *Milton Friedman's Monetary Framework*, Chicago: University of Chicago Press.

Friedman, M. (1974b), discussion in *Inflation: Causes, Consequences and Cures*, London: Institute of Economic Affairs.

Friedman, M. (1975), *Unemployment versus Inflation? An evaluation of the Phillips curve*, London: Institute of Economic Affairs.

Friedman, M. and A. J. Schwartz (1963), *A Monetary History of the United States, 1867–1960*, Princeton, NJ: Princeton University Press.

Galbraith, J. K. (1977), *The Age of Uncertainty*, London: BBC/André Deutsch.

Gordon, R. J., ed. (1974), *Milton Friedman's Monetary Framework*, Chicago: University of Chicago Press.

Hansen, A. (1953), *A Guide to Keynes*, New York: McGraw-Hill.

Hicks, J. R. (1937), 'Mr Keynes and the classics: a suggested interpretation', *Econometrica*, **5**, 147.

Hoover, K. D. (1988), *The New Classical Macroeconomics*, Oxford: Blackwell.

Hume, D. (1741 and 1742), *Essays Moral, Political and Literary*, ed. T. H. Green and T. H. Gross, London: Longman, Green (1882).

Jay, P. (1974), *Inflation: Causes, Consequences and Cures*, London: Institute of Economic Affairs.

Judd, J. P. and J. L. Scadding (1982), 'The search for a stable money demand function: a survey of the post-1973 literature', *Journal of Economic Literature*, **20**, 992.

Kahn, R. F. (1931), 'The relation of home investment to unemployment', *Economic Journal*, **41**, 173.

Kahn, R. F. (1975), 'Unemployment as seen by Keynesians', in G. D. N. Worswick, ed., *The Concept and Measurement of Involuntary Unemployment*, London: Allen and Unwin.

Kaldor, N. (1970), 'The new monetarism', *Lloyds Bank Review*, no 97, p. 1.

Keynes, J. M. (1923), *A Tract on Monetary Reform*, London: Macmillan.

Keynes, J. M. (1929), *Can Lloyd George Do It?*, reprinted in *The Collected Writings of John Maynard Keynes*, vol. IX, pp. 86–125, London: Macmillan.

Keynes, J. M. (1930), *A Treatise on Money*, London: Macmillan.

Keynes, J. M. (1936), *The General Theory of Employment, Interest and Money*, London: Macmillan.

Keynes, J. M. (1939), 'Relative movements of real wages and output', *Economic Journal*, **49**, 34, reprinted in *The Collected Writings of John Maynard Keynes*, vol. VII, London: Macmillan.

Keynes, J. M. (1940), *How to Pay for the War*, London: Macmillan.

Klamer, A. (1984), *The New Classical Macroeconomics*, Brighton: Wheatsheaf.

Laidler, D. E. W. (1974), discussion in *Inflation: Causes, Consequences and Cures*, London: Institute of Economic Affairs.

Laidler, D. E. W. (1981), 'Monetarism: an interpretation and assessment', *Economic Journal*, **91**, 1.

Layard, R. (1986), *How to Beat Unemployment*, Oxford: Oxford University Press.

Leijonhufvud, A. (1968), *On Keynesian Economics and the Economics of Keynes*, New York: Oxford University Press.

Leontief, W. (1936), 'The fundamental assumption of Mr Keynes' monetary theory of employment', *Quarterly Journal of Economics*, **51**, 192.

Lindbeck, A. and D. Snower (1986), 'Wage setting, unemployment and insider outsider relations', *American Economic Review*, Supplement, **76**, 235.

Lipsey, R. G. (1960), 'The relationship between unemployment and the rate of change of money wage rates in the UK: a further analysis', *Economica*, NS **27**, 1.

Lipsey, R. G. (1962), 'Can there be a valid theory of wages?', in B. J. McCormick and E. O. Smith, eds, *The Labour Market*, Harmondsworth: Penguin.

Lucas, R. E. (1973), 'Some international evidence on output–inflation trade-offs', *American Economic Review*, **63**, 326.

Lucas, R. E. (1975), 'An equilibrium model of the business cycle', *Journal of Political Economy*, **83**, 1113.

Lucas, R. E. (1976), 'Econometric policy evaluation: a critique', in K. Brunner and A. H. Meltzer, eds, *The Phillips Curve and Labor Markets*, Amsterdam: North-Holland.

Lucas, R. E. (1977), 'Understanding business cycles', in K. Brunner and A. Meltzer, eds, *Stabilization of the Domestic and International Economy*, Amsterdam: North-Holland.

Lucas, R. E. (1978), 'Unemployment policy', *American Economic Review*, Supplement, **68**, 353.

Malinvaud, E. (1980), *Profitability and Unemployment*, Cambridge: Cambridge University Press.

Malinvaud, E. (1985), *The Theory of Unemployment Reconsidered*, Oxford: Blackwell.

Meade, J. E. (1938), *Consumers' Credit and Unemployment*, Oxford: Oxford University Press.

Mill, J. S. (1862), *Principles of Political Economy*, New York: Appleton.

Modigliani, F. (1944), 'Liquidity preference and the theory of interest and money', *Econometrica*, **12**, 45.

Nickell, S. (1990), *Oxford Review of Economic Policy*, Winter, **6**, 26.

Nordhaus, W. D. (1983), 'Macroconfusion: the dilemmas of economic policy', in J. Tobin, ed., *Macroeconomics, Prices and Quantities*, Oxford: Blackwell.

Okun, A. M. (1981), *Prices and Quantities: A macroeconomic analysis*, Oxford: Blackwell.

Patinkin, D. (1948), 'Price flexibility and full employment', *American Economic Review*, **38**, 543.

Patinkin, D. (1965), *Money, Interest and Prices*, 2nd edn, New York: Harper and Row.

Patinkin, D. (1972), *Studies in Monetary Economics*, New York: Harper and Row.

Patinkin, D. (1976), *Keynes' Monetary Thought*, Durham, NC: Duke University Press.

Pigou, A. C. (1913), *Unemployment*, London: Williams and Norgate.

Pigou, A. C. (1933), *The Theory of Unemployment*, London: Macmillan.

Pigou, A. C. (1950), *Keynes's General Theory: A retrospect*, London: Macmillan.

Samuelson, P. A. (1947), *Foundations of Economic Analysis*, Cambridge, MA: Harvard University Press.

Samuelson, P. A. and W. Nordhaus (1985), *Economics*, New York: McGraw-Hill.

Samuelson, P. A. and R. M. Solow (1960), 'Analytical aspects of anti-inflation policy', *American Economic Review*, **50**, 177.

Schumpeter, Joseph (1954), *A History of Economic Analysis*, New York: Oxford University Press.

Shackle, G. L. S. (1967), *The Years of High Theory*, Cambridge: Cambridge University Press.

Sheffrin, S. M. (1983), *Rational Expectations*, Cambridge: Cambridge University Press.

Solow, R. M. (1979), 'Alternative approaches to macroeconomic theory', *Canadian Journal of Economics*, **12**, 339.

Solow, R. M. (1980), 'On theories of unemployment', *American Economic Review*, **70**, 1.

Tarshis, L. (1939), 'Changes in real and money wages', *Economic Journal*, **49**, 150.

Tobin, J. (1958), 'Liquidity preference as behavior towards risk', *Review of Economic Studies*, **25**, 65.

Tobin, J. (1981), 'The monetarist counter-revolution – an appraisal', *Economic Journal*, **91**, 29.

Trevithick, J. A. (1975), 'Keynes, inflation and money illusion', *Economic Journal*, **85**, 101.

Trevithick, J. A. (1976), 'Money wage inflexibility and the Keynesian labour supply function', *Economic Journal*, **86**, 327.

Trevithick, J. A. (1983), *Inflation: a guide to the crisis in economics*, Harmondsworth: Penguin.

Walters, A. A. (1971), *Money in Boom and Slump*, London: Institute of Economic Affairs.

Index

accelerationist hypothesis, 132, 134, 136,
    138–9, 150–1, 154–7
Ackley, Gardner, 212–13
adaptive expectations, 149–51, 154
aggregate demand, 6, 7, 18
    capital scrapping and, 207–8
    failures, 223–5
    Keynesian revolution, 51, 66, 74–5, 89–
        90
    money wages and, 98–103
    quantity theory, 33, 42, 117
    real wage and, 103–6, 114, 116–17
    -supply framework, 157–68, 178
    unemployment and, 139, 142, 173, 226,
        228–9
aggregate expenditure, 27, 46, 50, 68, 98
aggregate supply, 116–17, 157–68, 178
American Economic Association, 127,
    131, 144, 154
Azariadis, C., 210

Baily, N., 210
balance of payments, 121, 231
'bank' money, 46, 232–3
bargaining process, 96–7, 107, 110, 120,
    137–8, 201–5, 206
Barro, R. J., 101, 153, 175, 178, 182
barter economy, 17, 20, 142, 223–4
Baumol, W. J., 21
black box, 46–7, 232
Blackaby, F., 205, 212
Blanchard, O. J., 201
Blaug, M., 11
bonds, 32, 54–5, 89, 100–1
budget constraints, 126, 178
budget deficits, 89, 191, 226

business cycles, 157, 168–74

Cagan, Philip, 133
Cambridge equation, 24, 27–8, 34, 57,
    158, 163–4
capacity utilization, 113–14, 207–8
capital, 33, 41, 174, 181
    goods, 10
    scrapping, 207–8
    stock, 15, 24–5, 113–14, 207–8
Carlin, W., 138, 201, 206
cash-balances approach, 24, 27–9, 31–8,
    40, 46–7, 57, 158, 163–4, 232
central banks, 161, 176
    Keynesian revolution, 49, 66, 72, 77–80,
        89
    quantity theory, 25–6, 32, 34–7
Chicago School, 39
classical economics, 81–2, 92–4
classical/Keynesian macroeconomics, 118–
    19, 217–23
classical/Keynesian unemployment, 3, 180,
    181–96, 214–15
classical macroeconomics (new), 3
    business cycles and, 168–74
    involuntary unemployment, 143–4
    IS–LM model, 217–23
    Keynesianism and, 233–5
    rational expectations, 146–79
classical macroeconomics (old), 2
    Keynesianism and, 233–5
    quantity theory, 22–47
    Say's Law, 5–21
closed economy, 19–20, 25, 27, 49, 89, 214
Clower, Robert, 114, 115, 178, 182, 183,
    187

Coddington, R. A., 121
Coen, R. M., 193–6, 214
commodities, 5, 6, 54
commodity money, 25, 26, 41, 46, 47, 232
competition, 49, 97, 106, 113, 213
consumption, 8, 175
consumption goods, 10, 33
contracts, implicit, 209–14
correspondence principle, 122–3
cost-push inflation, *see* inflation
costs, marginal, 97, 104, 111, 125
credit money, 231–3
crowding out, 12, 69–71, 81–6

debt default, 99, 102
deflation, 224
    demand, 135, 198, 204
    price, 97, 99–103, 164
demand, 3, 6–8, 28, 29, 180
    deflation, 135, 198, 204
    see also aggregate demand;
        effective demand
demand management, 3, 66, 68, 102, 103,
    126, 128, 130–1, 135, 139, 152,
    162, 182, 215
demand for money function, 32–4, 40–1,
    43, 57, 73–81, 229–31
disequilibrium adjustment
    mechanism, 92, 96, 128–30
Dow, J. C. R., 192, 230–1
dual decision hypothesis, 178
Dunlop, J. G., 111, 112, 114

econometric modelling, 40–3, 73–4
    IS–LM system, 88, 118–19
    Phillips curve, 130, 148, 199
economic history, 1–4
economic policy, 126–7
    see also fiscal policy; monetary policy
effective demand, 49–51, 187, 234
    IS–LM model, 66–7
    liquidity preference, 52, 58–9
    wages, 97, 105, 114, 116
elasticity pessimists, 68, 218, 223
equivalence theorem, 101
Euro-pessimists, 196
excess supply, 91–3, 96–7, 102, 116
exchange equation, 24–7, 28, 163
exchange rate, 25, 42, 161, 188, 214, 229
exports, 1

fiat money, 100–1, 190, 191, 192
firm equilibrium, 184–6, 187
fiscal policy, 89
    IS–LM model, 66, 69–73
    labour market, 106, 131, 139, 152
    Treasury view, 11–14, 81–5 *passim*

Fisher, Irving, 24, 99, 103, 233
Fisher equation, 24–8, 163
fix-price, 60, 86–7, 147, 208
flow principle, 54, 59, 181, 225
French Keynesian School, 115, 182
Friedman, Milton, 17
    monetarism, 73, 81, 222–3, 227
    natural unemployment rate, 136, 138–
        44, 198
    Phillips curve, 3, 126–8, 131–5, 148, 149
    quantity theory, 39, 44–7, 232
    rational expectations, 146, 148–50, 154,
        161, 167, 171–2
    transmission mechanism, 35–8, 40
full employment, 5, 6, 14, 92
    Keynesian revolution, 48–53, 58–60, 87–
        9
    quantity theory, 2, 37, 119, 160
    target unemployment rate, 127–8
    wages and, 2, 19–20, 99–100, 102, 107,
        116, 120

Galbraith, J. K., 234
General Theory (Keynes), 1, 182, 189,
    217–18, 223–5
    labour market, 2, 120, 125, 128, 211
    quantity theory, 35, 37, 38
    rational expectations, 149, 165, 173, 179
    Say's Law, 7, 9, 15, 18, 19, 21
    see also Keynesian revolution
gold, 19, 25–6, 30, 47, 231–3
gold standard, 26, 31, 232, 233
Grossman, H. I., 175, 178, 182

Harrod, R. F., 60
Hawtrey, Sir Ralph, 11
Henderson, Hubert, 11
Hickman, B. G., 193–6, 214
Hicks, Sir John, 42, 56, 60, 90
    see also IS–LM model
household equilibrium, 184–7, 193
Hume, David, 2, 23, 46–7, 231–3
    analysis (output response), 30–1
hyperinflation, 36, 133, 139
hysteresis, 3–4, 180, 196
    capital scrapping, 207–8
    insider–outsider effect, 201–5
    long-term unemployed, 205–7
    NAIRU and, 197–200, 215, 228

implicit contracts, 209–14
imports, 30, 51
income, 14–15, 26–7, 61–2
    money income, 38–46, 73–81, 229
    national income, 49–50, 230
income–expenditure model, 1, 50–1, 120–
    1, 125, 148, 164

IS–LM, 44, 64–6, 95, 104, 227
income–output relations, 5
incomes policy, 79, 188, 215, 228–9
inflation, 1, 89, 90
  anti-inflation policies, 198–9, 215–16,
    228, 230
  cost-push, 42–3, 74–5, 77, 79–80, 124,
    136, 199–200, 228, 230, 231
  expected rate, 133–6, 154–5
  hyperinflation, 36, 133, 139
  money and, 226–8
  quantity theory, 36, 37, 42–3
  trade off, 126–7, 131–2, 134–5, 149
  unanticipated, 147, 148, 149–54
  see also hysteresis, inflation
    and labour market; non-
    accelerating inflation rate of
    unemployment
inflation and labour market, 2–3
  conclusion, 144–5
  involuntary unemployment, 143–4
  Keynesian approach, 118–21
  money illusion, 138–42
  NAIRU, 136–8
  Phillips curve, 121–36
inflationary gap, 33, 87, 125, 226
inside money, 100, 232
insider–outsider effects, 201–5
interest rate, 7–10, 98–9, 176
  classical theory, 11–14, 220, 225
  Keynesian revolution, 48–9, 58–9, 62–9
    passim, 72
  Keynesian theory, 52–7, 225
  natural rate, 32–4, 36–7, 58, 88, 161,
    163, 225
  neutral rate, 37–8, 58
  real/monetary phenomenon, 2, 65–6
  targets, 40–1, 161, 229–31
invariance proposition, 146–7, 157
investible funds, 8–9, 11–12, 54, 225
investment, 7–11, 33, 101
  decline (effect), 58–9, 61–3, 68
  Keynesian interest theory, 52–7
  private, 83–6
involuntary unemployment, 2, 95–8, 108–
    9, 136, 143–4, 164–9, 182, 210–11,
    224
IS–LM model, 75, 88, 181, 208
  classical model in Keynesian
    framework, 217–23
  fiscal policy in, 69–73, 104
  Hicks's development, 59–65, 103
  income–expenditure model, 44, 64–6,
    95, 104, 227
  labour market, 113, 116–19, 142
  monetary crowding out, 81–2, 83
  monetary policy in, 66–9

rational expectations, 147–8, 164, 175–
    6, 179
'island parable', 165–8

Jay, Peter, 80

Kahn, R. F., 50, 72, 120–1
Kaldor, N., 40–1, 43, 59, 68, 229
Kalecki, Michael, 120
Keynes, John Maynard, 40
  Can Lloyd George Do It?, 11, 84
  money and, 223–5
  Say's Law, 5, 7, 9–10, 14, 17–21
  Tract on Monetary Reform, 38
  transmission mechanism, 35–8
  see also General Theory (Keynes);
    labour market, Keynes and
Keynes effect, 98–9, 101–3, 125, 163–4,
    192, 214
Keynesian/classical macroeconomics, 118–
    19, 217–23
Keynesian/classical unemployment, 3,
    180–96, 214–15
Keynesian economics, 1–4
  inflation/labour market, 118–21
  rational expectations, 174–7
Keynesian macroeconomics (recent
    developments), 180
  conclusion, 214–16
  hysteresis and NAIRU, 197–208
  implicit contracts, 209–14
  prices and quantities, 208–9
  unemployment, 3, 180–96, 214–15
Keynesian revolution, 2, 48, 234–5
  concluding remarks, 88–91
  crowding out, 81–6
  effective demand, 49–51
  generalized quantity theory of money,
    86–8
  interest rate, 52–7, 65–6
  IS–LM model, 59–73
  liquidity preference, 58–9
  monetary accommodation, 73–81

labour market, 3
  adjustment, 48–9, 92–3, 95–6, 104, 122–
    4, 140–2, 144, 224, 227
  disequilibrium, 139–41, 227
  inflation and, *see* inflation and labour
    market
  Say's Law, 14–20
labour market, Keynes and, 2, 90
  aggregate demand, 98–106
  classical theory, 92–4
  concluding remarks, 115–17
  involuntary unemployment, 95–8
  money-wage stickiness, 109–11

labour market—*contd.*
  real wage and, 111–15
  wage stickiness and money
    illusion, 106–9
labour supply, 14, 15, 106–8
  excess, 91–3, 96–7, 102, 116
Laidler, David, 42, 77–8, 79–80
Layard, Richard, 137–8, 206, 229
Leijonhufvud, A., 68
leisure, unemployment as, 168–74
Leontief, W., 106–7, 164
Lindbeck, A., 201
Lipsey, R. G., 122–7, 129, 131, 134, 148
liquidity preference, 35, 52, 54–9, 65, 77,
    101, 192, 225
liquidity trap, 67, 68–70, 99, 223
loanable funds, 65, 225
London School of Economics, 11, 235
long-term unemployed, 205–7
Lucas, R. E., 80, 92, 120, 143–4, 146, 162,
    169–73, 179
  supply function, 154–7, 159, 168

macroeconomics, 1–4, 118–19
  see also classical/Keynesian
    macroeconomics; classical
    macroeconomics (new); classical
    macroeconomics (old); Keynesian
    macroeconomics (recent
    developments)
Malinvaud, E., 115, 182, 188, 190, 208
marginal
  analysis, 22
  cost, 97, 104, 111–12, 125
  disutility of employment, 128, 138
  product of labour, 15, 104, 183
  productivity theory, 19–20, 94–5, 104,
    106, 111, 113, 141, 172, 183
mark-up pricing, 75, 188, 212–13, 230
market-clearing approach, 143, 157, 162–
    3, 168–9, 172–4, 177–9
Marshall, Alfred, 27, 38, 92, 168, 181–2,
    233
Marshallian scissors, 8, 28, 29
Marshallian–Wicksellian
  transmission mechanism, 31–8, 40
Marx, Karl, 23, 233
maximization procedure, 90–1, 126, 138,
    174–5, 178
Meade, J. E., 60, 120, 130
Medium Term Financial Strategy, 229
Mill, J. S., 5
Modigliani, F., 102
monetarism, 1–4, 26, 144
  Keynesian revolution, 73, 77–8, 89
  quantity theory, 38–45, 46

monetary policy, 51, 223, 229
  accommodating, 72, 73–81
  expansionary, 64, 106
  IS–LM model, 66–9
money
  asset demand for, 55, 56
  'bank', 46, 232–3
  commodity, 25–6, 41, 46–7, 232
  credit, 231–3
  demand function, 32–4, 40–1, 43, 57,
    73–81, 229–31
  fiat, 100–1, 190–2
  income, 38–46, 73–81, 229–30
  inflation and, 226–8
  Keynes and, 223–5
  neutrality, 30–2, 34, 46, 140, 144–6, 158,
    160, 176
  outside, 100, 190–1
  stock, 25, 27, 54, 160–1
  supply-demand equilibrium, 63, 65, 70–
    1
  see also quantity theory of money
money illusion, 95, 172, 177
  natural unemployment rate and, 138–42
  wage stickiness and, 106–9
money supply, 72, 100, 229, 232–3
  -demand equation, 63, 65, 70–1
  quantity theory, 2, 23, 25, 36–8, 41,
    43–7, 223
  rational expectations, 147, 153, 155,
    158–63, 171–3, 176–7
money wage, 30–1, 90, 120–1, 129, 142,
    148
  aggregate demand and, 75, 98–103
  in *General Theory*, 94–8, 224
  long-term unemployed and, 205–7
  Say's Law, 17–20
  stickiness, 109–11, 177, 190, 211
multiplier, 50, 59, 61–2, 66–7, 72, 83, 85

national income, 49–50, 230
natural rate hypothesis, 162, 163–5
  see also interest rate; unemployment
neoclassical economics, 90–1, 106, 174–5
neoclassical synthesis, 98–103, 116, 131,
    163–4
non-accelerating inflation rate of
  unemployment, 43, 80, 136–8, 180,
    195–208, 215, 228
Nordhaus, W. D., 209

Okun, Arthur, 213, 215
open economy, 51, 188
open market, 31–4, 46, 66, 89
output, 5–6, 30–1, 50, 86–8
outside money, 100, 190–1

Pareto, Vilfredo, 91
partial equilibrium, 17, 189, 190
Patinkin, D., 60, 102–3, 113–15, 164, 165,
   192
permanent income hypothesis, 171
Phelps, Edmund, 148
Phillips, A. W., 121
Phillips curve, 90, 148–9, 199
   development, 3, 121–5
   disequilibrium adjustment
      mechanism, 128–30, 148
   economic policy and, 126–7
   expectations-augmented, 130–6, 139,
      226
Pigou, A. C., 11, 14, 18–19, 27, 38, 92,
      95–6, 130, 139–40, 142–3, 182–3,
      211, 224, 234
Pigou effect, 100–2, 125, 163–4, 191–2,
      214
policy inefficacy proposition, 146, 149, 162
price(s), 131, 202–3, 231
   absolute, 19–20, 37, 40, 44, 75, 102,
      148, 157–8, 165–6, 178, 190–1
   changes, 86–8, 90
   deflation, 97, 99–103, 164
   fixed, 60, 86–7, 147, 208
   and incomes policy, 188, 215
   inflexible, 212–14
   'island parable', 165–8
   Keynes effect, 98–9, 101–3, 192
   quantities and, 180, 208–9, 215
   relative, 49, 116–17, 157
   'prisoners' dilemma', 110, 212
private investment, 12, 83–6
private spending, 12–13, 69–71
product prices, inflexible, 212–14
production, 5–7, 15, 191
productivity, 32, 34, 75, 174
public works, 11–14
purchasing power, 5, 27

quantities, prices and, 180, 208–9, 215
quantity rationing (labour), 115, 187, 193
quantity theory of money, 2, 19–20, 57,
      73–4, 142, 158, 171–2, 181
   Cambridge equation, 27–8
   cash-balance transmission
      mechanism, 29
   classical dichotomy, 22–4
   conclusions, 45–7
   Fisher's equation, 24–7
   generalized, 86–8, 117, 160, 163, 208–9
   Marshallian–Wicksellian mechanism,
      31–8
   monetarism and, 38–45
   output responses (Hume), 30–1

Radcliffe Committee, 121
rational expectations, 198
   accelerationist hypothesis, 154–7
   aggregate demand, 157–68
   background, 146–9
   business cycles, 168–74
   concluding remarks, 177–9
   Keynesian context, 174–7
   unanticipated inflation, 149–54
rationality, 110–11, 149, 153–4, 156
real-balance effect, 100–3, 125, 163–4,
      191–2, 214
real wage, 94, 95–8, 224
   aggregate demand and, 103–6
   employment and, 111–15
   feasible, 137–8, 206–7
   in *General Theory*, 94, 95–8
   rates, 139–42, 165, 169–73, 182–3, 193,
      205–7, 220–2
Say's Law, 14–20, 30–1
   target, 137–8, 206–7
recession, 103, 192, 227–8
Reddaway, W. B., 60
Ricardo, David, 15, 23, 233
Robbins, Lionel, 11, 235
Robertson, Sir Dennis, 9, 86
Robinson, Joan, 120, 217
Royal Economic Society, 78, 95

Samuelson, P. A., 122, 123, 126, 127
Saville, I. D., 192, 230–1
savings, 7–11, 58–9, 61, 181
   crowding out, 12, 69–71, 81–6
   Keynesian interest theory, 52–7
Say's Law, 5–6, 48, 51, 220
   classical interest theory, 11–14
   conclusion, 20–1
   labour market, 14–20
   saving, investment and interest rate,
      7–11
Schumpeter, Joseph, 21
Shackle, G. L. S., 54
Sheffrin, S. M., 170
Shove, Gerald, 213
Smith, Adam, 211, 233
Snower, D., 201
social welfare function, 126, 127
Solow, R. M., 126, 127
Soskice, D., 138, 201, 206
stock-flow equilibrium, 54, 59, 181, 225
Stockholm School, 9
Summers, L., 201
supply, 8, 28, 29
   aggregate, 116–17, 157–68, 178
   function, Lucas, 154–7, 159, 168
   -side shocks, 173–4

Tarshis, L., 111, 112, 114
temporary equilibrium, 181–6, 188, 190,
    192, 193
terms of trade, 42, 188
Thatcher government, 198, 215, 230
Tobin, James, 56, 78, 196
trade cycle, 23, 111
trade unions, 42, 79–80, 93–4, 137, 170–1,
    183, 199, 204–5, 212
transactions approach, 24–7
Treasury view, 11–14, 81–5

unemployed, long-term, 205–7
unemployment, 45, 59, 60
    classical/Keynesian, 3, 180–96, 214–15
    frictional/structural, 17, 19, 128, 136
    inflation trade off, 126–7, 131–2, 134–5,
        149
    involuntary, 2, 95–8, 108–9, 136, 143–4,
        164–9, 182, 210–11, 224
    mass, 11–12, 48
    natural rate, 3, 134–6, 138–42, 146, 169,
        194–8, 228–9
    non-accelerating inflation rate, 43, 80,

    136–8, 180, 195–208, 215, 228
    rates, inflation and, 120–2
    rational expectation, 146, 148, 154–7,
        160, 168–74
    target rate, 126–8, 157
    voluntary, 144–5, 211
    wages and, 17, 19–20, 93–4, 103, 108–9,
        164, 210–11, 224

value theory, 22, 23

wage(s), 101, 103
    cost-pushing, 79–80, 199–200
    hysteresis, 197–208, 209
    rigidity, 209–14
    stickiness, 106–11
    see also bargaining process;
        money wage; real wage
Walras, L., 233
Walrasian auction model, 213
Walrasian equilibrium, 45, 60, 178, 184–8,
    190
Walters, A. A., 46
wealth, 54–6, 163, 192